Women and Transitional Justice

This book discusses the evolving principle of transitional justice in public international law and international relations from the female perspective at a time when the concept is increasingly recognised by the international community as an effective framework in which to negotiate and manage a community's post-conflict transition to peace and stability. The book adopts a gender lens with a particular focus on women's direct experiences and perceptions either as intended beneficiaries of transitional justice (TJ), protagonists in that process or as practitioners, in order to present a unique view in relation to the development of TJ. The range of experiences and knowledge in this collection provides a fresh and unique perspective through its blend of theory and practice.

This book will be of particular interest to students and scholars of law, political science and gender studies.

Lisa Yarwood specialises in transitional justice and state accountability. She is an independent consultant having worked in academic positions in Hong Kong and the United Kingdom and undertaken practical placements with the ICTR in Tanzania, Costa Rica and Panama.

Women and Transitional Justice

Justice

The experience of women as participants

Edited by

Lisa Yarwood

Routledge
Taylor & Francis Group

LONDON AND NEW YORK

First published 2013
by Routledge
2 Park Square, Milton Park, Abingdon, Oxon OX14 4RN

Simultaneously published in the USA and Canada
by Routledge
711 Third Avenue, New York, NY 10017

Routledge is an imprint of the Taylor & Francis Group, an informa business

British Library Cataloguing in Publication Data
A catalogue record for this book is available from the British Library

Library of Congress Cataloguing in Publication Data
A catalog record for this book has been requested

ISBN 978-0-415-69911-2 (hbk)
ISBN 978-0-203-07762-7 (ebk)

Typeset in Garamond
by Wearset Ltd, Boldon, Tyne and Wear

For Alexi's Papa, for Fabien.

Contents

Notes on Contributors

Dr Lisa Yarwood specialises in transitional justice and state accountability. She is an independent consultant having worked in academic positions in Hong Kong and the United Kingdom and undertaken practical placements with the ICTR in Tanzania, Costa Rica and Panama.

Amy Barrow is Assistant Professor in Law at the Chinese University of Hong Kong. She has a keen interest in inter-disciplinary research, primarily the intersection between public international law, gender and security policy and the development of Security Council Resolutions on Women, Peace and Security.

Catalina Díaz is a public interest lawyer with 12 years of professional and academic experience in the intersecting domains of law and social change. Catalina has concentrated in designing, implementing and assessing the impact of legal instruments for the promotion, defence and development of human rights in armed conflict and transitional contexts in Latin America. She has collaborated with various comparative research projects and published in English and Spanish on transitional justice issues in Colombia and on reparations for victims of political violence. She recently published the following book chapters: 'Challenging Impunity From Below: The Contested Ownership of Transitional Justice in Colombia' in Kieran McEvoy and Lorna McGregor (eds), *Transitional Justice from Below: Grassroots Activism and the Struggle for Change* (Hart Publishing, 2008); with Ruth Rubio-Marín and Clara Sandoval, 'Repairing Family Members: Gross Human Rights Violations and Communities of Harm' in Ruth Rubio-Marín (ed.), *Gender and Reparations* (Cambridge University Press, 2009); 'Colombia's Bid for Peace and Justice' in Kai Ambos, Judith Large, Marieke Wierda (eds) *Building a Future on Peace and Justice: Studies on Transitional Justice, Peace and Development* (Springer, 2008).

Lauren Fielder, JD, LL.M, is Assistant Professor of Law and Assistant Director of the Transnational Legal Studies Programme at the University of Luzern Faculty of Law, Switzerland.

Caroline Fournet (PhD LLM) is Associate Professor and Rosalind Franklin Fellow at the Department of Criminal Law and Criminology at the University of Groningen. Her research focuses on comparative and international criminal law and justice. Her list of publications includes *International Crimes: Theories, Practice and Evolution* (Cameron May, 2006) and *The Crime of Destruction and the Law of Genocide: Their Impact on Collective Memory* (Ashgate, 2007).

Sarah Maddox has been practising in criminal and refugee law in Australia for over ten years, has a Master of Laws from the United Nations Inter-regional Crime and Research Institute and works regularly with refugees at the Asylum Seeker Resource Centre in Melbourne.

Julissa Mantilla Falcón is a Lawyer and Professor of the Pontificia Universidad Católica del Perú (PUCP). She has a Gender Diploma by the PUCP and a LLM in International Human Rights Law at LSE. She is also an international consultant on Gender, Transitional Justice and International Human Rights Law. She was the Gender Director of the Peruvian Truth and Reconciliation Commission. She was a lawyer of the Peruvian Ombudsman Office and participated in the investigation of the cases of forced sterilisation during the Fujimori regime. She has given lectures around the world in universities and organisations like the IADB, the OAS, the World Bank, American University, Hunt Alternatives, George Washington University, George Mason University, University of Santiago de Compostela, University of Buenos Aires, University of Peace of the United Nations in Costa Rica, Iberoamericana in México, Universidad San Carlos de Guatemala, among others. She has also published several articles and documents on issues like sexual violence, armed conflict, truth commissions, transitional justice, gender and human rights. Currently, she is a Consultant on Gender Justice at UN Women in Colombia, where she advises the Truth, Justice and Reparation Programme for women of this UN agency. She is also a member of the Criminal Policy Commission created by the Minister of Justice in Colombia. She is a Professor of the Academy of Human Rights and Humanitarian Law of the Washingon College of Law at American University in Washington, DC.

Iris Marin is currently, Director of Reparations at the Unit for the Attention and Comprehensive Reparations for Victims (ACRUV), an executive body recently created within the Colombian Executive. Lawyer of the Universidad del Rosario and MA in Law from the Universidad Nacional de Colombia. With experience in international law of human rights and Colombian constitutional law. In addition, with experience in mainstreaming gender in public policies, elaboration of legal concepts and analysis of legislation in accordance with the Colombian constitutional law and international law.

Clotilde Pégorier is Senior Research Assistant at the University of Luzern. Her major research interests lie in international criminal and humanitarian law. She is currently working on a monograph on ethnic cleansing and has published further articles on the qualification of international crimes.

Annelotte Walsh is currently a PhD candidate at the University of Hong Kong researching the involvement of children in judicial proceedings at the International Criminal Court (ICC). Prior to this she was advocacy manager for UNICEF Australia and an intern at the ICTY, ICTR and Oxfam Australia.

Foreword

Over the past two decades the field of transitional justice has grown and evolved at a rapid rate. It has increased not just in the number of contexts in which it is being employed, but also in the types of contexts. Today transitional justice processes can be found in relation to countries which are in conflict, post-conflict, transitioning, non-transitioning, post-authoritarian and long established democracies. The use of transitional justice mechanisms has also grown out of a renewed commitment at the global level to the centrality of justice as a foundation for sustainable peace. Similarly the mechanisms themselves have evolved: the architecture of international justice, mandates of truth commissions and goals of reparations programmes, to name just a few, are all vastly different from their manifestations just some short years before.

What has been slower to evolve however has been a recognition of the differential impact of conflict on men and women, and as a result the differential needs in relation to the measures employed to deliver justice. This, too, is now shifting. Within the United Nations, the Security Council has established a normative framework through its five resolutions on Women, Peace and Security which affirm that women's participation in all aspects of post-conflict recovery is critical to the stability of a country. This includes measures for post-conflict redress. These same resolutions have acknowledged that conflict-related sexual violence is a threat to international peace and security, in addition to being the most serious of crimes under international law.

Perhaps one of the most important developments in recent years has been the seminal jurisprudence of the Inter-American Court on Human Rights as well as policy emanating from within the UN that affirms that, for women, the goal of transitional justice cannot be to simply address singular violations. Rather, these mechanisms must address underlying structural inequalities and further transformative justice.

At a national level and within transitional justice mechanisms themselves mandates have evolved to include in some cases quotas for women's representation, dedicated gender expertise on staff, specific mention of sexual and gender-based crimes in mandates, and efforts for gender sensitivity in witness protection, outreach investigations.

Too much of the focus to date however has been on increasing women's representation in existing mechanisms or including specific mention of gender-based crimes in mandates. In other words, the focus has been on reforming existing measures. It is here that this book, *Women and Transitional Justice*, is poised to make an important contribution to the continuing evolution of this field. This edited compilation as a whole points to the need not for piecemeal reforms, but for the measures themselves to be re-evaluated from a new perspective; that of women's own experiences.

A re-evaluation of transitional justice measures based on the experiences and voices of women might highlight the need to revise the range of violations for which we seek redress, not simply to include sexual violence but also, for example, to include socio-economic rights violations which disproportionately impact women. It may point to the need for new mechanisms of justice, or for shifting how these mechanisms operate at present. It would most certainly necessitate a rethinking of the very goals of transitional justice – including definitions of 'conflict-related' or 'guarantees of non-recurrence'. Last, a focus on women's voices would likely point to a need to reprioritise our emphasis on one mechanism over another, or the sequencing of these mechanisms. For example, women's demands for justice are frequently placed on comprehensive reparations, an area where there has been too little international focus or national implementation to date.[1]

This book reminds us of the critical importance of women's voice, participation and perspectives to all of the goals sought through transitional justice processes, and ultimately to their success. Most importantly, it brings to the forefront the contributions of women in this field and their views informed by their own experiences which can help to shape the transitional justice project going forward.

Ultimately, achieving gender justice through transitional justice measures will necessitate a broader approach and most importantly an engagement with all actors, in particular men. This book however points to the value of also creating spaces for dialogue between and amongst women transitional justice practitioners in order to share strategies, approaches and lessons learned to further the transformative potential of transitional justice.

Nahla Valji
Programme Specialist
Rule of Law and Transitional Justice
UN Women

---

1 UN Women, 'Making Transitional Justice Work for Women' (2012).

Acknowledgements

First and foremost thanks must be extended to all the contributors who gave time (in otherwise very busy lives) to put pen to paper and share their thoughts and reflections for this project.

A big thanks to Katherine Carpenter at Routledge for her support and optimism in getting the book to print. In addition, this book was largely due to the sponsorship of the Law Faculty at Chinese University Hong Kong. I am only sorry I did not get to spend more time working with you all.

Each contributor has been able to extend special thanks at the start of their respective chapters, as have I noting in particular the generosity of time and spirit shown by Dr Aroha Harris and Jacinta Ruru. However, I wish to make a more personal thanks here to all the women in my life who have provided inspiration including my grandmothers Anita Ritchie and Edith Yarwood; my aunts in particular Jenny and Liz; my very dear friends near and far (many of whom have also directly contributed to this book); my sisters Anita and Sally and of course my dear mother Judy who never ceases to amaze me.

Introduction

This book is concerned with transitional justice, which is an emerging feature of the international framework but which continues to escape definition given its organic and nebulous nature. A large proportion of commentary on transitional justice is provided by practitioners, NGOs and IGOs while only a small number of academics have undertaken research, although this is an increasing phenomenon to which the book aims to make a contribution. There is a significant body of academic commentary on international criminal justice and the work of the international courts, but this project is focused on a much broader notion adopting a working definition of 'transitional justice' that includes mechanisms of international criminal justice but also much more.

In the UN Secretary-General's 2004 Report on the Rule of Law and Transitional Justice in Post-Conflict Societies the notion of 'justice' was as 'an ideal of accountability and fairness in the protection and vindication of rights and the prevention and punishment of wrongs' and 'transitional justice' was considered to encompass 'the full range of processes and mechanisms associated with a society's attempts to come to terms with a legacy of large-scale past abuses, in order to ensure accountability, serve justice and achieve reconciliation'. The mechanisms listed in the Report were as diverse as short term peace operations, 'accounting for the past, building the rule of law and fostering democracy a[s] long-term processes' and at a minimum transitional justice was considered to secure 'political space for reformers, insulating law enforcement from political abuse and mobilizing resources for the strengthening of the justice sector'.[1] This book both adopts the definition as cited above while also leaving open the possibility that our understanding of transitional justice will adapt with time and as the principle itself evolves.

In fact, the Report indirectly forewarns that flexibility will be required when identifying what is required to ensure and facilitate transitional justice. It directly calls for dialogue with those groups most affected including

---

1 'Report of the Secretary-General on the Rule of Law and Transitional Justice in Conflict and Post-Conflict Societies' UN Doc. S/2004/616 (2004), paras 7 to 21.

minorities, the elderly, children, women, prisoners, displaced persons and refugees' in order to ensure the measures adopted ensure 'protection and redress in judicial and reconciliation processes'.[2] Thus, the second characteristic of this work is to focus on one of these groups and adopt a gender perspective to consider transitional justice from the perspective of women.

Just one general working definition of gender perspective (noting that each contributor has adopted and worked within her own definition) is that

gender perspective looks at the impact of gender on people's opportunities, social roles and interactions. Successful implementation of the policy, programme and project goals of international and national organizations is [therefore] directly affected by the impact of gender and, in turn, influences the process of social development. Gender is an integral component of every aspect of the economic, social, daily and private lives of individuals and societies, and of the different roles ascribed by society to men and women.[3]

One of the key characteristics therefore being that gender perspective is about social constructs relating to the different sexes whereas sex differences relate to the biological fact that females and males are different.[4] This definition captures the context in which the issue of gender is relevant in this work because it is not the difference in sex per se that is of interest rather it is the consequences faced by women because they are women that are at issue.

Statistics highlighting the prevalence of violence against women in times of conflict are extreme and cannot, and are not, avoided in this work but the emphasis in this project is on how women have been instrumental in the transitional justice process following conflict. This extends from the role of women in the international criminal justice framework in seeking greater recognition of sexual violence by international courts and tribunals to the role played by women in the instigation and implementation of more non-traditional mechanisms. Thus the focus is more on the role played by women than the theoretical issues faced by women in this field.

The substance of the book focuses on the experience of women in transitional justice, in terms of being beneficiaries of the transitional justice process, protagonists in that process for example by playing an instrumental role in negotiating what form justice is to take, as participants in that

---

2 'Report of the Secretary-General on the Rule of Law and Transitional Justice in Conflict and Post-Conflict Societies' UN Doc. S/2004/616 (2004), para. 25.

3 Economic and Social Development, FAO 'Agricultural Census and Gender Considerations', available at www.fao.org/DOCREP/003/X2919E/x2919e04.htm, Chapter Two, 'The Gender Perspective' (accessed April 2012).

4 Ibid.

process such as a court witness/conflict peace negotiator or as practitioners such as being legal counsel before one of the hybrid courts.

In addition, all the contributors to this work are women and are either direct or indirect practitioners of transitional justice – offering a unique perspective on the issue of gender and transitional justice. Virginia Woolf considered it was 'obvious that the values of women differ very often from the values which have been made by the other sex ... it is the masculine values that prevail'.[5] Gilligan was more expansive in arguing that the difference in perspective

> is rooted not only in [women's] social subordination but also in the substance of their moral concern. Sensitivity to the needs of others and the assumption of responsibility for taking care lead women to attend to voices other than their own and to include in their judgment other points of view.[6] *all women?*

This book tests both those perspectives aiming to indeed provide unique insight into the experience of women in the context of transitional justice.

The range of experience brought by the contributors to the book is formidable. Sarah Maddox has worked both at the international courts and in investigating and prosecuting high-profile organised crime leaders in Australia including their alleged relationship with the regime of Saddam Hussein, having studied at the United Nations Interregional Crime and Research Institute and the European Inter-University Centre for Human Rights and Democratisation, Italy. Practitioner based contributions are also provided by Julissa Mantilla Falcón who was former head of the Transitional Justice Unit at the Truth and Reconciliation Commission Peru and subsequently working for UN Women, Columbia. Dr Lisa Yarwood gained her experience at the ICTR, Catalina Díaz is an independent expert on transitional justice, Iris Marin is the Reparations Director of the Colombian Government Unit for the Integral Assistance and Reparations for Victims and Annelotte Walsh worked not only at the ICTR but also as an advocacy manager for UNICEF, Australia. Lisa subsequently completed her PhD in the UK before lecturing at the Chinese University of Hong Kong, Catalina is studying for an MPhil in sociology at the University of Oxford while Annelotte is currently a PhD candidate at Hong Kong University: thus these women have been able to combine their time working in practice with academic discipline in this work. The more theoretical sections are represented by Professor Amy Barrow, Dr Caroline Fournet, Dr Lauren Fielder and Dr Clotilde Pégorier writing from Hong Kong, Holland and Switzerland respectively. The international cross-section of participants is also intentional and avoids the allegation of

---

5 Woolf, V. A Room of One's Own (New York: Harcourt Brace and World, 1929) p.76.
6 Gilligan, C. In a Different Voice (Cambridge, MA: Harvard University Press, 1982) p.17.

cultural hegemony given that the book seeks to be a representation of gender perspective.

Given the variety of perspectives that is offered in a collected work of essays, such as this, it is somewhat axiomatic that there will be no one single argument to be made. Indeed, contrary to how it may otherwise appear when the title and perspective of the book is taken from one gender to suggest a pro-female stance, there is no over-arching hypothesis to be proven. Simply adopting a gender lens in terms of both content and form is insufficient to overcome the reality that 'experiences are often vague, contradictory and above all constructed',[7] thus if pressed to identify with a particular research methodology the editor would have to elect grounded theory where the theory is developed as the data is collected and analysed. Any themes that emerge as the book progresses will be extracted and discussed in the Conclusion. The Introduction, in contrast, is simply an insight into the book's contributors, content and structure without professing to present an argument to be subsequently proven.

The first part of the book focuses on non-traditional transitional justice measures before turning to consider developments that affect women in the context of the more formal mechanisms, such as the international criminal justice framework. The final chapters offer the insights and reflections of women who are practitioners working in the transitional justice field.

Yarwood looks at post-colonial New Zealand examining the relationship between the indigenous Maori and the colonial British settlors to consider whether the resulting settlement process of compensation and recognition of grievances is a non-traditional form of transitional justice. By referring to the four elements of transitional justice identified in the UN Secretary-General's Special Report on Transitional Justice, being truth, justice, reparation and guarantees of non-repetition, she seeks to identify instances where these goals have been attained and noting in what ways these features are still considered absent.

Arguing that the denial of rights and suppression of indigenous communities by colonial powers is a form of conflict and the steps taken to redress the grievance of these communities is a form of transitional justice, the author will focus on the experience of Maori and in particular the role of women in negotiating and implementing the Treaty of Waitangi settlement, which aimed to compensate Maori for the loss of legal, proprietary and cultural sovereignty. In particular, the extent to which Maori women played an integral role in ensuring the promotion and protection of Maori culture, rather than simply seeking monetary compensation, is considered.

Rather than focusing on hard law transitional justice mechanisms, being those that are entrenched and legitimated under the law, Barrow focuses on the role of UN resolutions. Barrow questions whether the criticism contained

---

7 Wells, C. 'Women Law Professors: Negotiating and Transcending Gender Identities at Work' (2002) Feminist Legal Studies 1, 6.

within UN Security Council resolutions effectively supports post-conflict responses to disarmament, demobilisation and reintegration, and accountability for sexual violence. She then specifically examines the impact of SCR 1325, which focuses on women, peace and security, as applied in Nepal. Barrow considers the extent to which, at a micro level, it has contributed to the participation of women within the community in peacebuilding.

In deconstructing the term gender analysis, Walsh concludes that it is the study of 'social relations, power structures and assumptions and how these influence the access to the enjoyment of rights'. She extends this analysis specifically to girls affected by armed conflict to highlight their gender-specific experiences and needs 'while at the same time identifying potentially differential and discriminatory impacts of policies and practices'. This is an important contribution as consistent throughout the book is the need to give a voice to those thus-far unheard. Girl children are easily one of the most marginalised groups in international society and Walsh seeks to illustrate this. Focusing on the criminal justice framework she addresses the different conflict context experienced by girls as opposed to boys and then addresses the extent to which these differences are recognised and taken into account within transitional justice approaches, namely the international criminal justice system. In doing so Walsh analyses the role of the Convention on the Rights of the Child, assessing its utility as a touchstone for practitioners when developing and implementing transitional justice practices.

Maddox establishes from the outset that her work is based on the premise that women and refugees have increased importance as subjects of transitional justice initiatives and then seeks to explore the extent of the participation of refugee women in those initiatives, the obstacles to their participation and any lessons for future initiatives that can be gleaned. Maddox's work is based on a series of interviews conducted with women who have worked with refugees in the field of transitional justice in order to highlight the importance of engaging with those directly affected by conflict in determining and implementing transitional justice measures and to seek the often overlooked (in academic works) and unique perspective of practitioners working in the field.

'Sexual violence and gender issues should definitely not become the monopoly of female lawyers and scholars' – Fournet takes a different approach in considering the role of gender in the increasing consideration of sexual crimes by the various transitional justice courts implemented at a more international level. Instead of focusing on the need to ensure that sexual crimes are included within the jurisprudence of international criminal law, Fournet looks at the advocates of such developments to consider whether the gender bias of women working in this area is of hindrance or help. This in itself is important because, as several of the contributions to this book consider, the failure to recognise sexual crimes has been anathema to the success of international criminal law as a tool of international criminal justice. Fournet investigates whether the best-intentioned advocates likewise undermine progress due to being female.

Pégorier examines the intersection of gender issues in the context of examining the extent to which transitional justice objectives such as reconstruction, recognition and reparation have been satisfied within the context of international criminal law, as the relevant overarching transitional justice framework. In particular, she focuses on the developments in legal jurisprudence recognising and prosecuting forms of sexual violence as international crimes, questioning the ongoing validity and role of international criminal law in the wider transitional justice framework.

Fielder examines the role of constitutional courts in transitional societies focusing on the African example. She seeks to illustrate how such courts are instrumental in the process of transforming customary law so that it reflects the principle of women's equality. Fielder will argue that women have an inherent right to participate in the transitional justice process as exercised in the context of constitutional courts.

From her work with the Transitional Justice Unit at the Truth and Reconciliation Commission in Peru, Mantilla Falcón considers the absence of gender differences in transitional justice processes focusing on the truth commissions to illustrate that where gender differences are taken into account a significant impact can be seen in relation to the experience of women victims. She first seeks to set out what exactly a gender approach to transitional justice entails before focusing specifically on the Peruvian Truth and Reconciliation Commission to illustrate the extent to which gender has been relevant to the process.

Likewise Díaz and Marin considered the extent to which a women's rights agenda was incorporated in a specific transitional justice context, this time being the reparations component of the transitional justice arrangement in Colombia. The authors explore whether engendering reparations is linked to the participation of women's rights organisations, relying on, amongst more traditional research sources, their first-hand experience in the field.

While there is no single argument to be made and the themes to be covered are several, it is worth noting that what this book does aim to do is to show that the traditional distinction between private and public when it comes to women should not be allowed to permeate the practice, development or study of transitional justice. While there are undoubtedly allowances for women's participation in aspects of public life there is seldom reciprocal relief given to ensure the traditional roles women take on in the home and community are satisfied. This book does not expressly argue that this must change, although implicitly several of the authors would share this view. Instead it seeks acknowledgement that those same characteristics that have led to the traditional distinction and attribution to women of certain roles due to perceived characteristics of nurturing, sensitivity and organisation (in contrast to 'men's competitiveness, ambition and toughness')[8] are

---

8 Cox, S. (ed.) Public and Private Worlds Women in Contemporary New Zealand (Sydney: Allen & Unwin, 1987) p.3.

likewise characteristics that make women suited to offering effective contributions in the framework of transitional justice. For example, women are more likely to identify what mechanism is best suited to meeting the direct and urgent needs of the affected community rather than men who may still be engaged in fighting or focused on more macro objectives associated with the conflict itself.

Although women are 'traditionally restricted to the private sphere, their identities are bound up in the new analysis',[9] in other words traditionally women are perhaps not considered to be active in negotiating or implementing transitional justice mechanisms, however as transitional justice is reconceptualised it is especially important to consider whether the role of women must be given new consideration to determine whether it too has developed. 'History is often remarkably arrogant. It can too frequently dismiss whole groups of people as lost causes or as merely irrelevant. Entire sections of society, usually the poor, the minorities, and the politically powerless are thereby obliterated from memory'.[10] This collection of works seeks to show, by focusing on the contributions of women with a strong background as transitional justice practitioners rather than basing the work in theory, what issues women continue to face in terms of making an active and strong contribution to transitional justice.

9 Ibid.
10 Binney, J. and Chaplin, G. Nga Morehu The Survivors (Auckland: Oxford University Press, 1986) p.3.

1 Women, transitional justice and indigenous conflict

The role of women in addressing New Zealand's colonial past

Lisa Yarwood[1]

Introduction – New Zealand and non-traditional transitional justice

According to the 2004 United Nations Secretary-General's report on transitional justice (TJ), the concept comprises 'the full range of processes and mechanisms associated with a society's attempts to come to terms with a legacy of large-scale past abuses, in order to ensure accountability, serve justice and achieve reconciliation'.[2] On the basis of the Secretary-General's definition, it is clear that TJ is not confined to addressing the aftermath of large-scale conflict and can be extended to non-traditional, indirect forms of conflict. This chapter adopts that premise to explore TJ in the context of addressing breaches of indigenous rights by colonial powers, in particular breaches of the Treaty of Waitangi signed in 1840 by Maori, the indigenous people of New Zealand, and representatives of the British Crown. In addition, the view of the former Special Rapporteur on Impunity, Louis Joinet, that TJ includes 'the right to justice, the right to truth, the right to reparation and the guarantee of non-repetition'[3] is also referred to here. Based on these four tenets, this chapter considers whether the Waitangi Tribunal,

1 The author wishes to thank Dr Claudia Orange (interview 17 March 2011), Dr Aroha Harris (interview 20 March 2011) and Tania Simpson (interview 22 March 2011). Appreciation is also expressed to the staff of the Library at Te Papa (in particular Victoria Boyack and Martin Lewis) and Otago University (in particular Toby Smrekar). Appreciation is also expressed to Sandy and Annabelle Ritchie for allowing me to crash their girlie time. The work described in this chapter was supported by a grant from the Research Grants Council of the Hong Kong Special Administrative Region, China (Project Code 2090010).
2 'Report of the Secretary-General on the Rule of Law and Transitional Justice in Conflict and Post-Conflict Societies' UN Doc. S/2004/616 (2004) 3.
3 'The Administration of Justice and the Rights of Prisoners' United Nations High Commission of Human Rights, Economic and Social Council UN Doc. E/CN.4/Sub.2/1997/20/Rev.1 (1997).

which makes findings about alleged Treaty breaches, and the Treaty settlement process,[4] which negotiates mostly financial settlements based on the Tribunal findings, have been effective TJ mechanisms in this context.

The research for this chapter was both by textual review and based on interviews, conducted by the author, including with members of the Waitangi Tribunal. All the interview subjects were women and in addition to examining the New Zealand context as an example of non-traditional TJ in action, this chapter considers the extent to which Maori women have played a role in the settlement process and whether any role played has been instrumental to its success, or not.

This chapter first discusses the conflict in question, providing a brief historical overview of the colonialisation of New Zealand by Great Britain and the impact colonisation had on the indigenous Maori population, in particular focusing on the period since the signing of the Treaty of Waitangi in 1840. It then outlines the settlement process and assesses whether the largely financial compensation given to Maori in recognition of Crown breaches of the Treaty has been effective in terms of transitioning New Zealand from a colonial society comprising divided indigenous and settlor populations to a unified post-colonial country. The chapter then focuses on the contribution of Maori women to the settlement process but starts by discussing the role and status of women in Maori culture generally to provide a benchmark for comparison when considering the extent and nature of any role given to Maori women in relation to the settlement process. The discussion considers the role Maori women have played, and continue to play, in the settlement process (as Tribunal members, negotiators on tribal settlements or as individuals who have influenced its adoption) as well as referring to some of the notable Maori women that have directly or indirectly influenced the transition of New Zealand to a post-colonial society. Finally the analysis turns to assess the effectiveness of the settlement process with reference to the four features of TJ identified in the UN Secretary-General's Report. In particular several questions are posed: whether Maori have received justice for the breaches of the Treaty by the Crown; whether the settlement process and airing of claims before the Tribunal has led to the truth about New Zealand's colonial history being identified and, if so, is the history a collective New Zealand history or representative of only a limited section of a still divided society; whether there has been reparation and in what form and from whose perspective; and, last, what guarantees the settlement process offers in terms of the New Zealand government upholding the principles of the Treaty in the future and ensuring a unified society comprising both Pakeha (non-native New Zealanders) and Maori.

4 Collectively referred to here as the settlement process.

Part one – the New Zealand experience

Identifying the conflict – New Zealand's colonial history

New Zealand's first settlors were believed to have arrived from Polynesia by the twelfth century, and certainly by the turn of the seventeenth century Maori colonies existed throughout New Zealand. The first documented sighting by Europeans was in 1642 when Abel Tasman sailed from Holland and sighted the land but retreated after sea clashes with Maori.[5] Captain James Cook of Great Britain led the first European expedition to actually land in New Zealand in 1769, which would start a period of intense commercial development both by European settlors and Maori in terms of exporting seal products and harvest commodities including flax and timber and importing commodities such as animals and medicines from the rest of the world.[6] At the time the Treaty of Waitangi was signed in 1840, it was only another 20 years before Pakeha would outnumber Maori.[7]

The establishment of a state of New Zealand was, as historian Michael King described, 'a subplot in the diaspora of Europeans that sent as many as 50 million people from the Old World to the New World over a period of 200 years'.[8] The Treaty of Waitangi represented the founding document of New Zealand society and brought the country within the sovereign dominion of the British Crown. The Treaty was signed by representatives of Queen Victoria and tribal chiefs, including at least 13 women,[9] although historian Dr Claudia Orange has speculated that women were only permitted to participate at the urging of missionaries, and only borne from a sense of Christian participation rather than in recognition that the consent of women was integral to the Treaty's legitimacy.[10]

---

5 The name New Zealand came from the Dutch Nieuu Zeeland: King, M. History of New Zealand (New Zealand: Penguin, 2003) p. 99.

6 Ibid., p. 127.

7 Ibid., p. 188.

8 Ibid., p. 170.

9 Being Takurua, Te Marama, Ana Hamu, Marama, Ereonora, Rangi Topeora, Kahe Te Rau o te Rangi, Pari, Te Kehu, Ngaraurekau, Te Rene o Maki, Hoana Riutoto and Te Wairakau (Rei, T. Maori Women and the Vote (Wellington: Huia Publishers, 1993)). In fact for a long time it was thought only five women signed and the final number remains unknown because of the gender neutrality of Maori names and the fact that 'over time people have become so conditioned to the Pakeha view that only men could have been political leaders that we have come to assume that the vast majority of the names were men's names' (Henare, M. 'Nga Tikanga me nga Ritenga o Te Ao Maori' in Report of the Commission on Social Policy (1988) 118). One woman was Rangi Topeoroa, Chieftainess of Ngati Toa Tribe on Kapiti Coast who signed the Treaty believing signing would promote cooperation with Pakeha and prosperity for her people. At the time, Rangi was one of few women to speak on the Marae and in 1846 she spoke of 'the aggressions of Pakeha and of the reluctant resistance of Maori at the time' (Ofner, S. New Zealand Women in the 19th Century (Auckland: Macmillan, 1993) 11).

10 Dr Claudia Orange (Te Papa Tongarewa: New Zealand, 17 March 2011).

The Treaty guaranteed the right of Maori to 'full, exclusive and undisturbed possession of their lands, estates, forests, fisheries and other properties that they may wish to exercise collectively or individually'.[11] However the English and Maori versions of the Treaty (as well as the several Maori versions that were circulated throughout the country for signing) contained different interpretations of the extent to which sovereignty was ceded in fact. For example, in Article I the word 'kawangatanga' was used in the Maori version rather than 'rangitiratanga' implying the ceding of something less than chieftainship as it was understood by Maori while in Article II Maori were promised retention of 'rangitiritanga' so that the subsequent land acquisitions were in blatant breach of that provision. Former Maori Land Court judge Eddie Durie, described the Treaty as joining Maori 'tangata tiriti' (people of the Treaty) with

> the people whose presence was authorised by the Treaty of Waitangi. And the face of New Zealand life would from that time be a Janus one, representing at least two cultures and two heritages, very often looking in two different directions.[12]

In addition to the differing interpretations of the Treaty, there were other issues which indicated the Treaty was not entered into or upheld with good faith by the Crown, including the fact that a declaration of sovereignty was made by the Crown prior to the Treaty being signed without the consent of Maori, not all chiefs were permitted to sign, some chiefs chose not to sign the document and 'missionary encouragement' led some Maori to believe that what they were signing was closer to an expression of guardianship by Queen Victoria than a legal contract ceding dominion over their lands.[13] The various issues became increasingly contentious as, within the following years, the Government imposed acquisition measures when Maori refused to sell land to Pakeha settlors. By the 1860s tensions escalated into a series of land wars, in which not only men but Maori women fought against the Pakeha,[14] including Heni Pore of Te Arawa who fought while holding her baby strapped to her chest in the Battle of Gate Pa in Tauranga in 1864.[15] The consequence of the wars was that the Government confiscated even larger chunks of Maori land in the regions of the Waikato and Tauranga.

A Native Land Court was established to deal with land grievances that arose before and as a consequence of the Treaty but in general the Court condoned the acquisitions. Maori women were again active in this process,

---

11 Article II, Treaty of Waitangi 1840.
12 King *supra*, note 5, 167.
13 Ibid., 164.
14 Mikaere, A. The Balance Destroyed: The Consequences for Maori Women of the Colonisation of Tikanga Maori (Auckland: International Research Institute for Maori and Indigenous Education, 2003) 119.
15 Ibid., 55.

bringing cases before the Court, including Maata Te Taiawatea of Ngati Awa and Airini Tonore of Ngati Kahungungu with the historian Ofner describing Airini's contribution in terms that her 'knowledge of land legislation, whakapapa and court procedures made her a powerful advocate on behalf of her people'.[16] Women were also active in petitioning the Crown seeking repeal of legislation that permitted wrongful acquisitions so that between 1886 and 1896 Maori women had brought in excess of 40 petitions to Parliament,[17] either on their own behalf or on behalf of their *iwi* (tribe/people).[18] Such attempts for redress were however ignored and the next decades were instead tarnished by the ongoing acquisition or confiscation of Maori land, and simultaneously a growing disparity between Maori and Pakeha in terms of socio-demographic statistics.

The mentality of the colonial settlors in the decades after the Treaty was signed has been described as being

> based upon notions of superiority of culture and process and supreme right over 'subordinate interests'. It denie[d] the right of the native tribes secured and guaranteed by the colonists' own Treaty process [but fought] feverishly for those same rights in pursuit of its own interests.[19]

Certainly, the consequences of colonisation for Maori have resulted in disparities in terms of education, health, employment, income, high representation in crime and reduced mortality – and in all those statistics Maori continue to fall behind Pakeha. The actions of the colonial settlors in the nineteenth century were spurious and motivated by the acquisition of land, but as time progressed the consequences of these actions and the marginalisation of Maori simply became normalised in society. For example, a belief that New Zealand had exemplary race relations has been heralded internationally by the Government, historically school children were taught that the Treaty of Waitangi was 'the fairest treaty ever made by Europeans with a native race',[20] and even the Governor General (the Crown's representative in Government) warned in 1938 that Maori ingratitude and protest could 'lead to the loss of that helpful assistance now being given'.[21]

The impact of colonialisation on Maori was particularly felt by women.

16 Ofner *supra*, note 9

17 Mikaere *supra*, note 14, 119.

18 Descent group consisting of many *hapu* (*whanau* groups, with *whanau* meaning family): Smith, L. 'Maori Women : Discourses, Projects and Mana Wahine' in Middleton, S. and Jones, A. (eds) *Women and Education in Aotearoa* (Wellington: Bridget Williams Books, 1992) Glossary.

19 O'Regan, H. 'Post-Colonialism: "Ko Te Mate Kururpopo – The Festering Wound"' (1995) *Womens Studies Journal* 11, 1, 55.

20 According to Our Nation's Story, which was a set of books given to all New Zealand schoolchildren and referred to in King *supra*, note 5, 471.

21 In King *supra*, note 5, 472.

Both men and women were subject to 'the colonial experience' in terms of the loss of land, property, cultural autonomy and political independence, accepting 'as inevitable the poverty in which they grew up' and witnessing 'the proletarianization of their kin ... the stripping-away of power from the Maori people created this sense of subordination'.[22] In addition, Maori women endured the consequences of 'a colonialization of the mind' as the Pakeha system of patriarchal hierarchy was also adopted creating a gender divide that had not previously existed. Traditionally, Maori men and women had enjoyed equal status with a division of roles but the labour and contribution of both were considered equal and necessary. Balance is central to *tikanga* (Maori tradition) and to ensure the harmony of the community in all aspects, men and women worked together in partnership.[23] The idea of female strength as a foundational pillar on which Maoridom was based has been represented throughout Maori cosmogony and mythology including creation legends such as Papatuanuku who advised her son on how he was to create humankind.[24] When Maori mythology was interpreted by Pakeha, however, it was brought more in line with the Christian tradition, making assimilation easier.[25] The adoption of patriarchal hierarchy that typified nineteenth century colonial society thus distorted the equilibrium in Maori society to the detriment of women.

The gender disparity may have been actively embraced by Maori men, for example women had to fight for the right to vote and stand as members in the Maori Parliament reflecting the traditional Westminster system, however it is not accurate to say that Maori acquiesced in relation to the increasing disparity between Maori and Pakeha. Although the land wars in the 1860s did not lead to gains, Maori have consistently petitioned the Crown for redress and relief from land acquisitions, such as in 1922 when the Ratana political movement sought a Royal Commission of Inquiry into Maori grievances although inevitably such requests were referred back to the New Zealand authorities. By the 1960s and 1970s, protest and discontent escalated in the face of Maori traditions and culture being submerged, potentially irretrievably, into Pakeha traditions such as in health and education. In addition to ongoing grievances relating to the loss of land, there was anger that Maori were expected to learn English but the obligation was not reciprocal, Maori were under-represented in the legal system and 'agencies of the state were committed to reflecting Western values, criteria, practices and priorities rather than Maori ones', all of which led to resentment and 'the rise of urban protest groups'.[26] Grievances also related to the suppression of

22 Binney, J. and Chaplin, G. *Nga Morehu The Survivors* (Auckland: Oxford University Press, 1986) 27.
23 Mikaere *supra*, note 14, 67.
24 See below for futher discussion on the role of women in Maori society.
25 Mikaere supra, note 14, 85.
26 King *supra*, note 5, 485.

culture, failure to respect the principles of the Treaty and 'denial of economic and political self-determination'.[27]

Increasingly high profile protests included land occupations in Raglan, the arrest of 200 protestors in the 'largest police operation in the country up until that time'[28] and the resignation of Maori MPs from Parliament. There were several notable features about the protests. First, in addition to Maori grievances being addressed, protestors sought severance of New Zealand's sporting ties with apartheid South Africa, drawing a parallel between the discrimination of native peoples in both countries. Second, the mode of protest adopted was Western using 'demonstrations, picketing, petitions to Parliament, press releases and appearances on television'.[29] One interpretation of the adoption of Western means of protest in order to express grievances about the denial of Maori traditions in New Zealand was that it indicated Maori accepted the inevitable assimilation of Maori into Pakeha traditions, although not to the extent capable of overcoming the vehemence with which the historical grievances of Maori were still felt. A second interpretation is that the protestors were largely led by a younger generation of Maori, influenced by increasing urbanisation and by a broader education that inspired awareness of human rights protests for example in the USA by the civil rights movement.[30] The third notable feature was that the protests were often led by Maori women, in particular the 1975 Maori Land March led by Whina Cooper who, at the age of 80, led protestors in walking the length of the North Island to Parliament in Wellington, and who was made a Dame six years later in recognition of her contribution to Maori. A Memorial of Rights was presented to Parliament calling for

> an enactment of Parliament which enshrines the spirit and intent of this Memorial [which] shall incorporate in it the protective principle of entrenchment whereby it shall not suffer repeal or amendment without the assent of the Maori people, such assent be forthcoming by the expression of a majority of those persons eligible to vote as Maori in a National Referendum [and] secondly, that all pernicious clauses in every statute of the present day or in new statutes in the future which have the power to take Maori land, alienate Maori land, designate Maori land of

27 Kelsey, J. *Rolling Back the State: Privatisation of Power in Aotearoa* (Wellington: Bridget Williams Books, 1993) 233.

28 King *supra*, note 5, 486.

29 Ibid., 484.

30 Protest groups that emerged during this time included the Maori Organisation of Human Rights clearly linking itself through its names to the more global cause of equality for all peoples rather than an isolated struggle for Maori grievances to be addressed: Orange, C. 'The Treaty of Waitangi: A Study of its Making, Interpretation and Role in New Zealand History' (Thesis submitted for PhD, University of Auckland, 1984) 610.

confiscate Maori land be repealed and never to be administered on the remaining Maori land.[31]

The profile of these protests and increasing public awareness of the injustice lingering in New Zealand society finally forced the Government to deal with Maori grievances, marking the start of an epoch in which the treatment of Maori in New Zealand would change. Over the following decades, changes included the 1981 adoption of *Kohanga Reo* (Maori language immersion programme) and adoption of the Race Relations Act 1971 outlawing discrimination. Yet most significant was the 1975 adoption of the Treaty of Waitangi Act and establishment of the Waitangi Tribunal.

The Treaty of Waitangi settlement: an exercise in monetary compensation or an example of cultural self-determination? Assessing the settlement as a transitional justice mechanism

Overview

Historian Claudia Orange described the Treaty as effectively creating New Zealand as a settlor's land with a place for Maori rather than providing Pakeha a place on Maori land.[32] In order to redress this imbalance, and due to the limitations that hindered the legal scope of the Treaty's application before the Courts, the Waitangi Tribunal was established in order to address grievances arising from alleged breaches of the Treaty and rifts in the relationship between Crown and Maori. The Tribunal is unique in comparison to traditional TJ mechanisms. It is not a court in the same fashion as other TJ courts, such as the Tribunals for the Former Yugoslavia and Rwanda. Its process is strictly inquisitorial, and it has no powers other than to make non-binding recommendations to the Government, although the Tribunal does have authority to determine conflicting interpretations in the English and Maori versions of the Treaty. This flexibility permits the Tribunal to adopt processes and take into account evidence that would otherwise be excluded under strict rules of evidence, for example the Tribunal may adopt Maori protocols and consider history recounted in the oral tradition. The maximum 20 member Tribunal, along with a chair and deputy chairperson, is composed of approximately 50 per cent Maori and Pakeha and 50 per cent women and men and members come from a range of backgrounds including members who are barristers, Maori Court judges, academics, historians and *kaumatua* (respected Maori elder).[33]

50% representation

---

31 Memorial of Rights 1975.
32 In King *supra*, note 5, 157.
33 See Office of Treaty Settlements (http://www.ots.govt.nz/); interview Tania Simpson (Waitangi Tribunal: New Zealand, 22 March 2011).

It is on the basis of recommendations made to the Government that settlements are negotiated between Maori and the Crown, a process managed by the Office of Treaty Settlements. The majority of Treaty claims relate to purchases of Maori land by the Crown including pre-Treaty purchases later investigated and validated, post-Treaty private purchases made during the Crown's waiver of its pre-emptive right to purchase Maori land, confiscation of Maori land under the New Zealand Settlements Act 1863 and transactions under various land laws.[34] In 1985 the mandate of the Tribunal was extended to allow any grievances arising from alleged breaches of the Treaty since 1840 and claims are not restricted to land claims. For example, the Te Reo Maori claim resulted in the Government adopting the recommendations of the Tribunal that language was a *taonga* (treasure) protected by the Treaty. The Government subsequently established Maori as an official language of New Zealand and founded the Maori Language Commission to facilitate assimilation.

Another example of a notable settlement and one beyond the realm of addressing land claims was the recognition of the effect of Government regulation over commercial fishing on Maori fisheries interests. The Crown has settled 10 per cent of New Zealand's fishing quota, shareholdings in various fishing companies (including 50 per cent of the country's largest company Sealords with the settlement being colloquially known as the 'Sealords deal'), 20 per cent of all new species brought within the quota system and a cash payout of $67 million on Maori. The total value of the deal was approximately $170 million.[35] Similarly, a settlement worth $170 million was made in relation to the land confiscations in the Waikato, which included a formal apology delivered by Queen Elizabeth II in a visit to New Zealand in 1995. Other notable measures by way of compensation were the renaming of Mount Cook to Aoraki, which was returned to the Ngai Tahu tribe who then regifted it back to the people of New Zealand. As of 2008, the total paid out in settlements exceeded $953 million.[36]

Praise

Given the considerable value of the settlements made thus far it is an easy assumption that the settlements process has been successful, but further consideration is needed to test its validity. Before addressing any criticism that has been made in relation to the settlement process, the ways in which the process has attracted praise will be considered.

One success has been the progressive flexibility of the Tribunal and the settlements process, for example in expanding its mandate to extend the

34 'The Negotiations Process' Office of Treaty Settlements: http://www.ots.govt.nz/.

35 Walrond, C. 'Fishing Industry' (2006) *Te Ara – the Encyclopedia of New Zealand*: http://www.teara.govt.nz/en/fishing-industry/7.

36 Office of Treaty Settlements: http://www.ots.govt.nz/.

period in which claims could be made despite the significant financial undertaking this required from the Government. Likewise, good faith on the part of the Government can arguably be interpreted in the decision not to adopt a fiscal envelope in terms of restricting the total amount payable to meet Maori grievances. Other progressive measures are the increasing incorporation of oral history to form part of the official record, so that the settlement process is more representative of a mechanism negotiated by both parties and respecting Maori traditions. One example of where departing from traditional Pakeha methods of evidence gathering has assisted is the realisation that the phrase 'tuku whenua' that Pakeha sett-lors interpreted as meaning land sales was inappropriate in Northland where Maori did not in fact have a concept of selling land, yet it was this phrase that the Crown relied on in land transactions to justify their claims to ownership.[37]

The primary success of the settlement process has been the opportunity for Maori grievances to be heard, both in terms of providing a public forum in which Maori have been able to express their grievances and in terms of highlighting forgotten grievances, for example the Te Uri-O-Hau settle-ment was vindication of a claim denied by the Crown for over 100 years.[38] Maori member of Parliament Sandra Lee considered that

---

37 Yates-Smith, A. 'Hine! E Hine! Rediscovering the Feminine in Maori Spirituality' (unpublished PhD Thesis, University of Waikato, 1988) 4.

38 As part of the settlement the Crown issued a formal apology. It is worthwhile including an excerpt from the settlement deed to illustrate that the settlements were not merely cursory and are a clear recognition by the Crown of wrongdoing:

> The Crown acknowledges Te Uri o Hau Historical Claims and the breaches of Te Tiriti o Waitangi/the Treaty of Waitangi and its principles by the Crown in relation to Te Uri o Hau Historical Claims as follows:
>
> (a) The Crown recognises that Te Uri o Hau endeavoured to preserve and strengthen their relationship with the Crown. In particular, the early land transactions for settlement purposes contributed to development of New Zealand and affirmed the loyalty of Te Uri o Hau to the Crown;
> (b) The Crown acknowledges that the benefits that Te Uri o Hau expected to flow from this relationship were not always realised. Early land transactions and twen-tieth century land development, including the Tai Tokerau Maori District Land Board and the Maori Affairs development schemes initiated in the 1930s, did not provide the economic opportunities and benefits that Te Uri o Hau expected . . .
>
> The Crown apologises to the ancestors of Te Uri o Hau and to their descendants for the breaches of Te Tiriti o Waitangi/the Treaty of Waitangi and its principles acknowledged above.
>
> The Crown unreservedly apologises and profoundly regrets that its actions, in failing to preserve sufficient lands for Te Uri o Hau, have had pervasive and enduring consequences, resulting in Te Uri o Hau losing control over the majority of their lands.
>
> (Formal Apology to Te Uri O Hau (5 July 2004): http://www.beehive.govt.nz/release/formal-apology-te-uri-o-hau)

one of the most positive things in the Waitangi Tribunal ... is not necessarily the cash that comes out the other end but the opportunity provided, at least, for our people to actually articulate those things that have caused sadness down through generations ... too few New Zealanders really understand what the Maori grievances are about.[39]

In addition to apologies being issued within settlement documents, the Prime Minister and even Queen Elizabeth II have made formal apologies in person to Maori.

The fact that such recognition occurs within the context of a policy driven, Pakeha dominated process can be interpreted as undermining the achievements, for example relying on a quasi-court like environment and utilising forms of monetary compensation arguably perpetuate the belief that contemporary New Zealand is a reflection of Pakeha traditions of dispute settlement. The more optimistic view is that irrespective of the method used, the settlement process represents an extrinsic agreement between 'Maori and the state ... to go forward'.[40] In other words, the settlement process has been 'as successful as a process driven approach can be',[41] but it is important not to view it as an end in itself. More is required, or, according to Dr Aroha Harris of the Waitangi Tribunal, more gains and 'returns for investment' are needed.[42] (verbiage)

A cursory reading of the Treaty of Waitangi Act 1975 illustrates the limits of the process because nowhere within the document is the term 'reconciliation' used, the word 'compensation' is used only twice and 'justice' is not referred to at all, except in referring to the Department of Justice. The Preamble states the Act aims to

provide for the observance, and confirmation, of the principles of the Treaty of Waitangi by establishing a Tribunal to make recommendations on claims relating to the practical application of the Treaty and to determine whether certain matters are inconsistent with the principles of the Treaty

but does not refer to the relationship of Maori to the Crown. Tania Simpson, interviewed in her role as both a Tribunal member and negotiator between *iwi* and the Crown, described the settlement process as 'doing what was needed to work' because ultimately the only way for Maori grievances to be aired and gains made in terms of compensation and recognition was for the

39 Lee, S. in Brown, A. (ed.) *Mana Wahine Women Who Show the Way* (Auckland: Reed Books 1994) 38–39.
40 Dr Aroha Harris (Waitangi Tribunal, University of Auckland: New Zealand, 20 March 2011).
41 Dr Claudia Orange (Te Papa Tongarewa: New Zealand, 17 March 2011).
42 Harris *supra*, note 40.

adoption of a dispute settlement mechanism that was tolerable for *iwi* while at the same time being palatable to the general public and Government.

Having recognised breaches of the Treaty by the Crown, the Government is under a continuing responsibility to ensure compliance with the Treaty principles. There has certainly been growth in the number of statutes that incorporate reference to the Treaty of Waitangi. For example, the Conservation Act 1987 provides that 'this Act shall be so interpreted and administered as to give effect to the principles of the Treaty of Waitangi', and pursuant to the Education Act 1989 'it is the duty of the Council of an institution, in the performance of its function and the exercise of its powers to acknowledge the principles of the Treaty of Waitangi'. The Courts increasingly look to the Treaty of Waitangi as an aid of statutory interpretation on the basis that the Treaty is part of the 'fabric of New Zealand society',[43] including references to Maori customary law for example after the disposition of fisheries assets following the Sealords deal.[44] Yet, such recognition is arguably insufficient to honour the Government's commitment to uphold Treaty principles unless policies are also adopted to meet the continuing discrepancy between Maori and Pakeha represented in terms of socio-demographic statistics. Sandra Lee described the ongoing obligation in terms of needing

> an ongoing commitment to policies which counter the fact that Maori found themselves at the bottom of what the economists love to call the socio-economic heap ... until such time as Maori are back up where they belong alongside their fellow New Zealanders, no true settlement has occurred.[45]

Criticism

It is the fact that despite hundreds of millions of dollars being granted in terms of compensation the social gap between Maori and Pakeha continues, which characterises the criticisms levelled at the settlement process. Aroha Harris reflected that in her experience it was Maori that continued to engage with their *iwi* organisation (*runanga*) that were often engaged with the settlement process in terms of its impact, benefits and costs to the relevant *iwi*, rather than focusing on the financial settlement at the end. She believes that what is missing from the process is a real commitment by both the Government and some Maori to airing the grievance itself, instead of merely

43 Huakina Development Trust v. Waikato Valley Authority [1987] 2 NZLR 188, 210) and viewed as being of constitutional importance Barton-Prescott v. Director-General of Social Welfare [1997] 3 NZLR 179.
44 McRitchie v. Taranaki Fish and Game Council [1999] 2 NZLR 139); Ngati Apa v. Attorney General (Attorney General v. Ngati Apa [2003] 3 NZLR 643).
45 Lee *supra*, note 39, 38–39.

designating a monetary figure with the view to resolving the settlements process as quickly as possible. The idea of full and final settlements is particularly of concern in terms of manipulating the history being recorded through the settlement process into a palatable agreed set of facts, an imperative potentially exacerbated by a political perception of Treaty fatigue amongst the public that intermittently inspires politicians to call for an end to the process, or Maori to settle rather than draw negotiations out for several more years. During times of economic hardship and recession such risks are greater.[46]

The danger in focusing on the financial settlement, or hurrying any settlement, is that the underlying purpose, being a commitment to upholding the principles of the Treaty that provided for Maori sovereignty and equality, is not achieved. There is a lack of public awareness of the settlement process typified by the fact that the majority of New Zealanders would not be aware of a distinction between the Tribunal hearing and negotiation of a settlement based on the Tribunal's report. Furthermore, the settlements that are reached fail to address underlying issues in relation to the socio-demographic gap between Maori and Pakeha whereby the life expectancy of the highest decile Maori remains lower than that of the lowest decile Pakeha.[47] There is no link drawn between the relevant breach and the status quo of Maori, nor is there any form of accountability between the settlements and the impact these settlements have in terms of addressing the underlying Treaty breach. Or, as Sandra Lee argues, there needs to be an 'audit' to make sure the settlements directly benefitted 'those Maori who are most marginalised and vulnerable … or whether the benefits [we]re only going to a handful of Maori who have been caught up in the web of corporate wheelings and dealings'.[48] Given that awarding millions of dollars in settlement fails to address basic inequalities, in breach of the Crown's guarantee to do so under the Treaty, there is increasing suggestion that what is required is for settlements to be dynamic and look to the 'trying out of Maori ways'.[49]

Obviously, this last suggestion has the potential to be controversial and Tania Simpson, also of the Waitangi Tribunal, advocates that Maori may instead have to be satisfied with 'incremental steps'.[50] The settlement process is already hindered by logistical problems relating to delays in bringing claims, attempting to consolidate the large number of potential claimants (as any individual Maori may bring a claim without requiring affiliation to a tribe) and the fact that the Tribunal remains constrained within a legal framework so there is an inevitable tension between the legalist and

46 Harris *supra*, note 40.
47 Robson, B. 'Economic Determinants of Māori Health and Disparities (A Report for the Public Health Advisory Committee)' Te Ropu Rangahau Hauora a Eru Pomare (2004): www.nhc.govt.nz/phac.
48 Lee *supra*, note 39, 35.
49 Harris *supra*, note 40.
50 Simpson *supra*, note 33.

culture-centred approaches taken. Simpson suggests that the settlement process is 'an imperfect contribution' in that it makes an important step in recognition of Maori grievances but she too concedes that it could make a 'better contribution to emotional healing' likening the process to the relief a victim may discover in giving evidence. Consistent throughout both the criticism and praise, therefore, is the need for more substantive acknowledgement of the relevant Treaty breaches so the settlement process is less of an exercise in monetary compensation and more an exercise in cultural self-determination as only then would the principles of the Treaty truly be upheld.

Part two – Maori women

The status of women in Maori culture

Principle III of the Treaty guaranteed equality between Maori and Pakeha, yet in 1993 the Mana Wahine claim was lodged before the Tribunal claiming that the Crown specifically breached this obligation in relation to Maori women. This part of the chapter discusses the Mana Wahine claim in more depth while focusing on the experience of Maori women throughout the settlement process. The basis of the claim is that the traditional equality historically characterising the relationship between Maori women and men was distorted through the imposition of patriarchal Pakeha societal constructs. This claim is examined first through understanding the role of Maori women in traditional compared with contemporary New Zealand society and, second, by analysing the extent to which Maori women have been effective (regardless of any patriarchal subjugation) in the settlement process.

Overview

Consistently, Maori women have been understood in New Zealand society as *whare tangata*, or possessors of wisdom, experience and knowledge that is passed on to succeeding generations and therefore shapes the world in which we live.[51] However, Maori women claim there is another layer that 'Christianity and colonisation effectively undermined and certainly damaged, and that is the warrior, the shaman, the initiator. The visionary, the groundbreaker – the women at the front'.[52] Certainly, as the Maori historian Aroha Harris points out, the portrayal of women throughout New Zealand's post-1840 history reflects the interests of those individuals who wrote it, who were largely male Pakeha academics. In recent decades exceptions have arisen and histories that are more inclusive of Maori women and sympathetic in their portrayals have emerged, highlighting the roles played in the suffrage

51 Ngangahu, H. in Brown, A. (ed.) *Mana Wahine Women Who Show the Way* (Auckland: Reed Books, 1994) 30–31.
52 Ibid., 30–31.

movement, the National Council of Maori Women and the Maori Women's Welfare League. This represents a start in identifying the lost women 'warrior' referred to above. In addition, the increasing number of Maori historians including Tania Rei,[53] has further expanded our knowledge of the roles Maori women have played throughout history. In so doing, a more comprehensive understanding is attained, which suggests that Maori women are fighters and have been a formidable influence in New Zealand's history.

Maori women in cosmogony and traditional society

Ancient Maori traditions, captured in the sacred text 'Kama ko Ra a Io', teach that 'all harmony and joy of life is to be found in women'. The Supreme Creator Io said 'the nature of all that I am is within women. No matter the nature of men in whom my creation also rests, it is women who have the gift of the sharing process of my being'.[54] In the 'Sacred Book of Wahine a Ra tu Atu – The Nature of Women's Relationship with the Gods' leadership was defined as giving 'women a natural advantage over men' in that 'for women intuitive knowing is a servant used well. For men it is misunderstanding of the role of the intuitive process of mind in action that defeats them' and 'because of this, women always lead from a position of strength and men from a position of weakness'.[55] The distinction between men and women is that man acts as the means (*Rangatira*) by which the sacred *mana* of the ancestors and the Gods may flow to reach the people, while women are the key (*Ruruarangatra*) to accessing that wisdom.[56]

> There was a clearly defined reciprocal process in the performance of all activities. Ko etahi mahi, e kore e taea e te tane, ko etahi mahi, e kore e taea e te wahine, some tasks are more appropriately performed by men and similarly some tasks are more appropriately performed by women. He rereke te mana o te wahine, he rereke te mana o te tane – the authority/prestige of women is different from that of men.[57]

Contrary to current beliefs, many Maori women are considered to possess both *mana* (authority, influence) and be *tapu* (sacred), including being able to act as *tohunga* (priests) such as Rimana Hii of Waihou. Rather than a society based on laws, as understood within Western society, Maori were governed by *tapu* which therefore gave women a lot of power. Birthrights within the *hapu*

---

53 Rei *supra*, note 9.
54 Page 20.
55 Ra, M. Wahine Ma Tapu a Io: The Role of Women in Leading Maori Through the Twenty First Century (Te Kauwhata: Mitaki Ra Publications, 2000) 20.
56 Ibid., 30.
57 Upenga, V., Rata, R. and Nepe, T. 'Whaia Te Iti Kahurangi: Maori Women Reclaiming Autonomy' in Puna Wairere (ed.) Essays by Maori (Wellington: New Zealand Planning Council, 1990) 10.

(tribe) could be traced through men or women and because of their *tapu* many women outranked their husbands so their children inherited their status from the woman, including the rank of chief. As chiefs, women could instigate and participate in war, as well as participating in the peace process. Some women had the authority to represent their tribe, such as Waitohi who persuaded her *iwi* to relocate to the Horowhenua District.[58] The *tapu* of women, as 'the channel between the realm of divine forces and the human realm' and their gender, which possessed them with special powers in relation to *tapu*, meant women even had the power to make people *noa*, or free from dangerous *tapu*.[59]

In daily life, women were traditionally responsible for child care, food preparation and weaving but shared the growing and gathering of food with men. This description should not detract from the fact that certain elements of Maori culture can be interpreted as patriarchal, for example few tribes permit women to speak on the *Marae* (meeting house), yet this must be balanced by the fact that other tribes do, including Ngati Kahungunu and Ngati Porou. What is clear is that traditionally Maori women were revered in society and carried out roles and functions that created a harmonious balance to the roles and functions of men. What is also clear is that the equilibrium between Maori men and women would be shaken with the arrival of the Pakeha settlors, inspiring claims that 'women's history, identity, spirit and confidence in themselves was taken over by the colonial mindset and the surge of Christianity and assimilation'.[60]

The status of Maori women in colonial times

The arrival and impact of the Pakeha settlors on the status of Maori women has been described thus: 'the white man came, imposing his god, wielding his technology, indulging his avarice and greed ... following what the missionaries taught — the defacement of women as unclean, the elevation of God the father, god as *man*'.[61] A second, equally disturbing description of colonial writers, such as Elsdon Best and Percy Smith, consolidates the picture that Pakeha settlement undermined the status of Maori women:

> the colonizer found a land of noble savages narrating his/her stories of the wonder of women. Their myths and beliefs had to be reshaped and

---

58 Rei *supra*, note 9.

59 Mikaere *supra*, note 14, 67.

60 'The Status and Autonomy of Māori Women as Viewed through Selected Kaupapa Māori Narratives' (MAOR 480: submitted by Henderson, M., Te Tari Māori, Te Whare Wānanga o Otāgo, Ōtepoti) 5.

61 Emphasis added in order to highlight the consistent theme in literature that one of the reasons the relative equality of Maori women was disturbed was in order to perpetuate Christian teachings which are premised on God the creator being male and thus divinity resting in the hands of men: Awekotuku, N. *Mana Wahine Maori* (Auckland: New Women's Press, 1993) 18.

retold ... in the retelling of our myths, by Maori male informants to Pakeha male writers who lacked the understanding and significance of Maori cultural beliefs, Maori women find their mana wahine destroyed.[62]

The 'industrialist mentality'[63] whereby women were chattels that characterised Western society was adopted by Pakeha historians with the resulting degradation of the role of Maori women in New Zealand history but more catastrophically 'the view Maori men have of women now appears no different from the non-Maori view of women of the last 150 years'.[64] Pakeha historians did not have an understanding of the nuances in Maori culture to understand the significance of the role played by women and throughout time these roles have been degraded so that even Maori men view the role of women as inferior. This was apparent by 1893 when the Maori Parliament debated the vote for Maori women which was originally rejected because 'what use is suffrage to women who comprehend even less than their Pakeha sisters their right to put in power an alternative government?'[65]

Despite the doubt expressed by men, Maori women did win the right to vote. In 1897, a motion by Meri Mangakahia of Te Rarawa that women could vote in the Kotahitanga Maori Parliament was passed. Mangakahia noted that men's efforts to change land legislation and address Maori grievances had thus far failed claiming it was time women were given the chance.[66] She speculated that perhaps it would be through the appointment of women members that Maori grievances may finally be heard as 'perhaps the Queen may listen to the petitions if they are presented by her Maori sisters, since she is a woman as well'.[67] This victory was twofold because Maori women had also won the right to stand as members of Parliament long before Pakeha women did and Maori women with the mandate of their *iwi* had always been permitted to speak on their behalf in the house. This victory represented not only the continuing spirit of Maori women in the face of Maori men having adopted the colonial patriarchal construct, it also highlighted that the struggle of Maori women was unique and borne alone. For example, in 1893, when women won the right to vote in New Zealand, the reform movement had to be conviced that Maori women equally merited the privilege. The battle faced by Maori women has been fought in isolation and has characterised and contributed to the status of Maori women today.

62 Mikaere *supra*, note 14, 71.

63 'The Status and Autonomy of Māori Women as Viewed Through Selected Kaupapa Māori Narratives' (MAOR 480: submitted by Henderson, M., Te Tari Māori, Te Whare Wānanga o Otāgo, Ōtepoti) 9.

64 Henare, D. in Brown, A. (ed.) *Mana Wahine Women Who Show the Way* (Auckland: Reed Books, 1994) 21.

65 Awekotuku *supra*, note 61, 45.

66 Mikaere *supra*, note 14, 120.

67 Ofner *supra*, note 9, 23.

The status of Maori women today

Maori women have never been short of a voice for the purpose of protest, but the manner in which that voice has been expressed has been consistently unique from the earliest days when women Maori chieftains expressed their anger by lifting their skirts. The lack of a 'universal sisterhood'[68] between Maori and Pakeha women, as each group faced different adversities, led to Maori feminists in the 1970s calling upon Pakeha women to think about the positions of power they held, as Pakeha, and the way the choices of these women impacted on Maori. For Pakeha feminists, their 'rage as an oppressed group was directed at [changing] dominant white structures' but because it was these very structures that were the source of oppression for Maori they were perceived to include 'white women as much as white men'.[69] The focus of struggle for Maori women has been aimed at the structure of Pakeha society itself, rather than certain participants within it.

Throughout the twentieth century Maori women were active in calling for the establishment of Maori educational reform, the introduction of Maori history and language in schools, the protection of Maori culture, such as conducting weaving workshops, when Government policy was pro-integration, seeking Maori housing and agitating for more rights for women on the *Marae*. Maori women were also politically active for example calling for a boycott on sporting links with South Africa at a time when the Maori Council still advocated these ties. Thus, it can be seen that Maori women were focused on equality and the end of all discrimination, not just the discrimination of women. Although the concerns of Maori women were unique there continued to be interaction with Pakeha women and all the women interviewed for this project (both Maori and Pakeha) acknowledged 'shared goals', a 'sense of responsibility' and the impact of 'women's activism' globally.

During the second half of the twentieth century, and commensurate to the increased pace of international feminism, the profile of Maori women in New Zealand society rose. Since the 1970s, at about the time the settlement process was initiated, more Maori women have occupied senior *iwi* positions and many have taken on roles at the Tribunal as participants, claimants, administrators, counsel and representatives. Increasingly Maori women are employed throughout the public service, for example Tania Simpson elected to enter the civil services in order to acquire necessary skills and knowledge for her subsequent role in facilitating the relationship between Maori and the Government.[70] However, Maori women continue to draw a distinction between themselves and their Pakeha sisters, disputing that the Maori culture traditional oppresses women. Instead, the struggle for Maori women is to gain equality between Maori and Pakeha, in turn protecting and

68 Simpson *supra*, note 33.
69 Smith *supra*, note 18, 47.
70 Simpson *supra*, note 33.

promoting the Maori way of balance between the sexes, which would then undermine lingering Pakeha patriarchal constructs. There is an acknowledgement that Maori men have enjoyed the fruits of gender disparity based on Pakeha systems, but instead of focusing on this colonial legacy, Maori women are striving to foster their self-professed strength and support men in a unified bid for equality and recognition of Maori as partners in New Zealand society.

The role of women in the Treaty of Waitangi settlement negotiation and implementation

As noted above, Maori women play varied roles within the settlement process, although in accordance with customs of talking and debating on the *Marae*, Simpson notes that women seldom take lead negotiation roles. The roles undertaken have been assumed with a 'huge amount of responsibility', given the dual necessities of both acting in an unbiased capacity as a functionary of the process and as a member of the Maori community.[71] For example, Dr Aroha Harris spoke of ensuring she was not overly emotive in the face of what can be harrowing evidence, because she did not want to behave in any way that fuelled the perception that she might be biased, particularly perceptions that that bias might be based on being Maori.

A particularly notable contribution to the settlement process that is expressly linked with the fact the relevant individuals are women and Maori, is in their contribution as orators. The recording of oral history which serves to remember and record 'the injustices of the colonial past'[72] is one of the most significant achievements of the settlement process and women as the bearers of *whanaungatanga* (family values and history) are primarily responsible for passing that history on.[73] Women are also the singers of *Waiata* (song) which was accepted as a mechanism for giving historical evidence in the Muriwhenua Fisheries Claim.

It is fair to characterise the various contributions of women to the settlement process as groundbreaking, irrespective of whether the Tribunal itself is evaluated in terms of success. Prior to the establishment of the Tribunal, the Maori Women's League had been fundamental in agitating for changes in Government policy towards Maori, coming up with practical solutions such as the establishment of Maori schools that would both educate Maori children but also protect Maori culture through the transmission of *Tikanga Maori* (the Maori ways of doing things) to younger generations. When the Government was slow to respond it was a march led by Whina Cooper from the top of the country on foot to Parliament in Wellington, rather than the land occupation at Parliament by protestors which the Government largely

Cultural retention (handwritten marginal note)

71 Harris *supra*, note 40.
72 Binney and Chaplin *supra*, note 22, 27.
73 *Whanaungatanga* means family values: Binney and Chaplin *supra*, note 22, 3.

ignored (after consulting with Whina Cooper as to whether the protests had any mandate from Maori), that was a major catalyst for the establishment of the Tribunal in 1975. Whina Cooper's contribution is one of, if not the, most notorious. Born 1895, Whina was an early pioneer for Maori women, for example frustrated by women's inability to speak on the *Marae*, she built her own *marae*, calling it a Parish Hall allowing anyone the chance to speak.[74] She was elected the first chairwoman of the Maori Women's Welfare League and in that role sought to address inequalities for women leading a report to the Government that resulted in the construction of 400 state houses for Maori in Auckland. The League was, until the establishment of the New Zealand Maori Council in 1962, the only national Maori body and non-political pressure group for representations to Government on Maori issues.[75]

Another notable woman was Whetu Tirikatene-Sullivan, who was the youngest woman, as well as being the first Maori woman elected to Parliament in 1967, and appointed to Cabinet aged 35. Whetu initiated private Members' bills to address injustice to Maori including the Maori Language Bill to put in place measures for the promotion and protection of Maori language. She was instrumental in a caucus investigation of the effects of Government policies on Maori, was a member of the Select Committee that worked to introduce the *Tangata Whenua* voting system that allowed Maori to vote anywhere within the Maori electorate rather than being required to cast special votes that often led to invalid votes and effective disenfranchisement.[76]

It was the incremental effect of efforts by women throughout the 1950s, 1960s and 1970s in thinking of solutions within the parameters of what would be politically feasible while also achieving forward momentum that made the changes in Government policy towards Maori possible. Maori women showed a willingness to work with the Government to seek solutions and only then did the Government reciprocate and for the first time actively consult Maori. In so doing, Tania Simpson speculates that an accord was reached whereby the settlement process is not simply about justice, but aims to move the relationship between Maori and Pakeha forward seeking 'progress and evolution [rather] than unity'.[77]

Maori women continue to play a role in the settlement process that can be characterised as groundbreaking. Instead of merely calling for monetary compensation, women have been instrumental in seeking to diversify the nature of settlements. For example, *Te Runanga Kuia* (a women's *hui*/meeting offering views on the relationship between the Government and Maori) called on the Government to 'listen to the cries of our people and realise that

74 Boon, K. *Whina Cooper* (Wellington: Kotuku Publishing, 1993) 11.
75 King *supra*, note 5, 479.
76 Boon, K. *Whetu Tirikatene-Sullivan* (Wellington: Kotuku Publishing, 2006).
77 Simpson *supra*, note 33.

we know what's best for ourselves' imploring that Maori be given 'resources to help ourselves ... because how can they supply a cure for our Maori ills, when they don't know anything about our aches and pains'.[78] This suggestion has been translated into a variety of proposals including calling on the Government to finance the television broadcast of the relevant *iwi*'s story and the financing of young Maori to dramatise the story of Maori grievances on stage and radio.

The roles of Maori women in, and preceding, the settlement process have been varied and can be described as non-typical in the various contributions made. The final question is whether the role played by those women can also be described as effective in terms of addressing New Zealand's colonial past and in relation to viewing the settlement process as a non-traditional TJ mechanism.

The effectiveness of the settlement process in addressing New Zealand's colonial past

It was noted above that both criticism and praise have been directed towards the settlement process. This final section breaks down the analysis by focusing on the four features of TJ identified in the Joinet Report on TJ to discuss the effectiveness of the settlement process and in particular the extent that women have been instrumental in any success.

Justice

The first feature of TJ is the attainment of justice and therefore the question is whether there has been justice for Maori as a result of Crown breaches of the Treaty. Yet, justice is a largely indeterminate concept due to its subjectivity, thus there can be no accurate determination of what justice entails and whether it has been attained unless the 'victim' party is consulted.

In the sense that for the first time Maori has received a national forum at which to air their grievances the settlement process can be seen as effective.[79] However, and as noted throughout this piece, the major criticism continues to be that the substance of the claims by Maori, being a loss of *tikanga* Maori (Maori ways of doing things), and disparity between Maori and Pakeha continues to be overlooked. It is in this way that the role of women is particularly notable because they have been consistently responsible for highlighting where the discrepancies between Maori and Pakeha arise, for example in health and education of children. While Maori men have more readily adopted Pakeha traditions and advocated for the financial settlements which have without doubt given Maori a much greater degree of financial

---

78 'Speaking from My Own Experience: Nga Mea I Whakairongia e Nga Tau Ki Toku Hinengaro' (New Zealand Runanga Kuia Proceedings, 1993) 25–28.

79 Simpson supra, note 33.

autonomy, it is women who have sought a return to or an assimilation of Maori traditions in New Zealand society in accordance with the promise made by the Crown under the Treaty to respect Maori sovereignty. As Simpson summarised 'there is no disability in Maori women's participation', there is only disability in the limited outcomes of that participation thus far.[80]

Truth and the development of collective history

In the same way that the capturing of New Zealand's history by Pakeha male historians can be described as a version of the truth, so too can the settlement process and airing of claims before the Tribunal be viewed as a version of the truth. As noted, the Tribunal is inquisitorial only and there is no advocacy function in which to test evidence, yet there is the flexibility for non-traditional forms of evidence such as the giving of oral history that expand the range of perceptions and experiences able to be captured. Arguably, it is an accumulation of all these forms of history that best capture a collective history of New Zealand in a way that had not happened before the settlement process began. Likewise the strong participation of women, for example in the traditional oral narratives used at the Tribunal, suggest that the history emerging is not gender biased in the same way that the history captured in textbooks had been for much of the twentieth century.

The role of women is also important because they have often led the calls within the settlement negotiations for public education of the settlement process and outcomes. Interestingly, the contributions of three Pakeha women are notable in terms of contributing to the telling of truth, creating a post-colonial collective New Zealand history and raising awareness of Maori grievances. As part of the settlements, the Crown has been required to apologise to Maori and in addition to capturing these apologies in the relevant settlement deeds, Queen Elizabeth II and both female Prime Ministers of New Zealand (being Helen Clark and Jenny Shipley) have made formal apologies acknowledging and admitting the wrongdoing by the Crown.[81]

Reparation

Financial reparation has been a strong characteristic of the settlement process reaching millions of dollars and incorporating a range of other measures such as the acquisition of state assets and giving of apologies. Yet, as with justice, reparation as a means for attaining justice is largely a subjective matter and it has been noted a number of times here that financial reparation is being eschewed in favour of more substantive recognition of the breach by the return or inclusion of Maori traditions into Pakeha society. Harris identified

---

80 Simpson *supra*, note 33.
81 'Formal Apology to Te Uri O Hau' (5 July 2004): http://www.beehive.govt.nz/release/ formal-apology-te-uri-o-hau.

the debate between the importance of establishing the historical record and return to Maori ways on the one hand and the economic cost on the other as being a generational one, while Simpson considered there was 'little space for creativity' within negotiations so, for example, the return of Maori relics is given little serious consideration. A second reason for this is that negotiating settlement is itself a long drawn out process conducted under the eye of the public, therefore the negotiated outcome is more a compromise reflecting the temporal and political context. Thus, while the provision of reparations in the financial sense is notable, the effectiveness of reparation in recognition of the breach is less so.

It is perhaps for this reason that the Mana Wahine claim was lodged in 1993. The claim was lodged in the context of all women having been recently removed from the shortlist of appointments to the Treaty of Waitangi Fisheries Commission and since 1987 the Government recognising 'the mandate of an extremely select group of Maori men to act as negotiators on behalf of all men' 'despite that mandate being challenged by *iwi* all over the country'[82] implying that Maori women had less value than Maori males or even Pakeha males. Thus the settlement process was at the time being blatantly dominated by men who were not taking into account the more substantive nature of the breach in question, opting instead for financial settlements with little *iwi* consultation.

The claim seeks to bring about a change in structure and process both of Maori women in society as well as a more substantive recognition of the grievances Maori hold towards the Crown. It seeks to affirm the status of the Maori Women's League asking for equal consultation in the same way the New Zealand Maori Council and Maori Congress are consulted.[83]

The claim alleged that the Crown breached its Treaty obligations to Maori women by failing to protect their *rangitiratanga* and status in Maori society, and is a departure from the more traditional claims relating to land acquisition. The response from the Government, expressed by then Minister of Maori Affairs Doug Kidd, was that the lack of status accorded to Maori women was not the Crown's responsibility or in other words 'in the Crown's estimation it is Maori society's definition of Maori women that renders them subservient'.[84] Thus, it would seem that the Mana Wahine claim highlights the limitations of the largely financial rubric of reparations employed thus far under the settlements process given the continuing failure to recognise the substantive nature of the breach of faith and racial oppression that underlies Maori grievances, rather than just monetary loss.

82 Mikaere *supra*, note 14, 130–131.
83 Henare *supra*, note 64, 22.
84 Mikaere *supra*, note 14, 131.

Guarantees of non-repetition

The principle guarantee given by the New Zealand Government to affirm its relationship with Maori and protect against the continuation or repetition of breaches of the Treaty of Waitangi is found in the 1975 Treaty of Waitangi Act, which states in the Preamble the aim to 'provide for the observance, and confirmation, of the principles of the Treaty of Waitangi'. In addition, the settlement process can be characterised in terms of a movement from grievance and anger to post-settlement development. The shift in focus from monetary compensation to the protection and assurance of equality for Maori and Pakeha in New Zealand society is arguably a more entrenched assurance that New Zealand's colonial history will not be repeated, and more than just the provision of financial compensation.

Conclusion: the contemporary conflict

It is difficult to measure with any accuracy the success of the settlement process, if for no other reason than because the process is an ongoing one. This chapter has attempted some form of analysis by referring to the four elements of TJ identified in the UN Secretary-General's Special Report on TJ, being truth, justice, reparation and guarantees of non-repetition identifying instances where these goals have been attained and noting in what ways these TJ features are still considered absent. In addition to the foregoing analysis, some concluding remarks are made here in the manner of reflecting on the extent to which Maori and Pakeha cultures have blended to form a post-colonial New Zealand culture. This exercise is appropriate given that it was the Crown's failure to respect Maori culture as obligated to under the Treaty that underpinned the conflict between Maori and Pakeha.

Certainly, in the first 100 or so years after the Treaty was signed, New Zealand was a colonial dominion of Great Britain. However, the escalating publicity in the 1970s that preceded the establishment of the Tribunal, as well as measures such as the adoption of *kohanga reo* (instituting Maori language), promoted awareness that New Zealand was no longer a colonial dominion but was an independent nation. There was both awareness that Pakeha New Zealanders were not merely English descendants, as well as a renaissance in terms of recognising Maori's place in New Zealand society. The increasing sympathy for the grievances of Maori and acceptance that over 100 years of colonial rule meant the Maori community was vulnerable in comparison to Pakeha, as borne out in countless statistics[85] relating to health, education, mortality, income and lifestyle justified the extraordinary means being taken to redress the balance in the form of the Tribunal and other means to adopt Maori culture into New Zealand culture. Historian

---

85 'Speaking from My Own Experience: Nga Mea I Whakairongia e Nga Tau Ki Toku Hinengaro' (New Zealand Runanga Kuia Proceedings, 1993) 29.

Michael King described the view of the Pakeha community being that 'the special measures undertaken as a Treaty obligation to protect and strengthen Maori language and culture were necessary because of their vulnerability and [because] such measures would not in any way threaten the viability of Pakeha culture'.[86]

The acceptance and understanding of Pakeha that measures in recompense were necessary was not, of itself, indicative that Maori culture was afforded the respect guaranteed to it under the Treaty. But, by the 1990s, there were increasing examples of a wider societal embracing of Maori culture. In 1998 Te Papa Tongarewa (the national museum of New Zealand) refused to remove an exhibit the Christain community claimed to be offensive while at the same time an exhibit was taken from the Museum of Art and History that *Tainui kaumatua* (respected elders of the Tainui tribe) considered offensive. Similarly, in 2002 Transit New Zealand ended work on a section of state highway that the local tribe considered would disturb a guardian spirit.[87]

It is an inescapable fact that, as this is written in 2012, New Zealand society comprises Maori and Pakeha communities, which have evolved in a complementary manner.

> Pakeha culture continues to borrow and to learn from Maori. That was one of the features that made it different from its European culture of origin. It took words and concepts (mana, tapu, whanau, taonga, haka, tuangwwaewae), attitudes (the tradition of hospitality which, in the early nineteenth century, was so much more visible in the Maori community), ways of doing business (an increasing willingness to talk issues through to consensus), and rites of passage (relinquishing formal, structured funeral services).[88]

And of course, whether rightly or wrongly, Maori have been required to adopt Pakeha culture in all facets of life.

This adoption of Pakeha culture started with the arrival of the first colonial settlors whose gun power left Maori with little choice but to assimilate and there are countless examples of Maori being forced to accept Pakeha standards, including the adoption of more conservative modes of dress to escape the tag of being savage. There are examples where Maori unilaterally elected to adopt Pakeha ways into the Maori community including the establishment of a Maori Parliament and a Maori King mirroring the British Parliamentary system. Such examples can be seen as acts of good faith on the part of Maori, accepting the Pakeha presence and permitting the address of grievances through channels and forums that reflect the Pakeha tradition

86 King *supra*, note 5, 516.
87 All examples taken from King *supra*, note 5, 517.
88 Ibid., 519.

rather than insisting that traditional Maori means of dispute settlement be used. However, it is the adoption of Pakeha standards that lies at the heart of the Mana Wahine claim currently before the Waitangi Tribunal, and the women who brought this claim are in fact seeking compensation on the grounds that Maori and Pakeha cultures were forced to assimilate.

The basis of the Mana Wahine claim is that the Crown failed in its Treaty obligation to ensure equality between Maori and Pakeha, in particular as that obligation was owed to women. The claim is that the patriarchal nature of Pakeha culture in 1840 was one of the many features adopted by Maori and that as a result Maori women were excluded from many decision-making processes, one of the consequences being that Maori men have been largely unsuccessful in seeking to have Maori grievances addressed. In so doing, Article III of the Treaty, which states Maori were to be granted 'all the rights and privilege of British subjects', was breached. It would be going too far to argue that the Mana Wahine claim is a condemnation of the fact that Maori and Pakeha cultures have blended into modern New Zealand society, which in itself is contended here to be evidence that the settlement process has resulted in a degree of success. Instead, the reference to the Mana Wahine claim aims to highlight that to the extent the settlement process remains deficient, the exclusion of women may be a contributing factor.

The engagement of civil society was recognised by the UN Secretary-General as a fundamental factor in the success of TJ and this overview of New Zealand's experience illustrated that the participation of many elements of New Zealand society in terms of negotiating and implementing the settlement process is key to the achievements thus far. However, it has also been shown that the roles played by Maori women were often overlooked, marginalised or the women in question had to be forceful in seeking recognition for their views. It will remain speculative whether greater recognition of the Maori system of equality between genders would have led to a reduction in the scope of Maori grievances because women were afforded the chance to speak and to a greater extent given formal rules in the settlement process. But it can be stated that while New Zealand is an effective example of non-traditional TJ to be studied for consideration in other conflict situations, it remains another reminder of the fact that the participation of women must be ensured, as an essential component of TJ.

2 Women, peace and security

Mainstreaming gender in transitional justice processes

Amy Barrow[1]

Introduction

For societies emerging from conflict or an era of repressive rule, the transitional period offers an opportunity to negotiate peace agreements, determine transitional justice mechanisms to seek accountability for past human rights abuses as well as lay the foundation for institutional reforms. Since the inception of 'transitional justice'[2] in the early 1990s, the mechanisms through which accountability has been sought have expanded and evolved beyond traditional mechanisms such as prosecutions, truth commissions, institutional reform and reparations to broader notions of nation-building and regime change. However, the intersection between gender and transitional justice has often been overlooked.

Bell and O'Rourke suggest that feminist unease with transitional justice mechanisms stems from concern over 'what exactly transitional justice is transiting "from" and "to,"' rather than the institutional design of transitional justice mechanisms.[3] Women are often excluded from the forums which settle upon and design transitional justice mechanisms,[4] exacerbating normative legal gaps, which result in further exclusion throughout all stages of transition.[5] This exclusion is particularly detrimental given that post-conflict transitions potentially provide a critical juncture to reorient traditional gender roles and advance the status of women.

The transitional feminist movement of the 1990s pushed for significant reforms to counter the culture of impunity towards violence against

1 Amy Barrow is Assistant Professor in the Faculty of Law at the Chinese University of Hong Kong. The author would like to thank Angela Kar Yee Tsui for her research support.
2 The term 'transitional justice' was coined by Neil Kritz in reference to a range of mechanisms employed during post-conflict transitions including trials, commission of enquiry and reparation. See Bell, Christine 'Transitional Justice, Interdisciplinarity and the State of the "Field" or "Non-Field"' (2009) *International Journal of Transitional Justice* 3(1), 7.
3 Bell, C. and O'Rourke, C. 'Does Feminism Need a Theory of Transitional Justice: An Introductory Essay' (2007) *International Journal of Transitional Justice* 1(1), 35.
4 Ibid., 23.
5 Ni Aolain, F. 'Women, Security and the Patriarchy of International Transitional Justice' (2009) *Human Rights Quarterly* 31(4), 1057.

women during post-conflict transitions, by recognising gender-based violence as a crime of war. In 1995, the International Committee of the Red Cross (ICRC) declared that rape represented a 'grave breach' under Article 147 of Geneva Convention IV, though there has been no explicit amendment to the text of the Convention to support this acknowledgement. The ad hoc criminal tribunals of the mid-1990s addressed gross human rights violations which took place in the former Yugoslavia and Rwanda, securing greater acknowledgement of the use and extent of sexual violence in armed conflict. The International Criminal Tribunal for the former Yugoslavia (ICTY) was instrumental in advancing accountability for sexual violence.[6] Recognition of rape as a crime against humanity in the landmark case of *Akayesu*[7] at the International Criminal Tribunal for Rwanda (ICTR) further supported the integration of gender in transitional justice mechanisms.

A principal drawback of these reforms, however, has been the tendency to focus narrowly on sexual violence,[8] effectively equating sexual security with security, which could have negative repercussions for women.[9] The development of soft law mechanisms including the unanimous adoption of Security Council Resolution 1325[10] (SCR 1325), which focuses on women, peace and security in October 2000, created renewed optimism that the Security Council was moving beyond a victim-centred rhetoric to the recognition of women's roles as actors and protagonists in conflict prevention, conflict resolution and peacebuilding.

This chapter will consider the development of soft law mechanisms at the Security Council, focusing on SCR 1325 and subsequent resolutions on women, peace and security to evaluate the role of these instruments in mainstreaming gender in transitional justice processes. First, the chapter will analyse and critique SCR 1325 to consider the normative impact of the resolution. Second, subsequent resolutions on women, peace and security (SCR 1820,[11] 1888,[12] 1889,[13] 1960[14]) will be examined with a view to considering how these soft law mechanisms, along with SCR 1325, support gender justice including responses to disarmament, demobilisation and reintegration, accountability for sexual violence and broader aims including women's

---

6 Campbell, K. 'The Gender of Transitional Justice: Law, Sexual Violence and the International Criminal Tribunal for the Former Yugoslavia' (2007) International Journal of Transitional Justice 1(3), 412.

7 *Prosecutor* v. *Jean Paul Akayesu*, 2 September 1998, ICTR-96-4-T, para. 585. As noted by the judgment, rape is classified as a Crime against Humanity under Article 3(g) of the Statute of the International Tribunal for Rwanda.

8 Bell and O'Rourke *supra*, note 3, 34.

9 Ni Aolain *supra*, note 5, 1066.

10 SCR 1325, 31 October 2000.

11 SCR 1820, 19 June 2008.

12 SCR 1888, 30 September 2009.

13 SCR 1889, 5 October 2009.

14 SCR 1960, 16 December 2010.

participation in peacebuilding. This chapter will also consider how these soft law mechanisms filter down to the micro level, by examining civil society's engagement with SCR 1325 in Nepal.

Mainstreaming gender in transitional justice mechanisms: the role of the Security Council

Prior to the adoption of SCR 1325, the UN Security Council had largely overlooked the intersection between gender and armed conflict and in many ways has been resistant to engaging with feminist visions of peace and security including broader considerations of human rights and social justice.[15] During the Cold War in particular, the security sector proved impervious to women peace activists, which Enloe links to a deeply militarised understanding of security premised on specific notions of masculinity.[16] Further, the majority of peace processes instigated through the Security Council have been based on the negative peace paradigm (absence of military warfare, restricted to peace agreements and high-level negotiations), which focuses on the cessation of conflict. Although the negative peace paradigm's limited objectives will produce tangible outcomes in the sense that warfare will end or continue, without addressing the root causes of war, there is a risk that underlying power imbalances are overlooked during the transition from conflict to 'peace'.

Criticism of the negative peace paradigm may in part stem from the Security Council's organisational set-up, which is perceived to be 'state-centred, militaristic and male dominated'.[17] From the gendered articulations of subjects and objects which run through policy documentation, to the rules of procedure of the Security Council, Shepherd suggests that men are positioned in a way which dictates their role as the power holders.[18] Similarly, the state and non-state protagonists of peace agreements are predominantly male, which influences the design of transitional justice mechanisms,[19] leading to the exclusion of gender at all stages of transition. However, since the end of the Cold War, a number of developments in public international law may support the integration of a gender perspective in transitional justice processes including the empowerment of women as protagonists.

---

15 Otto, D. 'Security the "Gender Legitimacy" of the UN Security Council: Prising Gender from its Historical Moorings' (Faculty of Law Studies Research Paper No. 92, University of Melbourne, 2004) available at http://ssrn.com/abstract=585923 (last accessed 3 January 2011), 7.

16 Enloe, C. *The Morning After: Sexual Politics at the End of the Cold War* Berkley, CA; London: University of California Press (1993), 3.

17 Shepherd, L. 'Power and Authority in the Production of United Nations Security Council Resolution 1325' (2008) *International Studies Quarterly* 52(2), 389.

18 Ibid., 395.

19 Bell and O'Rourke *supra*, note 3, 25.

gender mainstreaming

The adoption of the Beijing Declaration and Platform for Action (BPFA) in 1995[20] was instrumental in formalising the concept of gender mainstreaming, in addition to drawing attention to the position and experience of women in armed conflict and its aftermath. Gender mainstreaming is the process of assessing the implications of legislation, policies or programmes on both men and women at all stages of design, implementation and monitoring.[21] In contrast with other gender equality initiatives such as equal treatment, the central purpose of gender mainstreaming is to achieve equality of outcome rather than equality of opportunity, which could strengthen the inclusion of women during post-conflict transitions. Further, the Security Council adopted a number of thematic resolutions focused on civilians and children in armed conflict.[22] In line with these developments, the creation of the NGO working group on women, peace and security[23] provided the impetus to push for formal recognition of women's roles through the adoption of a thematic Security Council resolution on women, peace and security.[24]

Initially comprising a select alliance of civil society organisations including the Women's International League for Peace and Freedom (WILPF), Amnesty International, International Alert, the Women's Commission for Refugee Women and Children (WCRWC) and the Hague Appeal for Peace (HAP), the NGO working group was heavily involved in the drafting of SCR 1325. The initial goal of the NGO working group was to secure recognition of women's role as peacebuilders, but the legitimacy of this aim may be undermined by the suggestion that SCR 1325 along with other similar thematic resolutions, instead merely provided the Security Council with an opportunity to 'arrest its flagging legitimacy' in the post-Cold War period.[25]

Though the objectives behind the Security Council's adoption of SCR 1325 may be contentious, for women activists the unanimous adoption of

20 Strategic Objective E on women and armed conflict sets out a number of strategic objectives: Strategic objective E1, 'Increase the participation of women in conflict resolution at decision-making levels and protect women living in situations of armed and other conflicts or under foreign occupation'; and Strategic objective E4, 'Promote women's contribution to fostering a culture of peace'. Fourth World Conference on Women, Declaration and Platform for Action, A/CONF.177/20, 15 September 2005.
21 Report of the Economic and Social Council for the year 1997, A/52/3/Rev.1, 18 September 1997, 24.
22 See for example SCR 1261, 25 August 1999 and SCR 1314, 11 August 2000 on children and armed conflict.
23 The NGO working group continues to advocate for the full and equal participation of women in international peace and security affairs, including monthly action points (MAP) on women, peace and security, available at www.womenpeacesecurity.org/ (last accessed 15 December 2011).
24 Shepherd, *supra*, note 17, 388.
25 Otto, D. 'The Exile of Exclusion: Reflections on Gender Issues in International Law Over the Last Decade' (2009) *Melbourne Journal of International Law* 10(1), 11, 21.

SCR 1325 signalled the 'strongest expression'[26] given to women, peace and security. The centralisation of gender at the highest echelon of the United Nations (UN) proved encouraging and gave women peace activists a renewed sense of optimism that the Security Council was shifting away from a victim-based rhetoric to instead focus on the empowerment of women, by recognising the role of women in conflict prevention, conflict resolution and peacebuilding. Interpretation of the scope and content of the Resolution give a sense of SCR 1325's potential in supporting the integration of a gender perspective during post-conflict transitions.

Scope and content of SCR 1325

The preamble and 18 clauses which comprise SCR 1325 address the empowerment and protection of women in four distinct areas of peace and security process: access to decision-making, strategies to address gender-based violence, peacekeeping operations and disarmament, demobilisation and reintegration (DDR). SCR 1325's preamble makes specific reference to conflict prevention and recalls a number of Security Council resolutions that have addressed both the position of children and armed conflict[27] and the protection of civilians in armed conflict.[28]

Reference is also made to the Namibia Plan of Action on Mainstreaming a Gender Perspective in Multidimensional Peace Support Operations,[29] which identifies practical ways that women can be better integrated into peace processes. Building on the commitments made in the BPFA and the General Assembly Report, 'Women 2000: Gender Equality, Development and Peace for the Twenty-First Century',[30] the substantial focus on gender creates an additional dimension in the UN system's understanding of armed conflict.

Although not creating any substantive rights as such, SCR 1325 is underpinned by substantive legal provisions. Importantly, reference is made to existing international human rights provisions and international humanitarian law. These include particular obligations under the Geneva Conventions

---

26 Cockburn, C. *From Where We Stand: War, Women's Activism & Feminist Analysis* London & New York: Zed Books (2007), 142.

27 See SCR 1261, 25 August 1999 and SCR 1314, 11 August 2000 on children and armed conflict.

28 See SCR 1265, 17 September 1999 and SCR 1296, 19 April 2000 on the protection of civilians in armed conflict.

29 Namibia was instrumental in taking SCR 1325 forward at the Security Council backing NGOs and women's organisations' calls to adopt the resolution. Windhoek Declaration: Namibia Plan of Action on Mainstreaming a Gender Perspective in Multidimensional Peace Support Operations, Windhoek, Namibia, 31 May 2000.

30 Report of the Ad Hoc Committee of the Whole of the twenty-third special session of the General Assembly Women 2000: Gender Equality, Development and Peace for the Twenty-First Century, A/S-23/10/Rev.1, 2000.

of 1949[31] and the Additional Protocols of 1977;[32] the Convention on the Elimination of all forms of Discrimination Against Women (CEDAW)[33] and the Optional Protocol of 1999, and relevant provisions of the International Criminal Court. Operative paragraph 10 of SCR 1325, for example, is directed at the protection of women and girls from rape, sexual abuse and other violence, echoing gender-specific protection provisions under international humanitarian law.

SCR 1325 encompasses a number of gender mainstreaming strategies and several of the provisions focus on increasing gender sensitivity both at a field level and in military operations. The process of gender mainstreaming could take a number of forms including the adoption of a gender lens in pre-deployment peacekeeping training. For example, under operative paragraph 6, which focuses on peacekeeping operations, the Secretary-General should provide guidelines to Member States on training, which will reflect the particular needs and experiences of women during conflict and its aftermath including HIV/AIDS awareness training. Additionally DDR processes should be planned in a way which take account of the complexity of women's multiple support roles in conflict. Many female unarmed ex-combatants are unable to access traditional DDR processes, which are designed on the basis of post-conflict reintegration support in exchange for a weapon. Significantly, the resolution also identifies the importance of integrating a gender perspective when negotiating and implementing peace agreements, the principal mechanism utilised to end violent conflict.[34]

There is, however, significant debate over what exactly a 'gender perspective' entails. While SCR 1325 encourages gender to be mainstreamed through peace and security operations, the nature of the resolution's focus on women's experience of armed conflict, risks gender being perceived as a synonym for women with a gender perspective similarly perceived as such. This alignment proves inherently problematic but is perhaps not to be unexpected. Gender mainstreaming strategies have largely adopted an integrationist approach, often referred to as 'add women and stir'. This

---

31 Geneva Conventions of 1949, e.g. Geneva Convention Relative to the Protection of Civilian Persons in Time of War, adopted 12 August 1949, 75 U.N.T.S 287 (entered into force 21 October 1950).

32 Additional Protocols to the Geneva Conventions of 1977, e.g. Protocol Additional to the Geneva Conventions of 12 August 1949, and Relating to the Protection of Victims of International Armed Conflicts (Protocol I), adopted 10 June 1977, 1125 U.N.T.S 3 (entered into force 7 December 1978) and Protocol Additional to the Geneva Conventions of 12 August 1949, and Relating to the Protection of Victims of Non-International Armed Conflicts (Protocol II), adopted 8 June 1977, 1125 U.N.T.S 609 (entered into force 7 December 1978).

33 Convention on the Elimination of All forms of Discrimination against Women, adopted 18 December 1979, 1249 U.N.T.S 13 (entered into force 3 September 1981).

34 Bell, C. and O'Rourke C. 'Peace Agreements of Pieces of Paper: UN SCR 1325 and Peace Negotiations and Agreements' (Research Paper No. 11-01, Transitional Justice Institute, University of Ulster), 9 March 2011.

integrationist approach fails to adopt a more radical means of deconstructing the gender bias that runs through UN systems, structures and operational policies, and falls short of challenging the masculine standard against which women's experiences are measured.

While there appears to be increasing awareness of women's participation and role in peacebuilding at the macro level, which may in part be related to the adoption of SCR 1325,[35] it is difficult to point to the implementation of any concrete norms regarding how women should be engaged in decision-making processes. Within SCR 1325, there is little exploration of tangible measures that could be used to improve accessibility, such as micro level educational campaigns, quotas or affirmative action. Pragmatically, NGOs and gender mainstreaming advocates have lobbied the UN and state actors using the BPFA, which stipulates that women should form a critical mass of 30 per cent in decision-making processes. Despite this provision, the majority of public officials involved in high-level peace negotiations, a central premise of the negative peace paradigm, continue to be predominantly male. Women are rarely included in formal peace processes.

While potentially opening up spaces for women's participation and the inclusion of a gender lens in policymaking, it is unlikely that SCR 1325's adoption indicates a shift away from militaristic and state-centric conceptions of security. The Resolution lacks enforcement mechanisms and the language is weak with SCR 1325 only able to 'call' upon parties to adopt measures to redress imbalances and foster a gender perspective that will deepen understanding of the gender bias that operates in conflict, thus seeking to strengthen gender equality.

Under operative paragraph 8, SCR 1325 also calls upon actors involved in peace negotiations and agreements to consider the 'special needs of women and girls during repatriation and resettlement and rehabilitation, reintegration and post conflict reconstruction'. Despite the scope to advocate for the increased protection of women and girls, SCR 1325 is not sophisticated enough to respond to structural and less overt forms of violence. If transitional justice mechanisms fail to broach uneven power relations, Bell and O'Rourke suggest that women risk losing 'the perverse equality gains of war and returning to the home and perhaps other forms of abuse'.[36]

A lack of engagement with women's structural inequality within SCR 1325 potentially avoids more probing questions including why the Security Council continues to follow a militaristic-centred approach to peacekeeping activities,[37] rather than longer term peacebuilding processes. As a result, it is

---

35 Bell, C. and O'Rourke C. 'Peace Agreements of Pieces of Paper? The Impact of UN SCR 1325 and Peace Processes and their Agreements' (2010) *International and Comparative Law Quarterly* 59, 942.

36 Bell and O'Rourke *supra*, note 3, 41.

37 Otto *supra*, note 25, 20.

unclear whether SCR 1325 succeeds in securing its protagonists vision of a transformative mechanism designed to empower women as central actors in peace and security processes during post-conflict transitions.

Implementing SCR 1325

There has been significant debate regarding the enforceability of SCR 1325 and whether the Resolution is legally binding. Though many NGOs refer to SCR 1325 as legally binding in their advocacy campaigns, the Resolution does not invoke Chapter VII of the UN Charter which enables the Security Council to enforce the implementation of resolutions. Under Article 25 of the UN Charter, Member States must adhere to decisions of the Security Council, and should therefore be encouraged to fulfil the aims and objectives of SCR 1325.[38] In practice, however, it is very difficult to hold international actors to account given the lack of enforceability for Security Council resolutions falling outside the remit of chapter VII.

NGOs and grassroots organisations have routinely called for identifiable and tangible benchmarks that will assist implementation but this will not necessarily enforce SCR 1325. To date, the majority of human rights instruments directly related to women's experiences of armed conflict have been 'soft law' in character, comprising General Assembly resolutions and declarations, which are legally unenforceable. However, soft law can enable greater cooperation by creating a space or entry point for the involvement of non-traditional actors with different values and objectives.[39] Further, soft law instruments, such as the BPFA, have exposed gaps within the international framework which over time could crystallise into hard law, thus allowing increased enforceability and accountability.

The transformative potential of SCR 1325 to provide either a systematic or operational shift in the functioning of the peace and security sector is debatable. Certainly, since the end of the Cold War, peace processes appear to be dependent not only on formal negotiation and mediation, but also on the inclusion of third party contributions including civil society actors.[40] These changes may be connected to a rise in non-traditional armed conflicts involving non-state actors such as militia and armed opposition groups, and not specifically tied to new developments in public international law such as SCR 1325. It appears that the diversification of armed conflict, involving multiple actors, may potentially allow for greater flexibility in how peace negotiations are broached.

---

38 UN Charter, Article 25. 'The Members of the United Nations agree to accept and carry out the decisions of the Security Council in accordance with the present Charter.'

39 Abbot, W.K. and Snidal, D. 'Hard and Soft Law in International Governance' (2000) *International Organisation* 54(3) 421, 423.

40 Haffar, W. 'Emergent Peacemakers: Cataloguing New Patterns of Activity in Post-Cold War Conflict' (2002) *PEPS* 8(2), 32.

Space may be created to incorporate a gender perspective, taking account of women and men's experiences of conflict, in contrast to traditional peace processes, which have generally proved restrictive. A multilayered approach to peacebuilding potentially has the capacity to engage civil society and women's organisations more effectively than high-level negotiations, centred on brokered peace agreements which do not necessarily afford space to third party actors and often seem removed from day to day recovery. However, the Security Council largely adopts militarised responses and economic sanctions, which often have a disproportionate impact on women, rather than actions centred on sustainable development and health.[41] Given that many institutions and specifically the UN Security Council favour the negative peace paradigm this may impact on the effectiveness of SCR 1325 as a feminist transitional justice mechanism if long-term peacebuilding objectives are overlooked in preference for narrowly applied peace negotiations and settlements.

Since the adoption of SCR 1325, there have been increasing references to women in peace agreements, with greater references recorded in those processes where the UN is engaged.[42] The 'inclusive language' running through UN documentation may, however, mask the reality on the ground, where women continue to be excluded. Bell and O'Rourke suggest that further consideration should be given to how SCR 1325 can be effectively implemented including what a 'gender perspective' truly entails in peace agreements.[43] While SCR 1325 has had a wider impact on institutional activity at the UN, Otto cautions activists against allowing SCR 1325 to be 'fully harnessed by the institution', which may conversely hinder the transformative effect of the resolution.[44]

Despite SCR 1325's overarching focus on armed conflict and the institutionalised approach to peacebuilding which perpetuates UN operational policies, SCR 1325 holds great promise in terms of its cross-cutting thematic engagement with gender equality and empowerment. For example, operative paragraph 1 of SCR 1325 *urges* Member States to ensure increased representation of women at all decision-making levels in national, regional and international institutions and mechanisms for the prevention, management and resolution of conflict'. This type of provision is significant as it points to the importance of women's inclusion not only in conflict resolution, but conflict prevention, which could strengthen SCR 1325's applicability to women's lives on the ground.

Further, operative paragraph 15 seeks to ensure that Security Council missions take gender considerations into account and the rights of women,

41 Charlesworth, H. 'Transforming the United Men's Club: Feminist Futures for the United Nations' (1995) *Transnational Law and Contemporary Problems* 4, 448.
42 Bell and O'Rourke *supra*, note 35, 954.
43 Ibid., 978.
44 Otto *supra*, note 25, 19.

through means including consultation with local and international women's groups. However, this provision solely applies to Security Council missions and fails to outline NGOs' wider consultative role in general peace and security affairs. The increased physical representation of women, does not necessarily translate into gender-sensitive policy outcomes, and may conversely lead to the essentialisation of 'women as peacebuilders' who appear characteristically equipped with such predisposed function to address the 'gender gap'.[45] Nevertheless the formal inclusion of women as peacebuilders is in itself significant.

SCR 1325 protagonists involved in the initial drafting of the resolution have recognised SCR 1325's transformative potential, but question whether SCR 1325's implementation may instead lie in a radical re-examination of masculinity, identity and peace and security processes. As Hill states:

> 1325 is potentially revolutionary as it could transform ways of understanding how security is conceived, protected and enforced ... But for this to happen, the focus has to move from women to men and this still hasn't happened. Perpetually problematising women, placing women, their absence or their victimhood at the centre of the problem of women, peace and security fails to notice the problematic role of masculine identities in security discourse and actual wars or the systematic overrepresentation of men.
>
> (Felicity Hill)[46]

This is not to undermine civil society women's organisations who have proactively lobbied the Security Council and Member States in an effort to recognise women's multiple roles during conflicts and strengthen the participation of women in peacebuilding processes. Examples of women's multiple roles and resilience both during and after armed conflict have been examined,[47] but still remain under-researched. However, the intersection between masculinity, peace and security needs to be examined alongside these examples of women's engagement to evaluate why there is sustained resistance to women's participation in decision-making processes.

As the Security Council is the governing body and authority behind SCR 1325, the key issue becomes whether peace processes based on the negative peace paradigm are appropriately tied to the aims and objectives of a Resolution

---

45 Ni Aolain, F. and Rooney, E. 'Underenforcement and Intersectionality: Gendered Aspects of Transition for Women' (2007) *International Journal of Transitional Justice* 1(3), 350.

46 Cohn, C., Kinsella, H. and Gibbings, S. (2004) *International Feminist Journal of Politics*, 6(1), 137.

47 See for example Coulter, C. 'Female Fighters in the Sierra Leone War: Challenging the Assumptions?' (2008) *Feminist Review*, 88(1); Moser, C.O.N. and Clark, F.C. (eds) *Victims, Perpetrators or Actors? Gender, Armed Conflict and Political Violence* London, Zed Books (2001); Al-Ali, N. and Pratt, N. 'Women's Organising and the Conflict in Iraq since 2003' (2008) *Feminist Review*, 88(1).

that seeks to transform women from victims to actors in the transition from conflict to peace. It is unlikely that SCR 1325 represents a radical shift in the Security Council's agenda to allow a more liberal understanding of peace and security. A number of follow-up thematic resolutions have been adopted, but the extent to which these resolutions build upon the commitments made in SCR 1325 is open to scrutiny.

Follow-up resolutions on women, peace and security

SCR 1325 has spurred a number of policy initiatives, stemming from the macro level. Several Member States have adopted National Action Plans (NAPs) on SCR 1325, which are designed to strengthen the implementation of SCR 1325 in peace and security operations on the ground, particularly peacekeeping operations. Further, a number of Member State driven Security Council resolutions have been adopted since SCR 1325, which reaffirm the Security Council's commitment to a woman, peace and security agenda. In 2008, a US-sponsored resolution on sexual violence in conflict was adopted (SCR 1820), followed in 2009 by two further resolutions (SCR 1888 and 1889) and most recently by SCR 1960 adopted in December 2010. Significantly SCR 1889 was adopted to help reinforce the implementation of SCR 1325. A major concern among advocates of SCR 1325, however, is that these new resolutions may effectively dilute SCR 1325's aims, by re-situating women as victims thus effecting a step back from the transformative potential of SCR 1325. Without any substantive focus on women's empowerment in subsequent resolutions on women, peace and security, the Security Council risks paying lip-service to women's participation in decision-making processes.

SCR 1325 was driven by a network of civil society organisations, who sought recognition of the empowerment of women as protagonists in peacebuilding. The language of the Resolution was framed in a way which spoke to key concerns held by women, peace and security advocates, specifically women's exclusion from decision-making processes. In contrast, the follow-up resolutions are Member State driven, and do not necessarily reflect the same strength of commitment to women's empowerment as contained within SCR 1325. Although prevention of sexual violence is undoubtedly a major critical concern to be addressed in peace and security processes, the nature and format of these additional resolutions overlook the multiple and complex factors which need to be addressed during transitions in order to smooth the way for women's participation in decision-making processes. Focusing on sexual violence reinforces Hill's concern that situating women's victimhood at the centre of women, peace and security discourses detracts from analysis of the complex intersection between masculinity, peace and security which needs to be unpacked and understood before a gender perspective can be effectively integrated in post-conflict transitional justice processes. In some respects, these additional resolutions are detrimental to the spirit and intention of SCR 1325, and there is a risk that Security Council resolutions focused primarily on sexual violence will risk the development of broader norms on women's participation in decision-making processes and other empowerment strategies during post-conflict transitions. The substantive content of the follow-up resolutions to SCR 1325 give a sense of the direction in which the women, peace and security agenda is developing at the UN.

Shifting away from the transformative potential of SCR 1325? Security Council resolutions centred on sexual violence in conflict

Adopted in 2008, SCR 1820 focuses on sexual violence in conflict and diverges significantly from the aims and objectives of SCR 1325. The preamble explicitly affirms the important role of women in the prevention and resolution of conflicts and peacebuilding, including the obstacles preventing women's capacity and legitimacy to participate. However, the central aim of the Resolution is to draw attention to the forms of sexual violence employed during conflict as well as the targets of sexual violence. SCR 1820 refers to the use of sexual violence as a 'tactic of war', which may reinforce concerns that the recognition of rape as a 'weapon of war' has effectively created a high threshold against which all acts of sexual violence will be measured, thus undermining accountability for individual acts of sexual violence during armed conflict.

Significantly, SCR 1820 builds upon and strengthens existing provisions contained within the Geneva Conventions regarding accountability for sexual violence in armed conflict. The Resolution outlines a series of detailed provisions which indicate a shift towards preventative strategies. For example, women and children at imminent risk of sexual violence should be evacuated to safety. Otto suggests, however, that the abhorrence of sexual violence, which underscores this provision, perpetuates sexual violence as a 'male-perpetrator and female-victim'[48] paradigm, effectively stigmatising sexual violence carried out by men against men.[49] The Resolution's focus on protection fails to engage with the root causes of gender-based violence in conflict, suggesting that SCR 1820 is not radical enough to respond to structural violence, inequality and the role of hegemonic masculinity including how it impacts on both men and women during armed conflict and its aftermath.

SCR 1888 chiefly supports the aims and objectives of SCR 1820, and again places emphasis on the particular victimisation of women and girls in armed conflict. Compared to SCR 1820, the Resolution's language is somewhat broader, instead referring to 'women and children' rather than 'women and girls'. Further, under operative paragraph 15, the Resolution recognises

---

48 Linos, N. 'Rethinking Gender-based Violence during War: Is Violence against Civilian Men a Problem worth Addressing?' (2009) *Social Science and Medicine* 68(8), 1549.
49 Otto *supra*, note 25, 24.

the role of multiple actors including national, local and religious leaders in sensitising communities to sexual violence to allow for improved social reintegration and avoid stigmatisation of victims. Significantly, SCR 1325 requested the UN Secretary-General to appoint a Special Representative on Sexual Violence in Conflict, and in early 2010 Margot Wallström of Sweden was appointed to the role.[50]

More recently, SCR 1960 was adopted in December 2010. Again the Resolution focuses on sexual violence in conflict, drawing attention to the systematic use of sexual violence as a tactic of war, which may impede the restoration of international peace and security. The Resolution builds upon commitments made in SCR 1820 and SCR 1888, by incorporating a range of concrete strategies including the establishment of monitoring, analysis and reporting arrangements as well as encouraging health care service providers and women's groups to enhance their data collection procedures documenting incidents of sexual violence.

Similarly to the thematic resolutions relating to children in armed conflict, each resolution on sexual violence builds progressively upon earlier commitments, with the inclusion of accountability mechanisms including a zero tolerance policy towards sexual violence and abuse in UN peacekeeping operations as well as by humanitarian personnel. While the development of accountability mechanisms for sexual violence is to be commended, the substantive content of the resolutions shifts away from the transformative potential of SCR 1325, which could effectively dilute the women, peace and security agenda at the UN.

The resolutions do not build upon SCR 1325's commitments nor seek to develop broader accountability mechanisms for women's inclusion in peace-building and decision-making processes. Paradoxically, the resolutions expand upon commitments contained within international humanitarian law, while effectively reinforcing similar constraints by focusing primarily on women as victims of conflict. Despite the limitations of these resolutions focused on sexual violence, which fail to effectively support women's inclusion as protagonists in post-conflict transitions, the adoption of SCR 1889 potentially develops the commitments contained within SCR 1325.

Strengthening the implementation of SCR 1325?

SCR 1889 perhaps holds the most promise for strengthening the implementation of SCR 1325. Under operative paragraph 17, the Security Council requests the Secretary-General to submit a set of global level indicators to track SCR 1325's implementation within six months of the Resolution's adoption, and additionally a report containing specific information relating

---

50 'Secretary-General Appoints Margot Wallström of Sweden as Special Representative on Sexual Violence in Conflict', 2 February 2010, available at www.un.org/News/Press/docs/2010/sga1220.doc.htm (last accessed 29 February 2012).

to SCR 1325 with recommendations for how coordination on SCR 1325 could be improved across the UN system. The Resolution places the burden upon the Secretary-General to interpret the implementation of SCR 1325 to date, but the development of the global level indicators, as with similar bureaucratic tools, has lagged behind target.

SCR 1889 is certainly more detailed in its aims than SCR 1325. For example, Member States in conflict zones are encouraged to consult civil society, and the Resolution details specific ways in which the needs and priorities of women and girls can be addressed. While the Resolution helps to flesh out SCR 1325's provisions by considering women and girls' access to justice, education, health and decision-making during post-conflict transitions, SCR 1889's role is undermined by a lack of clarity on measures to improve women's participation.

Though the Resolution explicitly states that women should be included in political and economic decision-making, again, there is little indication of tangible mechanisms which could actually be adopted, suggesting that the inclusion of women is still very much determined by the political will of the parties involved. SCR 1889 also includes reference to the Peacebuilding Commission and Peacebuilding Support Office in a bid to cement the inclusion of gender equality and empowerment in broader reform of the UN Peacebuilding architecture.

Is SCR 1325 an effective transitional justice mechanism?

Despite being driven by the NGO working group on women, peace and security, and thus underpinned by a feminist vision of peace and security, SCR 1325's influence at the macro level, reveals the restrictive parameters of the highly masculinised domain of peace and security, which may undermine the transformative potential of SCR 1325 as a feminist transitional justice mechanism. SCR 1325 is neither radical enough to reorient patriarchal institutionalised responses to peace and security threats, nor able to broach broader critical concerns including structural violence which extend beyond the confines of the public sphere.

Underlying the tensions which stem from SCR 1325's implementation is the role of the Security Council, which continues to sustain a restrictive interpretation of peace and security, failing to address structural violence or sustainable peace. SCR 1325 is not sophisticated enough to respond to structural and less overt forms of violence. The ensuing state-sponsored resolutions on women, peace and security, such as SCR 1820, demonstrate a reversion to narrow conceptions of gender identity in peace and security by focusing on sexual violence in armed conflict. Even SCR 1889, which was intended to support SCR 1325's implementation does not broach what type of transformative mechanisms need to be in place to support women's empowerment and inclusion as protagonists in conflict prevention, conflict resolution and peacebuilding. The progressive development of monitoring mechanisms only applies narrowly to incidents of sexual violence, failing to strengthen women's access to participation. Conversely, SCR 1325's real transformative potential appears to lie in bottom-up peace and security processes.

Civil society's use of soft law mechanisms in transitional justice processes

At the micro level, SCR 1325 has transcended the high level policy arena by engaging the commitment of multiple actors, working towards women's empowerment and gender mainstreaming, which is unique given that Security Council resolutions are usually sustained at the bureaucratic level. The use of SCR 1325 as an advocacy tool by women's civil society organisations demonstrates the versatility of soft law. Generally the adoption of SCR 1325 has reinforced women's organisations' existing work, which aims to strengthen women's empowerment and human rights. While lacking the financial capital to implement the framework in a systematic and consistent manner, civil society organisations demonstrate the 'living' nature of the Resolution through their campaigns and advocacy. The Resolution has been translated into over 100 languages.[51] Efforts have been made to contextualise SCR 1325 in order to make it applicable and relevant to the lives of men and women on the ground. For example, provisions within the framework have been employed at the grassroots level in Nepal in campaigns to reduce intra-personal violence, reflecting the Resolution's broader potential. The following analysis of SCR 1325's potential as a transitional justice mechanism in Nepal draws upon research undertaken by the author with Nepalese civil society organisations from January to February 2007.

Gender and conflict in Nepal: assessing the potential of SCR 1325

From 1996–2006 Nepal experienced a protracted conflict between Government forces and Maoist rebels. Gender-based violence including rape and intimidation was instigated by both the Security Forces and Maoist Insurgents. The conflict also increased the number of single women, exacerbating discriminatory cultural and social practices towards widows, including lack of access to resources and failure to secure Government compensation.[52] As with other conflicts, changing social roles meant that responsibility for households and agriculture shifted to women, and in some instances women's

51 For translations of SCR 1325 see http://peacewomen.org/translation_initiative/security-council-resolution-1325 (last accessed 20 December 2011).

52 Raj Upreti, B. *Armed Conflict and Peace Processes in Nepal: The Maoist Insurgency, Past Negotiations and Opportunities for Conflict Transformation* New Delhi: Adroit Publishers (2006), 274.

direct participation in the armed conflict; with women making up an esti- mated 30–35 per cent of the Maoist army fighting forces.[53]

[handwritten: women combatant]

While Nepal has signed and ratified CEDAW, the internal armed conflict has had a significant impact on women and hindered implementation of the convention as noted by the CEDAW committee,[54] yet CEDAW does not contain any explicit provisions on women and armed conflict. For transitional justice mechanisms to be successful in Nepal, D'Aguirre and Pietropaoli suggest the adoption of a dual strategy that will allow for serious human rights violations to be addressed as well as the creation of a rights-based development programme.[55] Accordingly, any development priorities must be explicitly linked to women's human rights in order to support women's participation and empowerment, particularly given that inequality within Nepalese society has been exacerbated by underdevelopment.[56]

SCR 1325's specific focus on women and armed conflict potentially bolsters the implementation of CEDAW in Nepal by strengthening consideration of women's human rights, status and roles in situations of armed conflict and its aftermath, and is particularly applicable given the specific gendered consequences of the conflict in Nepal. A good illustration of SCR 1325's use in practice lies in the activities of Women's Human Rights (WHR) Single Women Group, an NGO which seeks to address the rights of widows in Nepal. WHR uses the term 'single women' rather than widows because of the negative social attitudes and discrimination towards widows in Nepalese society. In Nepal single women are exposed to violence at the family, community and state level.[57] In terms of objectives WHR aims to raise the social and economic status of single women and to mainstream their rights in development, humanitarian and peacebuilding initiatives. With a membership of 14,000 single women, 115 Village District Committees have been established in 38 districts of Nepal. WHR has organised training of single women to act as agents of change within their communities. This network is extensive given that Nepal has been affected by a violent Maoist insurgency for the past decade, damaging infrastructure and creating a culture of violence and intimidation.

WHR has specifically used SCR 1325 as a framework for its own activities and work, documenting how SCR 1325 has been implemented within its own organisation as well as by the Nepalese Government. For example, under operative paragraph 1 of the Resolution, which urges member states to increase representation of women at all decision-making levels, WHR

---

53 Ibid., 274.
54 CEDAW/C/2004/I/CRP.3/Rev.1, para. 202.
55 Aguirre, D. and Pietropaoli, I. 'Gender Equality, Development and Transitional Justice: The Case of Nepal' (2008) *International Journal of Transitional Justice* 2(3), 358.
56 Ibid., 358.
57 Action Aid and Single Women Group, Women for Human Rights *Problems and Challenges of Single Women (Widows) in Nepal* (2006) Action Aid Nepal and Single Women Group, Women for Human Rights.

organises Capacity Building Workshops, designed to give leadership training to single women (widows), including information on CEDAW, BPFA
and SCR 1325.

WHR also formulated a Widows Charter in response to operative paragraph 15 regarding consultation with local and international women's
groups, which was submitted to the Ministry of Women in Nepal. Based on
provisions in CEDAW, the BPFA and SCR 1325, Article 8 of the Widows
Charter is aimed at addressing the status of widows in conflict and post-
conflict situations, 'recalling UNSCR 1325 and recognizing increasing
number of widows and wives missing as a consequence of armed conflict'.
Further, under operative paragraph 9, WHR analysed state obligations
under CEDAW and other UN conventions, to identify 17 discriminatory
laws within the Civil Code (*Muluki Ain*) and to date has successfully lobbied
the Nepalese Government to repeal a number of laws. Male consent is no
longer required to obtain a passport, the property of a deceased husband no
longer needs to be returned after marriage and women no longer need to
obtain the consent of their sons or unmarried daughters to be able to sell or
hand over property ownership.

Other organisations in Nepal, such as the Institute of Human Rights
Communication Nepal (IHRICON) have also used SCR 1325 as a tool at the
district level in four districts of Dang, Sindhuli, Gorkha and Kailali. More
than 4000 women have benefited from the programme of Village District
Committees and IHRICON has also established women peace volunteers in
villages. IHRICON has provided thematic training on women's rights,
media monitoring and a human rights and sustainable peace programme for
women and empowerment to both the Security Forces and Maoists.[58] Additionally, IHRICON has monitored human rights violations by both Security
Forces and Maoists against women and children including killings, sexual
violence and rape.

Though it is difficult to determine the extent to which the programmatic
objectives and goals of international NGOs influence this type of bottom-up
process, these grassroots initiatives help to develop the broader remit of the
Resolution. For example, the framework of SCR 1325 does not directly
engage with the relationship between international and national legal
regimes, or direct that gender-based discriminatory laws or policies should
be repealed, which would breach the principle of sovereignty. SCR 1325
lends itself to support advocacy and awareness campaigns aimed at reducing
examples of gender-based discrimination, which although linked to armed
conflict, have broader social repercussions. Employing SCR 1325, a universal
transitional justice mechanism, to localised contexts should give some cause
for optimism that the provisions contained within the framework resonate

58 IHRICON Our News Media Monitoring Report Kathmandu: Institute of Human Rights
Communication in Nepal Anamnagar (2005).

with women's civil society organisations working on the ground, where immediate social and political problems are most acute.

Women's civil society organisations lobbied the Nepalese Government for several years to adopt a national level strategy to support the implementation of SCR 1325. In February 2011, the Ministry of Peace and Reconstruction adopted a National Action Plan on SCR 1325 and SCR 1820, which will span a five year period.[59] Significantly, the National Action Plan also makes reference to legal amendments under the *Muluki Ain*, including consideration of structural as well as direct violence, though some of these standards may still not fully comply with the Government's obligations under CEDAW and the strategies for implementing SCR 1325 and SCR 1820 do not appear particularly cohesive or clear.

There have been some significant developments in the post-conflict period which support women's participation. The House of Representatives passed a resolution proposal to ensure that each organ of the state would include 33 per cent representation of women. The Constituent Assembly Elections of 2008 resulted in women gaining 33.2 per cent of 575 elected positions, a significant achievement for women's participation in decision-making processes. These developments may not be tied specifically to SCR 1325, but may instead relate to the broader lobbying and advocacy campaigns of women's civil society organisations.[60] Women still continue to experience inequality and exclusion, however, with discrimination further exacerbated by the complex intersections between caste, ethnicity and gender. The adoption of any rights-based development programme needs to carefully consider the intersection between indigenous and minority rights with women's human rights to address inequality.

Conclusion

While transitional justice mechanisms have expanded and evolved, the intersection between gender and transitional justice has often been overlooked. Given that women are largely absent from the design of transitional justice mechanisms, SCR 1325 holds great promise as a soft law instrument. First the drafting of the Resolution was driven by a network of women's civil society organisations, pointing to women's inclusion in SCR 1325's design. Second, the Resolution actively seeks to engage with women's experiences of armed conflict including their role in conflict prevention, conflict resolution and peacebuilding as well as mainstreaming gender in peace and security

---

59 *National Action Plan on Implementation of the United Nations Security Council Resolution 1325 and 1830 2011/2012–2016/17*, Government of Nepal, Ministry of Peace and Reconstruction, Singhadurbar, Kathmandu, 1 February 2011.

60 The Women's Alliance for Peace, Power, Democracy and the Constituent Assembly (WAPPDCA), an alliance of ten women's organisations representing a diverse range of interests including indigenous and minority rights provided the impetus to push for women's participation in the Constituent Assembly.

operations, thus directly confronting the perceived absence of gender in post-conflict transitions.

The protagonists of SCR 1325 envisaged that a thematic Security Council resolution would provide the strongest support for women's participation in peace and security processes. On paper, SCR 1325's principal objectives as a transitional justice mechanism include the reduction of gender-based violence and empowerment of women at all levels of decision-making. Within that framework concessions have been made. For instance, WILPF's strong anti-military stance is not reflected within the resolution. WILPF continues to advocate for the implementation of SCR 1325, but inevitably some provisions do not sit easily with the wider aim of WILPF, which is to weed out the root causes of war by means of total disarmament and demilitarisation. For example, SCR 1325 could be used to increase the numbers of female security personnel, which would be in direct opposition to the anti-militaristic aims of some feminist organisations. Indeed, the recently adopted SCR 1960 encourages Member States to deploy greater numbers of female military and police personnel under operative paragraph 15.

Read narrowly, the framework is restricted to gender, peace and security within the context of armed conflict and transitional justice. For example, gender mainstreaming is only specifically identified in relation to peacekeeping missions. Further, the inclusion of progress reports on gender mainstreaming remains discretionary, and then only applies to peacekeeping missions. Gender-specific indicators such as levels of violence against women, which could be used to measure whether gender-sensitive training has had any impact in practice, are not included. Equally, without clear gender indicators in place to measure the representation of women at a policy level, it is difficult to determine any tangible or broader advances in gender equality which may have occurred indirectly outside the realm of armed conflict.

Certainly, the link between resolutions on women, peace and security and existing women's rights conventions including CEDAW needs to be strengthened to help to drive the development of broader norms based on women's equality and empowerment in the period of transition from armed conflict. If civil society's expectations for SCR 1325 are not mirrored by policymakers, it leaves open the question of whether the development of the women, peace and security agenda at the UN is being steered away from the feminist vision of peace and security, envisaged by its protagonists. If such is the case, advocates may consider how SCR 1325 can be reclaimed and operationalised in the way in which it was perceived, to avoid SCR 1325's use as a transitional justice mechanism being undermined.

Despite SCR 1325's restricted focus on armed conflict, multiple actors have not deterred from using SCR 1325 to mainstream gender in peace and security processes in localised contexts. Civil society organisations currently apply a broad interpretation to SCR 1325's provisions, implicitly contributing to the development of important international norms on women's role as protagonists in conflict prevention, conflict resolution, peacebuilding and gender relations more broadly during post-conflict transitions. While policymakers call for regular consultation with civil society, stronger links need to be forged between the Security Council and civil society if SCR 1325 is to extend beyond its restricted focus on the negative peace paradigm to operate as a transformative transitional justice mechanism.

3 International criminal justice and the girl child

Different needs, equal opportunities

Annelotte Walsh[1]

Introduction

International criminal justice has only recently started to focus on specifically prosecuting grave crimes committed against children during armed conflict and on the inclusion of children in processes of accountability, truth-seeking and reconciliation.[2] At the first international tribunals in Nuremberg and Tokyo very little attention was paid to crimes committed against children and it was only decades later that the plight of children in the context of armed conflict and its aftermath gained widespread international visibility. This was largely the result of two international developments. First, there was the increased recognition of the legal rights of children under international law, culminating in the adoption of the Convention on the Rights of the Child (CRC) in 1989. For the first time, a minimum standard for the protection of the human rights of children was established. The other significant development was the release of a United Nations (UN) report on the impact of armed conflict on children.[3] The report was groundbreaking as it was the first initiative to capture the devastating impact of armed conflict on children and to provide a clear agenda for action. Importantly, the study also paid attention to gender specific effects of armed conflict on girls and women which had previously been neglected in other UN studies. Following these developments several international and hybrid courts started to focus on the sanctioning of crimes committed against children and to involve children as victims and witnesses in international

---

1 PhD Candidate, University of Hong Kong, formerly Advocacy Manager UNICEF Australia, Intern at Oxfam, ICTR and ICTY.
2 The Convention on the Rights of the Child defines a child as anyone below the age of 18 years. Convention on the Rights of the Child, UN Doc. A/44/49 (20 November 1989), Article 1.
3 Graça Machel, 'Report of the Expert of the Secretary-General, Ms. Graça Machel, Submitted Pursuant to General Assembly Resolution 48/157', UN General Assembly, 51st session, UN Doc. A/51/306 (26 August 1996) ('Graça Machel Report').

criminal justice processes.[4] Yet, these developments have been painstakingly slow and in reality children have remained largely sidelined. This has particularly been the case with girls as international courts have not sufficiently recognized, investigated and prosecuted crimes committed against girls and current policies and practices within the courts have not adequately taken into account gender and age specific vulnerabilities.

This chapter adopts a gender perspective to look critically at the ways in which girls have been considered by international criminal justice processes as victims and witnesses to date.

The term 'gender' refers to the socially constructed roles played by men and women that determine the functions and responsibilities of each sex as well as their access to resources and opportunities for social and economic advancement.[5] A gender analysis thus looks at gendered social relations, power structures and assumptions and how these influence the access to the enjoyment of rights.[6] Applying such a gender lens to examine girls affected by armed conflict and their involvement in international criminal processes will highlight their gender specific experiences and needs while at the same time identifying potentially differential and discriminatory impacts of policies and practices.

The first section of the chapter examines the legal framework protecting the rights of girls, most importantly the protection provided by the CRC. It argues that the CRC provides the most effective framework for the protection of rights of all children, boys and girls, while at the same time addressing their gender specific needs and interests. The following section discusses how boys and girls experience armed conflict in very different ways, outlining their specific vulnerabilities in terms of sexual and gender based crimes, recruitment into armed forces and 'generic' crimes committed against civilians. The chapter then goes on to examine the extent to which girls have been considered by international courts to date drawing from experiences of recent international courts and identifying areas in which reform is needed. The final section addresses the importance of a girl-friendly international criminal justice system both for the individual and for the wider community. The chapter draws the conclusion that international criminal justice institutions have not adequately considered gender specific differences between

---

4 The term 'international criminal justice processes' refers to all international criminal fora including but limited to international criminal courts and hybrid courts. The terms 'international criminal mechanisms', 'international criminal courts', 'international criminal processes', 'international courts' and 'processes of individual accountability' are all used interchangeably. For a general discussion on children and international criminal justice see: Sharanjeet Parmar, Mindy Jane Roseman, Saudamini Siegrist and Theo Sowa (eds), Children and Transitional Justice: Truth-Telling, Accountability and Reconciliation (Cambridge, MA: Harvard University Press, 2010).

5 'Report of the UN Secretary General on the Implementation of the Fourth World Conference on Women', UN Doc. A/51/322 (3 September 1996).

6 P. Spees, 'Gender Justice and Accountability in Peace Support Operations' (2004) International Alert Policy Briefing.

girls and boys in the recognition, investigation and ultimately prosecution of crimes committed against children as well as the participation of girls in these processes. It argues that these institutions must adopt a child rights-based approach to ensure that girls' age and gender specific experiences, needs and rights are fully understood and addressed. A few recommendations on how the implementation of such a child rights based approach may manifest itself in practice are proposed in the conclusion.

The international legal framework for the protection of girls

As both a woman and a child, the two main international legal frameworks that are applicable to girls are the Convention on the Elimination of Discrimination against Women (CEDAW) and the CRC. While both afford some degree of protection to girls, they don't fully overlap and girls risk falling between the cracks of the 'age neutral' provisions of CEDAW and the 'gender neutral' provisions of the CRC.[7] This section takes a closer look at both frameworks, identifying their weaknesses in addressing girls' needs and determining the most appropriate legal framework protecting girls' rights.

Adopted in 1979, CEDAW is the definitive international legal instrument protecting the rights of women.[8] It is aimed at advancing and empowering women as well as protecting their civil, political, economic, social and cultural rights. While CEDAW is applicable to all women regardless of age, it seems to do very little to protect the rights of girls. The phrase 'girls' for example is only used once in the entire Convention, in reference to school drop-out rates (Article 10). Taefi adds that many provisions of CEDAW make reference to parent–child relations (Articles 9, 5 and 16) which 'deepens the division between girls and adult-women, and compromises a reading in which girls are elevated to the status of equal rights holders'.[9] Furthermore, in her examination of CEDAW, Cohen concludes that the Convention mainly aims 'at correcting inequalities between adult men and women' rather than between boys and girls.[10] The girl child thus largely fails to benefit from the legal protections for women as provided by CEDAW

---

7   See also: Ladan Askari, 'Girls' Rights under International Law: An Argument for Establishing Gender Equality as *Jus Cogens*' (1998–1999) 8(3) *Southern California Review of Law and Women's Studies*; Kirsten M. Backstrom, 'The International Human Rights of the Child: Do they Protect the Female Child?' (1996–1997) 30(541) *George Washington Journal of International Law and Economics*; Cynthia Price Cohen, 'The United Nations Convention on the Rights of the Child: A Feminist Landmark' (1997) 3(1) *William and Mary Journal of Women and the Law*; Nura Taefi, 'The Synthesis of Age and Gender: Intersectionality, International Human Rights Law and the Marginalisation of the Girl-Child' (2009) 17(3) *International Journal of Children's Rights*, 345.

8   'Convention on the Elimination of All Forms of Discrimination against Women', UN Doc. A/34/46 (18 December 1979).

9   Taefi *supra*, note 7, 356.

10 Cohen *supra*, note 7, 39.

because she is too young. But what about the protection provided to her because she is a child?

The most widely accepted framework for the protection of rights of children is laid out in the CRC. Adopted in 1989, the CRC is progressive in many ways. It is the first human rights treaty to recognize civil and political rights as well as economic and social rights and it remains one of the only human rights treaties to do so. The CRC also provides a new interpretation of children, as they are no longer simply considered as passive recipients in need of protection, but as human beings with specific rights and responsibilities and the ability to exercise these rights in a manner consistent with a child's evolving capacities. The Convention further bridges relevant standards enshrined in humanitarian and human rights law as the provisions of the CRC are always applicable, including during times of emergency or armed conflict.[11]

The CRC goes further than any other human rights instrument in recognizing the potential needs of the girl child. For Cohen, the CRC even represented a feminist landmark in that 'in its text, boys and girls are truly treated as equals'.[12] Others however are less optimistic in their assessment of the CRC arguing that it has fallen short of its potential and that girls' interests are not adequately addressed.[13] Taefi for example notes that, although intended to establish gender equality, 'the gender-neutral language of the CRC is detrimental to the development of girls because it cannot articulate their experiences'.[14] Askari further notes that loopholes in the international legal system result in the inadequate protection of girls' rights. While both arguments hold some truth, it is argued here that the CRC does in fact provide the most appropriate framework for addressing girls' interests and that the failure to recognize and address girls' interests in practice is not so much the result of the inadequacy of the legal framework but rather of the failure to translate this framework into effective action. A closer look at the substance and meaning of the CRC is thus warranted.

The Committee on the Rights of the Child (hereafter Committee) has outlined a set of general principles that underpin the CRC: non-discrimination (Article 2); the best interests of the child (Article 3); the right for children to have their views heard and be given due weight in all decisions affecting them (Article 12); and the rights to life, survival and development (Article 6).[15] Based on these principles, the CRC provides the strongest legal

11 Committee on the Rights of the Child, 'Report on the Second Session', 2nd session, UN Doc. CRC/C/10 (19 October 1992), para. 67.
12 Cohen *supra*, note 7, 45.
13 See e.g.: Backstrom and Cohen *supra*, note 7; Michael Freeman, 'The Future of Children's Rights' (2000) 14(4) *Children and Society*, 277.
14 Taefi *supra*, note 7, 357.
15 Committee on the Rights of the Child, 'General Comment No. 5: General Measures of Implementation of the Convention on the Rights of the Child', 34th session, UN Doc. CRC/GC/2003/5 (27 November 2003) ('General Comment No. 5'), at para. 2.

framework for protecting the interests of girls. If implemented correctly, a child rights-based approach understands that children are active holders of rights, that they have essential experiences to offer in matters that affect them and that their best interests should always be at the forefront of decisions that affect them. It provides for the equal protection between boys and girls while at the same time addressing their specific needs and interests and allowing for their full participation in the processes. While international courts are not party to human rights treaties and are therefore not bound by their provisions,[16] treaties can nevertheless provide important guidance on policies and practices for non-state actors such as international criminal courts. The Committee has confirmed this, stating that: 'while it is the State which takes on obligations under the Convention, its tasks of implementation – of making reality of the human rights of children – needs to engage all sectors of society'.[17] International criminal courts must therefore put more effort into implementing and operationalizing a child rights based approach throughout their policies and practices in order to ensure equal access to justice for all children, and particularly girls.

Girls and armed conflict

The effect of armed conflict on vulnerable groups such as women and children is increasingly being recognized and documented.[18] The changing nature of modern warfare has increasingly exposed women and children to its affects and in addition to the thousands of children killed and wounded as a direct result of the fighting, many more suffer from indirect causes of the fighting such as malnutrition, disease and being denied access to education, healthcare and recreation. Girls suffer in many of the same ways as boys and women in armed conflict. They are forcibly displaced, killed, injured, abducted, deprived of education and healthcare, uprooted from their homes and they suffer the same trauma. But there are also important differences and their age and gender makes girls particularly vulnerable during times of armed conflict.

One of the main differences between boys and girls during armed conflict is that girls are much more likely to be targeted for sexual violence and

16 Vienna Convention on the Law of Treaties (1969), Article 1.
17 'General Comment No. 5', 1.
18 See for example: 'Graça Machel Report'; Graça Machel, 'The Impact of Armed Conflict on Children: A Critical Analysis of Progress Made and Obstacles Encountered in Increasing the Protection of War-Affected Children' (September 2000) presented at the International Conference on War-Affected Children, Winnipeg, Canada; Dyan Mazurana and Kristopher Carlson, 'The Girl Child and Armed Conflict: Recognizing and Addressing Grave Violations of Girls' Human Rights', United Nations Division of the Advancement of Women in collaboration with UNICEF, UN DocGM/DVGC/2006/UP.12 (September 2006); World Vision International, 'The Effects of Armed Conflict on Girls' (1996) *World Vision Staff Working Paper No. 23*.

exploitation. Gender based violence and sexual abuse – including rape, forced pregnancy, forced marriage, sexual slavery, forced prostitution, trafficking and mutilation of sexual organs – have increasingly become strategic weapons in modern-day warfare.[19] Sexual crimes are used as instruments of war to destroy women's psyches, to isolate them from their families or communities, to humiliate their families or husbands, or simply to boost morale among the fighting men. Often, women and girls are raped by people they know, such as neighbours, teachers or community members, making it extremely difficult for women to continue to live in their community. Young girls are particularly vulnerable to sexual violence because of their size and age and because they are often thought to be less likely to be infected with HIV/AIDs or other sexually transmitted diseases.[20] Rape has become so commonplace during most armed conflicts that few girls and women escape. Research has found that almost every female older than 12 who survived the 1994 Rwandan genocide was sexually assaulted.[21]

Rape and sexual violence has devastating effects on the general and reproductive health of girls as they suffer from increased risk of HIV/AIDs and other STDs, severe damage to their reproductive systems, and high maternal and infant mortality rates due to lack of appropriate healthcare. Girls subjected to sexual violence are often forced to suffer in silence as they fear stigmatization and rejection by their families and communities, not to mention the personal pain and humiliation. In addition to the obvious physical and psychological distress, sexual violence can also have long-term socio-economic implications. The Graça Machel Report found that sexual violence against women and girls during times of conflict can become endemic within society after the war is over.[22] Furthermore, girls who have been rejected by their families and communities may face trouble getting married and may be forced into prostitution as a means of survival.

While girls are particularly vulnerable to sexual violence, they are also victims of 'generic' acts of violence such as maiming, killing, abduction, hostage taking, forced labour, exploitation and trafficking. While not targeted specifically against girls, their age and gender make them particularly vulnerable to becoming victims of such crimes. For example, girls are often responsible for fetching food, fuel and water, requiring them to leave the relative safety of their homes, communities or refugee camps and thereby putting themselves at increased risk of being raped, killed, tortured or wounded by landmines. Moreover, societal and cultural interpretations of gender roles may also adversely influence the impact of war on girls, for

---

19 'Graça Machel Report', 22–26.
20 S. McKay, 'The Effects of Armed Conflict on Girls and Women' (1998) 4(4) *Peace and Conflict: Journal of Peace Psychology*, 381–392.
21 International Panel of Eminent Personalities to Investigate the 1994 Genocide in Rwanda, 'Rwanda: The Preventable Genocide' (2000), 148.
22 'Graça Machel Report', 97.

example cultural practices that prioritize boys over girls when it comes to education, healthcare and distribution of food are exacerbated during times of conflict. Thus, even though these 'generic' crimes are not specifically directed towards girls, they often result in disproportionate suffering for girls.

Girls are also affected by armed conflict as child soldiers. Most people automatically think of boys when they think of child soldiers yet nearly 40 per cent of all children associated with armed groups are girls.[23] They serve as armed combatants, wives, cooks, sex slaves, cleaners, messengers and porters. The Cape Town Principles (1997) recognizes the varied roles played by children in armed forces and defines a 'child soldier' as 'any person under 18 years of age who is part of any kind of regular or irregular armed force or armed group in any capacity, including but not limited to cooks, porters, messengers and anyone accompanying such groups, other than family members. It includes girls recruited for sexual purposes and forced marriage'.[24]

While some girls are forcibly abducted, conscripted or coerced into joining armed forces, others may decide to join 'voluntarily' driven by economic, cultural, social and/or political pressure. When recruited as child soldiers, girls suffer in many of the same ways as boys in terms of being held against their will, being subjected to physical and psychological violence, being forced to witness or participate in killings and torture, and being denied food and water. In addition, girls often suffer additional mistreatment as they are forced to serve as sexual slaves, suffer sexual violence and mistreatment or are forced to provide the majority of domestic labour to support the fighting forces.

The suffering of girl child soldiers does not end when the fighting does. While all child soldiers are likely to experience a wide range of difficulties when returning home, such as physical disabilities, mental problems and socialization issues, the situation for girls returning home is often worse. Shepler's research on reintegrating female child soldiers found that it is often much more difficult for girls to reintegrate into their communities as a result of embedded cultural practices and beliefs: 'in many cases it is easier for a boy to be accepted [by his community] after amputating the hands of villagers than it is for a girl to be accepted after being the victim of rape'.[25] Furthermore, girl child soldiers may not be released as commanding soldiers may prefer to keep 'their' women, particularly if she has borne a child.

Despite the explicit reference to girls in the Cape Town Principles and

23 Save the Children, 'Forgotten Casualties of War: Girls in Armed Conflict' (2005), vi.
24 UNICEF, 'Cape Town Principles and Best Practices on the Recruitment of Children into the Armed Forces and on Demobilization and Social Reintegration of Child Soldiers in Africa' (1997) ('Cape Town Principles').
25 Susan Shepler as quoted in: S. McKay and D. Mazurana, Where are the Girls? Girls in Fighting Forces in Northern Uganda, Sierra Leone, and Mozambique: Their Lives During and After War (Montreal, Canada: Rights & Democracy, 2004), 37.

research showing that girls make up to 40 per cent of all child soldiers, girls are consistently overlooked in Demobilization, Disarmament and Reintegration (DDR) programmes.[26] For example in Sierra Leone, Save the Children estimated that only 4 per cent of girls known to have been involved with fighting forces passed through formal DDR programmes.[27] The reasons for this are diverse. Some of the girls interviewed said they were put off by the military orientation of the DDR process while others said that openly participating in such programmes highlighted the fact that they were involved with armed groups and increased the risk of being stigmatized.[28] Furthermore, DDR programmes often have strict criteria for participation which exclude girls. For example, a DDR programme in Sierra Leone featured a 'cash for weapons' approach under which children were required to turn weapons in to authorities in order to qualify for financial benefits, which rendered many girls ineligible for participation as most of them had no weapon of their own.[29]

Overall, it can be seen that over the past few decades the knowledge base among academics, NGOs, the UN and practitioners in relation to the impact of armed conflict on women and children, including girls, has strengthened significantly. Unfortunately, as will become clear in the following section, the international criminal justice community has failed to translate this knowledge into effective intervention and action for girls.

Girls and international criminal courts

Girls are primarily involved with the international criminal justice processes in three ways: as victims, as witnesses and as perpetrators. While it is true that many children, including girls, actively participate in hostilities around the world and that they may be guilty of committing grave international crimes, child protection advocates often argue that these girls are also victims and that international courts are not the appropriate mechanism to deal with juvenile offenders and they should be dealt with using other judicial or non-judicial mechanisms. This position has consistently been shared by all international criminal courts to date and in practice no international court has prosecuted any child combatants.[30] The Rome Statute of the ICC

---

26 The United Nations Disarmament, Demobilization and Reintegration Resource Centre defines DDR processes as a means to contribute to security and stability in post-conflict environments so that recovery and development can begin. By removing weapons from the hands of combatants, taking the combatants out of military structures and helping them to integrate socially and economically into society, DDR seeks to support ex-combatants so that they can become active participants in the peace process.

27 Save the Children *supra*, note 23, 1.

28 Ibid., 2.

29 McKay and Mazurana *supra*, note 25.

30 See, Cécile Aptel, 'International Criminal Justice and Child Protection' in Sharanjeet Parmar, Mindy Jane Roseman, Saudamini Siegrist and Theo Sowa (eds), *Children and Transitional Justice: Truth-Telling, Accountability and Reconciliation* (Cambridge, MA: Harvard University Press, 2010).

even explicitly limits its jurisdiction to prosecute crimes committed by persons aged 18 and above.[31] This chapter will therefore focus on the two other main forms of involvement by girls before the international courts: as victims and witnesses. The first section will examine progress made by international courts in holding perpetrators of crimes committed against girls responsible, distinguishing between sexual crimes and the recruitment and use of girl child soldiers. The second section will then focus on the participation of girls as witnesses, identifying some of the successes and failures achieved by international courts to date. It must be noted that an in-depth examination of all legal provisions, procedures and the jurisprudence of all international courts is beyond the scope of this chapter and this section will instead focus on highlighting a number of relevant examples.

Crimes committed against girls

Sexual crimes

Rape and other sexual crimes have long posed a threat to women and girls during armed conflict. For centuries rape was considered an unfortunate but inevitable side effect of armed conflict necessary to boost soldier morale and to intimidate the enemy. Only in the last few decades has significant progress been made in recognizing, prohibiting and prosecuting rape and sexual crimes albeit at a very slow pace.[32]

Although evidence of rape and other sexual crimes was extensively documented, these crimes were largely ignored by both the Tokyo and Nuremberg Tribunals. It took several decades, until the establishment of the four flagship international criminal institutions – the International Criminal Tribunal for the Former Yugoslavia (ICTY), the International Criminal Tribunal for Rwanda (ICTR), the Special Court for Sierra Leone (SCSL) and the International Criminal Court (ICC) – before international criminal law started to acknowledge sexual crimes such as rape, forced marriage, sexual slavery and forced prostitution as war crimes, crimes against humanity and even as acts of genocide. The ICTR led the way in this area with the groundbreaking case of Jean-Paul Akeyesu in 1998, which was the first time an international court held that rape constituted an act of genocide. In many of its following indictments, the ICTR included charges of sexual violence in various forms and although this reflects the mass rapes that occurred during the 1994 genocide, the prosecutors at the ICTR have encountered much dif-

---

31 Rome Statute, Article 26.
32 For a comprehensive historical overview of the treatment of gender-related crimes under International Law see, Kelly D. Askin, 'Prosecuting Wartime Rape and other Gender-Related Crimes under International Law: Extraordinary Advances, Enduring Obstacles' (2003) 21(288) *Berkeley Journal of International Law*.

ficulty in procuring convictions for rape and sexual violence due to lack of substantive evidence.[33]

The ICTY followed suit with several decisions adding to the jurisprudence relating to sexual crimes with several cases even referring explicitly to girls as victims of these crimes. In 1996, the *Tadic Case* was the first case where a defendant was specifically charged with rape and sexual violence as a crime against humanity and war crimes.[34] Furthermore in the so-called *Celebici Case*, the ICTY characterized the rape of Bosnian Serb prisoners at the Celebici prison camp as acts of torture.[35] The *Celebici Case* was also important as it recognized command responsibility for sexual crimes committed by subordinates. Moreover, the *Kunarac (Foca) Case* was the first trial of multiple accused to focus exclusively on various forms of sexual violence committed against women and girls resulting in the first international conviction for rape, torture and enslavement of girls as crimes against humanity.[36]

The SCSL has probably been the most progressive in addressing sexual based crimes charges and crimes committed against girls and women were included in most of its indictments.[37] Importantly, in the *RUF Case*, the SCSL became the first international court to recognize forced marriage, a crime mainly affecting adolescent girls, as a crime against humanity. Similarly the Appeals Court in the *AFRC Case* acknowledged that children, and specifically girls, were victims of forced marriage as part of the AFRC's systematic attack on the civilian population. Notably, the SCSL also mentioned girls as a distinct victim group in some of its charges, for example, in the indictment of Charles Taylor, who was charged *inter alia* with rape and sexual slavery.

The move towards ending impunity for sexual crimes continues with the ICC, both in terms of substantive law as well with the structure of the Court. The 1998 Rome Statute, which established the ICC, explicitly recognizes rape, sexual slavery, enforced prostitution, forced pregnancy, gender based persecution, sexual enslavement, enforced sterilization and sexual violence as war crimes and crimes against humanity. Consequently, all current trials before the ICC include charges of sexual crimes or rape and of the 23

---

33 See, e.g. *Prosecutor* v. *Musema* (ICTR, Case No. ICTR-96-13-A, 16 November 2001); Prosecutor v. Kamuhanda (ICTR, Case No. ICTR-95-54A-T, 22 January 2004); *Prosecutor* v. *Nahimana* (ICTR, Case No. ICTR-99-52-T, 3 December 2003); *Prosecutor* v. *Kajelijeli* (ICTR, Case No. ICTR-98-44A-T, 1 December 2003).

34 *Prosecutor* v. *Tadic* (ICTY, Case No IT-94-1-A, 15 July 1999).

35 *Prosecutor* v. *Delalic (Judgment)* (ICTY, Case No. IT-96-21-A, 20 February 2001) ('Celebici Judgment').

36 *Prosecutor* v. *Kunarac (Trial Judgment)* (ICTY, Case No. IT-96-23-T and IT-96-23/1-T, 22 February 2001) ('Foca Trial Judgment').

37 See, e.g.: *Prosecutor* v. *Sesay* (RUF Accused) (SCSL, Case No. SCSL-2003-15-I-001-B, 7 March 2009); *Prosecutor* v. *Brima* (AFRC Accused) (SCLR, Case No. SCSL-2004-16-PT-006, 5 February 2004); *Prosecutor* v. *Taylor* (SCSL, Case No. SCSL-2003-01, 7 March 2003).

individuals indicted by the Court, 12 have been charged with gender-related crimes. Perhaps the most important case in this respect is the *Bemba Case*, in which former Congolese Vice President Jean-Pierra Bemba is charged with rape as a war crime as a crime against humanity.[38]

The *Bemba* trial is also remarkable for the presence of female legal practitioners in the Court with the case being presided over by three female judges and a female trial attorney taking the lead in prosecuting the case. The presence of women in judicial processes is an important issue when it comes to prosecuting gender based and sexual crimes. The presence and participation of women in all stages of judicial processes is fundamental, both as a gender equity goal in itself and because women are often more likely to investigate and prosecute gender based crimes. For example in the *Akayesu Case*, Judge Navi Pillay, the only female judge on the ICTR was instrumental in getting additional charges of sexual violence added to the original indictment which ultimately led to the first conviction of rape as an instrument of genocide and crimes against humanity. The equal representation of women and men with appropriate training and experience in sexual and gender violence, in all stages of the judicial process is the first step to an environment in which women and girls feel more comfortable and at ease to share their stories. The ICC has taken important steps in this regard and the Rome Statute requires the Court to include fair representation of women in all of its organs and that staff with specific expertise in sexual and gender violence are included in the Court's staff at all levels.[39]

While international criminal law has come a long way in acknowledging the sexual crimes affecting women and girls, rape and sexual violence continues to be systematically committed against women and girls around the world and relatively few perpetrators have been held accountable. It is estimated that between 250,000 and 500,000 women and girls were raped during the 1994 Rwandan genocide, 40,000 women and girls were raped in 1993 in Bosnia-Herzegovina and as many as 215,000 to 257,000 women and girls were sexually attacked during the Sierra Leone conflict.[40] Yet, despite these appalling numbers the number of individuals held responsible for such crimes by the international courts is shamefully disproportionate with only 34 successful prosecutions for sexual violence across the ICTR, ICTY and SCSL.[41] As the Special Rapporteur on Violence Against Women

---

38 *Prosecutor* v. *Bemba* (ICC, Case No. ICC-01/05-01/08, 23 May 2008).

39 'Rome Statute of the International Criminal Court', UN Doc. A/CONF.183/9 (17 July 1998) ('Rome Statute'), Articles 36(8)(a)(iii), 38(b), 44(2), 42(9), 43(6).

40 UNFPA, 'Sexual Violence against Women and Girls in War and its Aftermath: Realities, Responses, and Required Resources' (A Briefing Paper Prepared for the Symposium on Sexual Violence in Conflict and Beyond, Brussels, 2006).

41 See, UN Department of Peacekeeping Operations (DPKO), 'Review of the Sexual Violence Elements of the Judgments of the International Criminal Tribunal for the Former Yugoslavia, the International Criminal Court for Rwanda and the Special Court for Sierra Leone in the Light of Security Council Resolution 1820' (2010).

rightly observed: 'rape in times of conflict remains one of the least-condemned war crimes'.[42]

A major issue relating to the failure to prosecute sexual crimes is the failure to adequately investigate these crimes. Stigma, shame and threats to personal safety are only some of the reasons why the victims of sexual crimes may be reluctant to come forward. Moreover, the lack of consistent attention to sexual crimes during the investigation phase and the lack of appropriately trained investigators have constrained the prosecution of rape and sexual crimes in the aftermath of conflict. Gender imbalance in the investigation teams can also result in the obscuring of sexual crimes as many girls and women feel more comfortable sharing their experiences with female investigators. A dedicated and appropriately trained team of both male and female investigators is therefore important to ensure that sexual crimes are adequately investigated and documented.

It is recognized here that many serious crimes are committed against civilians during armed conflict and, with limited available resources, it is of course not possible for international courts to prosecute all of them. However, in light of the systematic use of rape during modern day armed conflicts and the devastating physical and psychological effects of sexual violence on women and girls, sexual and gender based crimes should be given due consideration by international courts.

Recruitment and use of child soldiers

Positive steps have also been taken towards criminalizing the recruitment and use of child soldiers. Over the past few decades a number of international human rights treaties have set a minimum age for the participation in armed conflict, including the CRC, the Optional Protocol to the CRC on the Involvement of Children in Armed Conflict, the Additional Protocols to the Geneva Conventions, and the International Labour Organization's Convention Concerning the Prohibition and Immediate Action for the Elimination of the Worst Forms of Child Labour. But it was in 1998, with the adoption of the Rome Statute, that the recruitment and use of child soldiers was expressly criminalized under international law.[43]

The criminalization of recruiting child soldiers was also expressed in the 2002 Statute of the SCSL.[44] Subsequently the SCSL has charged, and ultimately convicted, a number of individuals for the unlawful recruitment and

---

42 ECOSOC Commission on Human Rights, 'Preliminary Report Submitted by the Special Rapporteur on Violence against Women' (22 November 1994).
43 Rome Statute Article 8(2)(b)(xxvi) and 8(2)(e)(vii).
44 Statute of the Special Court for Sierra Leone (adopted 16 January 2002) ('Statute of the SCSL') Article 4(c).

use of child soldiers.[45] The ICC has also devoted considerable energy to investigating and prosecuting crimes related to the recruitment and use of child soldiers by armed groups. Of the 23 individuals thus far indicted by the Court, seven have been charged with crimes related to the recruitment of child soldiers.

Despite these positive developments problematic issues remain in addressing girl child soldiers. The main problem relates to the interpretation of 'participating actively' in the legal definition of the prohibition of the use of child soldiers. While the well-established definition of child soldiers, as laid out in the Cape Town Principles, aims to include all children associated with armed forces regardless the nature of their involvement, this broad definition is not reflected in the language of the Rome Statute. Article 8 of the Statute recognizes the use of child soldiers as a war crime but its definition only includes children that 'actively participate in hostilities'. While this provision clearly encompasses children who participate directly in the fighting, it is less clear if it also includes children in non-combatant roles as often performed by girls. The restricted language of the Statute thus threatens to exclude a large number of girls from coverage under the prohibited crimes. In recognition of this, UN Secretary-General's Special Representative for Children and Armed Conflict, Ms Radhika Coomaraswamy has urged the Court to '[a]dopt a case-by-case approach when determining whether a child "participated actively" in the hostilities with the relevant question in each case being whether the child's participation served an essential support function to the armed force or armed group during the conflict'.[46] Such an interpretation would be in line with the definition used by the SCLS Trial Chamber in the *AFRC Case* which held that '[a]ny labour or support that gives effect to, or helps maintain, operations in a conflict constitutes active participation'.[47] Whether or not the ICC will follow Ms Coomaraswamy's recommendations in the *Lubanga Case* remains to be seen.

Participation of girls in international courts

When addressing the rights of girls affected by armed conflict, it is not only important to hold those who have committed crimes against girls responsible but also to address the interests and needs of girl witnesses in these processes. Many obstacles prevent girls from taking part in judicial processes.

---

45 See: *Prosecutor v Fofana (the CDF Accused) (Trial Judgment)* (Special Court for Sierra Leone, Case No. SCSL-2004–14-T, 2 August 2007); *AFRC Appeals Chamber Judgment* (Special Court for Sierra Leone, Case No SCSL-2004–15-A, 26 October 2009), *RUF Trial Chamber Judgment* (Special Court for Sierra Leone, Case No SCSL-2004–15-T, 2 March 2009).

46 Radhika Coomaraswamy, 'Written Submission of the United Nations Special Representative of the Secretary-General on Children and Armed Conflict – submitted in Application of Rule 103 of the Rules and Procedure and Evidence' (18 February 2008), 20–21.

47 *AFRC Trial Judgment* (Special Court for Sierra Leone, Case no SCSL-2004-16-T, 20 June 2007), 737.

They may be too young or not have enough money to travel. They may be intimidated by the programme or prevented from participating by their parents. When girls are provided with the opportunity to take part in international judicial processes, a balance needs to be found between child participation and child protection. On one hand being a witness can be extremely important for girls as it provides important recognition of their suffering and it can help girls regain control over their lives. However, without appropriate support and protection mechanisms, recalling traumatic events such as sexual violence and abuse, can provoke intense emotions and can be extremely stressful.[48]

Dealing with vulnerable witnesses such as victims of sexual crimes or children can be an extremely challenging issue for international courts and practice to date leaves much room for improvement. The earlier international courts, the ICTY and ICTR, struggled in providing adequate protection for female victims and both Courts have been subject to criticism regarding problems with training investigatory staff, providing adequate witness protection before, during and after the trial, implementing confidentiality agreements as well as for inappropriate cross-examination and inadequate counselling.[49]

In an attempt to learn from the experiences of the ICTY and ICTR, the SCSL developed a comprehensive support and protection strategy for children and other vulnerable witnesses.[50] This strategy included short- and long-term plans for children's protection and support, including medical assistance, physical and psychological rehabilitation, and special protective courtroom measures for child witnesses. The SCSL also included a special provision in its Statue outlining that

> given the nature of the crimes committed and the particular sensitivities of girls, young women and children, victims of rape, sexual assault, abduction and slavery of all kinds, due consideration should be given in

---

48 A. Michels, 'Psychosocial Support for Children: Protecting the Rights of Child Victims and Witnesses in Transitional Justice Processes' (2010) Innocenti Research Centre Expert Paper Series on Children and Transitional Justice, 6.

49 See, e.g., Human Rights Watch, 'Struggling to Survive: Barrier to Justice for Rape Victims in Rwanda', www.hrw.org/en/reports/2004/09/29/struggling-survive; Elizabeth Neuffer, The Key to my Neighbor's House: Seeking Justice in Bosnia and Rwanda (New York: Picador, 2002); Elisabeth Rehn and Ellen Johnson Sirleaf, Women, War, Peace: The Independent Experts' Assessment on the Impact of Armed Conflict on Women and Women's Role in Peace-Building, Progress of the World's Women (New York: United Nations Development Fund for Women, 2002), at 9; Connie Walsh, Witness Protection, Gender and the ICTR (Montreal, Canada: Coalition for Women's Human Rights in Conflict Situations, 1997); and Committee on Human Rights, 'Report of the Special Rapporteur on Violance Against Women, its Causes and Consequences, Ms. Radhika Coomaraswamy, Addendum, Report of the Mission to Rwanda on the Issues of Violence against Women in Situations of Armed Conflict', UN Doc. E/CN.4/1998/54/Add.1 (4 February 1998), III.

50 *Statute of the SCSL*, Article 16.

the appointment of staff to the employment of prosecutors and investigators experienced in gender-related crimes and juvenile justice.[51]

The ICC aimed to further improve support and protection strategies for children and the Statute contains several Articles referring directly to the protection of children interacting with the ICC. For example, Article 68 requires that the Court take 'appropriate measures to protect victims and witnesses and in doing so to take into account all relevant factors including age and gender, in particular where the crimes involved sexual or gender violence or violence against children'.[52] The Article further allows for the Court to conduct any of the proceedings via camera link or other special means in order to protect victims, witnesses or an accused, particularly in cases of victims of sexual violence of child witnesses.[53] Articles 36, 42 and 43 of the Statute also require that judges, legal advisers in the Prosecutor's Office and staff at the Victims and Witness Unit have special expertise in issues relating to sexual and gender violence and violence against children. Furthermore the Victims and Witnesses Unit is required to provide protective measures, counselling and other appropriate assistance for witnesses.

Article 54 of the Statute further calls for the Prosecutor to

> take appropriate measures to ... respect the interests and personal circumstances of victims and witnesses, including age, gender, ... and health, and take into account the nature of the crime, in particular where it involves sexual violence, gender violence or violence against children.

To assist with this the Office of the Prosecutor has established a specific Gender and Children's Unit to strengthen the link between the investigation of crimes committed against women and children and support and protection strategies. Finally, the ICC allows the unique opportunity for victims, including children, to participate in the criminal proceedings without being a witness.[54]

The *Lubanga Case* was the first trial at the ICC where several former child soldiers have taken the stand to testify and it has been a learning experience for the Court. The first child soldier to testify recanted his story soon after he started his testimony, arguably as a result of having to testify in clear view of his former commander. The former child soldier was excused from the stand but he later returned to continue his testimony after additional protective measures were put in place including being shielded from the direct view of

51 Ibid., Article 15.
52 *Rome Statute*, Article 68(1).
53 Ibid., Article 68(2).
54 The participatory rights of victims are outlined in Articles 15(2), 15(3), 19(3), 75(3), 82(4), 68 of the Rome Statute and Rules 85–933 of the Rules of Procedures and Evidence (RPE).

the accused.[55] The ICC subsequently reviewed its Court procedures for vulnerable witnesses including reducing the number of people in the courtroom, shielding the witness from the accused and non-confrontational questioning. The example illustrates that even the best intentions on paper may not have the desired outcomes in practice and that stringent efforts need to be put into understanding precisely what children, particularly girls, require in order to fully and effectively participate in the judicial process.

The importance of justice for girls

It must be noted at the outset that justice for girls is important for exactly the same reasons as justice is important for boys, women and men. The argument here is not that justice for girls is somehow more important than for other members of the community but rather to highlight that, despite increased efforts of international criminal justice mechanisms to consider and involve women and children, girls tend to fall between the cracks. Girls affected by armed conflict represent a particularly vulnerable victim group that requires special advocacy, attention and protection. As a minor, legal protections for women often do not apply to her and as a female, legal provisions for children often fail to address the specific discrimination she suffers on the grounds of her gender. In the masculine realm of post-conflict reconstruction and international criminal justice, girls affected by armed conflict thus tend to remain sidelined in terms of their ability to access international criminal justice mechanisms.

Girls are not just passive victims of human rights abuse; they are survivors, activists, caregivers, peace-builders and often members of the workforce. They are active agents of their own welfare who can contribute valuable views, opinions and experiences to the process of international criminal justice. If we accept this intrinsic agency of girls, we must then adjust international criminal justice mechanisms in ways that enable and encourage their participation. Involving girls in international criminal justice processes empowers them and gives them a sense of control over their lives. Only when the status of the girl child is recognized and the crimes committed against her are given due weight by international courts, will the girl child be able to reap the benefits that international criminal justice has to offer participants such as associations with justice, accountability, reconciliation, empowerment, healing, truth and redress.[56] While these potential benefits of

---

55 Rachel Irwin, 'Interview with Fatou Bensouda, ICC Deputy Prosecutor' (2009), The Lubanga Trial at the International Criminal Court (Lubangatrial.org).

56 For a detailed discussion on the functions of international criminal law see, Payam Akhavan, 'Beyond Impunity: Can International Criminal Justice Prevent Future Atrocities?' (2001) 95(1) *American Journal of International Law*, 7; Stephan Landsman, 'Alternative Responses to Serious Human Rights Abuses: Of Prosecution and Truth Commissions' (1996) 59(4) *Law and Contemporary Problems*, 81; Diane F. Orentlicher, 'Settling Accounts: The Duty to Prosecute Human Rights Violations of a Prior Regime' (1991) 100(8) *Yale Law Journal*, 2537.

international criminal justice apply equally to all victims and witnesses, the positive impact may be more significant for girls.

Many girl victims, particularly victims of sexual crimes, suffer from societal stigmatization and even rejection. Recognition of their victimization by international courts can be an extremely important process for helping girl victims reintegrate into their families and communities. Moreover, international criminal justice processes can also help transfer guilt from the victim to the perpetrator thereby helping the girl realize that she is not to blame for what has happened to her or her family. Access to reparation can also be particularly important for girls as armed conflict is likely to have significant adverse effect on the livelihood of girls.[57] Their education is likely to have been disrupted and the loss of a support structure through the loss of family members may have forced them to take care of themselves. Victims of sexual violence may also face discrimination as a result of cultural beliefs as the loss of virginity may prevent girls from getting married.

The potential of international criminal prosecutions to deter future violence and address the culture of violence that is often embedded within societies can also be particularly important for girls. At an individual level, girls can find reassurance in the thought that perpetrators will not be able to do them any further harm. However, deterrence also serves at the societal level as the threat of future prosecutions may deter future violent and oppressive behaviour.[58] Moreover, negative external influences during a child's formative years, such as exposure to a culture of violence, undermines the formation of identity, values and political beliefs. If injustice is not addressed, this can have far-reaching effects on their ability to function as leaders and decision makers in the future which in turn has negative implications for long-term peace and stability.[59] Until sufficient focus is concentrated on crimes committed against girls, both the crimes themselves and impunity for these crimes will continue.

As shown earlier, the impact of armed conflict on girls and their ability to attain justice in its aftermath is largely influenced by discriminatory gender relationships within society. International criminal justice mechanisms provide a vehicle to address these issues by establishing an accurate account

---

57 Reparations are material or symbolic measures granted in recognition of wrongdoing to the victim and their harm suffered. For a general discussion on reparation and children see, Cécile Aptel and Virginie Ladisch, 'Through a New Lens: A Child-Sensitive Approach to Transitional Justice' (International Center for Transitional Justice, 2011); Dyan Mazurana and Khristopher Carlson, 'Children and Reparation: Past Lessons and New Directions' (June 2010) *UNICEF Innocenti Working Paper No. 2010–08*.

58 However, the connection between international prosecutions and deterrence of future atrocities is much debated and remains largely unresolved. For the purpose of this chapter it is assumed that prosecutions have at least some potential to prevent individuals from committing further crimes. See for full discussion on deterrence: Akhavan *supra*, note 56.

59 No Peace Without Justice and UNICEF Innocenti Research Centre, 'International Criminal Justice and Children' (UNICEF Innocenti Research Centre, September 2002), 137.

of past wrongdoings and exposing underlying discriminatory gender construction. Moreover, through the development of jurisprudence the depth and scope of crimes committed against girls can be consolidated, which is particularly important in light of future prosecutions for the use and recruitment of girl child soldiers. The potential of international criminal mechanisms to address such gender relationships is, in large part, also dependent on *who* participates in them. Experience has shown that unless women and girls have the opportunity to participate in the traditionally male-dominated realm of post-conflict reconstruction it is unlikely that the specific needs of women and girls will be appropriately addressed.

The importance of justice for girls should also be considered in light of the wider transitional justice process. The UN Secretary-General has defined transitional justice as 'the full range of processes and mechanisms associated with a society's attempts to come to terms with a legacy of large-scale human rights abuses, in order to ensure accountability, serve justice and achieve reconciliation'.[60] These measures can include, but are not limited to, international criminal prosecutions, truth-telling, reparations and vetting. It is clear from the definition that regardless of the chosen transitional justice measure, or combination thereof, the ultimate goal of transitional justice is to serve the affected population, a large part of which is usually made up of girls.

As we have seen in the above, international criminal justice has the potential to deliver justice, healing, reconciliation and empowerment for girl victims and can prevent further disenfranchisement within her community. This in turn will lay the foundation on which girls can positively contribute to the rebuilding of their society. As a large part of the population affected by these crimes, girls cannot and should not be ignored. Not only do they have the right to be heard and participate in decisions that affect them under the CRC, but they are also active agents of their own welfare who can provide a unique and important contribution to transitional justice mechanisms. As Graça Machel asserted

> children have an important and unique role in processes that seek truth, justice and reconciliation. Adults can act on behalf of children and in the best interest of children, but unless children themselves are consulted and engaged, we will fall short and undermine the potential to pursue the most relevant and most durable solutions.[61]

International criminal justice that marginalizes girls, thus not only threatens the emotional and social well-being of the girl victim but also long-term peace and development prospects for the wider community.

---

60 'The Rule of Law and Transitional Justice in Conflict and Post-Conflict Societies: Report of the Secretary General', United Nations Security Council, UN Doc. S/2004/616 (2004).
61 Parmar *et al. supra*, note 4, foreword by Graça Machel, x–xi.

Conclusion: towards a girl-friendly international criminal justice system

The adoption of the CRC and the increased recognition of the impact of armed conflict on the lives of children have contributed significantly to the increased focus on crimes committed against children within the jurisdiction of international courts and their participation in these processes. Yet, this process has been slow, particularly when it comes to girls, and they remain largely marginalized in this field. Subsumed either within the categories 'women' or 'children', the gender and age specific experiences and needs of girls affected by armed conflict are not adequately recognized, investigated and prosecuted. Girls represent a significant part of the affected population of modern day conflict that cannot be ignored. In addition, while boys and girls may experience similar 'generic' human rights abuses, cultural norms and gender relationships embedded in society can aggravate the consequences of such experiences for girls. This discrepancy between the impact of armed conflict on boys and girls continues after the fighting has ended as girls are often marginalized in DDR programmes and other post-conflict recovery efforts.

Over the past few decades international courts are slowly starting to address this exclusion and positive steps have been advanced in several areas. International courts have increasingly recognized gender based violence against women and girls as war crimes, crimes against humanity and genocide and a number of prosecutions for such crimes have been secured. Moreover, the recognition of the specific vulnerabilities of women and children has resulted in institutional reform within international courts including efforts to address gender imbalances among staff, the requirement that staff with specific expertise in gender violence and violence against children are amongst the court's staff, and changes in courtroom policies and procedures to address the needs and interests of vulnerable witnesses. Unfortunately, practice to date has shown that girls have failed to really benefit from these improvements as relatively few individuals have been prosecuted for sexual crimes committed against girls and even fewer girls have been given the opportunity to participate in international criminal justice mechanisms.

International criminal justice has the potential to fulfil a number of important functions for the girl victim and the wider community. It can serve to recognize victimization and help girls understand that they are not to blame for what has happened to them or their families. It can further provide girls the opportunity to share their story which can be an important aspect to the process of healing and forgiveness. Addressing accountability for crimes committed against girls is also an important part of long-term peacebuilding as it may prevent such crimes from happening again and can end the cycle of violence. Furthermore, excluding girls from international criminal justice mechanisms denies them access to reparations, a crucial mechanism for recognizing victimization to the victim and broader society and for healing damaged relationships within society. International criminal justice processes can thus serve as a vehicle for truth, justice and reconciliation for girl victims while at the same time addressing discriminatory societal structures and behaviours that contributed to the violations suffered by girls in the first place.

It is recognized that there may be significant logistical and security difficulties in prosecuting cases concerning child-victims and that there may be concerns that children will not be credible witnesses. While these concerns are real and should be carefully addressed, they do not warrant children being sidelined and evidence from domestic criminal courts shows that these obstacles can be overcome with appropriate child protection policies and procedures in place. It is important for international courts to grant due priority to cases concerning child victims, rather than neglect them because of perceived difficulties.

The involvement of girls in international criminal justice mechanisms is extremely important but this should always conform with relevant international legal standards as laid out in the CRC and related documents.[62] A child rights-based approach to international criminal justice ensures that children are treated equally while at the same time acknowledging their specific needs and interests. It allows for their participation in aspects of the judicial process while recognizing that the appropriate level of engagement should vary from child to child, depending on the age and the individual desire to participate. A child rights based approach further requires that concerns for the best interests of the child and their physical and psychological well-being must be always be at the forefront of the decision-making process. International courts must therefore aim to fully operationalize a child rights based approach as it is the most likely path towards enhanced recognition of the status of the girl child and endowing her with rights and a voice.

International Courts must strive to fully integrate children's rights into their institutional culture. There is no clear roadmap on how to achieve this but crucial aspects include: explicit and consistent inclusion of children's issues on the agenda of internal discussions and debates; incorporating child rights issues into mandatory staff training; conducting an internal audit of the institutional child right's climate to identify areas in need of improvement; ensuring adequate staffing and funding for units or departments dealing with child victims and witnesses; and adopting new strategies for the promotion and protection of children's rights throughout all levels of the institution and all phases of the trials. In practice, this means that courts

---

62 Including: UN Office on Drugs and Crime (UNDOC), *Handbook for Professionals and Policymakers on Justice Matters Involving Child Victims and Witnesses of Crime* (Vienna: UNDOC, 2009); 'Guidelines on Justice in Matters involving Child Victims and Witnesses of Crime', ESC Res. 2005/20, 36th plenary meeting, UN Doc. E/2005/20 (22 July 2005); 'United Nations Standard Minimum Rules for the Administration of Juvenile Justice', GA General Assembly, 40th session, UN Doc. A/40/53 (29 November 1985).

must adopt or revise existing child protection policies and ensure that these policies are reflected in the statutory framework of the international court to ensure that they are developed, implemented and adequately resourced. Furthermore all staff involved with girl victims and witnesses must receive appropriate training and adequate screening of witnesses needs to be established to ensure that the girls who do participate are empowered rather than harmed by the experience. Once witnesses have been identified, individual support or counselling before, during and after the testimony is also crucial. This will help establish trust, identify their needs and wishes and the girls' sense of control over the process. Finally, plans for long-term follow-up of girl witnesses and possible referral to specialized health services should be an integral part of the support strategy. The ICC has taken positive steps towards implementing these components in its statute and proceedings but it remains to be seen if it can deliver on full and effective participation of girls in the judicial process.

Only when international criminal justice mechanisms automatically consider the experiences, rights and needs of girls alongside those of boys, women and men, will girls be able to reap the full benefits that are theoretically provided to them by the international criminal justice system.

4 Lessons from the field

The inclusion of refugee women in transitional justice initiatives

Sarah Maddox[1]

Introduction

The importance of the participation of women, refugees[2] and particularly refugee women in transitional justice processes cannot be overstated.

In his 2004 report to the United Nations Security Council, "The rule of law and transitional justice in conflict and post-conflict societies", the then United Nations Secretary-General Kofi Annan stated that transitional justice processes should pay special attention to abuses committed against groups most affected by conflict and establish particular measures for their protection and redress in judicial and reconciliation processes. Among those the Secretary-General specifically listed women and refugees as being most affected by conflict.

Transitional justice is primarily at work within communities that are emerging from generalised violence, internal turmoil or civil war. Refugees however, by definition, have fled their country of origin to seek asylum in a third country, been forced across a border into a neighbouring country or been forced into refugee or IDP camps. Therefore refugees are often no longer within the territory in which the generalised violence, internal turmoil or civil war took place and consequently are also no longer within the territory in which transitional justice and peace initiatives are taking place. However it is a mistake to think that the absence of refugees from

---

1 Sarah Maddox is an Australian legal practitioner with ten years' experience practising in criminal and refugee law in Australia. She has a Masters degree in international criminal law from the United Nations Interregional Crime and Research Institute, worked for a short time as a volunteer solicitor with the United Nations International Criminal Tribunal for Rwanda and completed a course in human rights and the media with the European Inter-University Centre for Human Rights and Democratisation. She has worked with refugees in Australia for over two years at the Asylum Seeker Resource Centre in Melbourne.

2 In this chapter I will use the term "refugees" to refer not just to a refugee as defined in the 1951 Convention Relating to the Status of Refugees and its Additional Protocols, but as encompassing the broader range of displaced persons the United Nations High Commissioner of Refugees is mandated to protect, including asylum seekers, refugees, internally displaced persons (IDPs), returnees and stateless persons.

these territories, excludes their right to be included in transitional justice initiatives. In fact it is quite the opposite.

In addition to repatriation, the transitional justice initiative most explicitly inclusive of them, refugees are also greatly in need of what other transitional justice initiatives can offer, because they are among those that are most affected by conflict. Refugees are likely to have also experienced discrimination or abuse due to their race, ethnicity, religion, political opinion, sex or membership of a particular social group prior to a conflict erupting, increasing their vulnerability during conflict.

In addition to what transitional justice initiatives can offer them, refugees' experiences of the failure of the structures of society and governance in a community prior to the outbreak of conflict give them a unique insight into the issues that should be addressed by any comprehensive transitional justice strategy.

The inclusion of refugee women in transitional justice initiatives is of particular importance. This is because, first, women currently make up 50 per cent of the refugee population.[3] Second, while male refugees were not equal rights holders in the societies from which they fled, women refugees often had even fewer rights than their male counterparts. If refugee women are not included in transitional justice initiatives, there is a risk that gender inequities that existed prior to a conflict will be reinforced in post-conflict societies. Third, although women are increasingly becoming voluntary participants in armed conflict, the conduct of war and other conflict is still predominantly the arena of men,[4] leaving women as survivors of the conflict to pioneer peace and transitional justice initiatives. Fourth, women's experiences of conflict differ greatly from that of men, not only in physical acts of violence committed against them, but also through socio-economic exclusion. Research also indicates that military peace may not necessarily result in the cessation of violence against women as private acts of violence, such as domestic violence, has been shown to increase during times of greater societal unrest.[5]

Despite this, the participation of refugee women in transitional justice initiatives in the past and present has been limited or non-existent.

Given the recognised importance of women and refugees as subjects of transitional justice initiatives, this chapter explores the extent of the participation of refugee women in those initiatives, the obstacles to their participation and any lessons for future initiatives that can be gleaned. This includes a consideration of the interrelationship between conflicts and the causes of

3 United Nations High Commissioner for Refugees 'Global Trends 2010', 33: www.unhcr. org/4dfa11499.html.
4 International Committee of the Red Cross, 'Women Facing War: ICRC Study on the Impact of Armed Conflict on Women', October 2001, 2: www.icrc.org/eng/assets/files/other/icrc_002_0798_women_facing_war.pdf.
5 Ibid., 44–45.

displacement, and the status and experiences of women in conflict societies prior to and during a conflict. This exploration occurs by way of interviews conducted with three women who are transitional justice or refugee practitioners and who have worked with refugee women from a wide range of countries transitioning from conflict over an extended time period.

The field practitioners

The first interviewee (FP1) worked for the Italian Refugee Council[6] from 1998 to 2002 and as a legal adviser for asylum seekers, refugees and migrants with a local non-governmental organisation (NGO), the JRS Project[7] in Catania, Sicily, Italy.[8] She predominantly assisted Eritrean refugees fleeing military conflict in Eritrea from 1998 to 2000, Iraqi refugees fleeing persecution on the basis of political activism or political affiliations, and refugees from Sierra Leone fleeing the civil war fought between government forces and rebel groups from 1991 to 2002. She currently works for the International Catholic Migration Commission.

The second interviewee (FP2) worked from October 2006 to May 2007 with Palestinian refugees in the Neirab and Ein el Tal refugee camps in Syria on community development projects with the United Nations Relief and Works Agency (UNRWA). From April 2008 to December 2009 she worked repatriating Mauritanian refugees returning from Senegal after 20 years in exile who were settling in the river valley towns of Kaedi, Boghe and Rosso for the United Nations High Commissioner for Refugees (UNHCR). After this, from March 2010 to February 2011 she worked with IDPs from the Zalingei area in Western Darfur where she undertook protection work and the monitoring of returnees, also for the UNHCR.

The third interviewee (FP3) worked with the United Nations Mission in Sudan (UNMIS) as the head of the field office in Torit, Eastern Equatoria, Sudan, from August 2009 until April 2011. From May 2011 to October 2011 she worked with the new United Nations Mission in South Sudan (UNMISS) stationed in Juba, South Sudan, as a reporting and analysis officer and as the human rights liaison officer for the Joint Operations Centre. In

---

6 Consiglio Italiano per i Rifugiati – CIR onlus.
7 Ass. Centro Astalli Catania.
8 FP1 monitored the local reception centres and facilities for asylum seekers and irregular migrants. She acted as legal counsel for asylum seekers and vulnerable groups of migrants such as women and children. She provided legal assistance and individual social counselling to asylum seekers and refugees and made regular assessments on the handling of incoming irregular migratory flows in the reception centres in the east coast of Sicily. As part of her work she had regular interaction with public authorities, including prefettura, police stations, NGOs and other local associations. A key part of her work was the promotion of better policies and admission procedures for asylum seekers and refugees. She served mostly as legal counsel to asylum seekers and vulnerable groups of migrants (women and children).

both missions, her work involved investigation of human rights issues and violations.⁹ She worked with a number of groups who had been displaced for a variety of reasons, including Southern Sudanese who had been living in the north and were returning to the newly created South Sudan, ethnic groups targeted as part of violence occurring in particular areas, including members of the Dinka Ngok, Nuban, Uduk, Funj and Maban ethnic groups, and also refugees whose homelands were experiencing violence so they could no longer live there safely.

The interviews with the field practitioners took place between September and December 2011. It should be stated from the outset that the number of refugees each field practitioner worked with was enormous and they each stressed they were providing general views gained from their work and that such views could not and do not reflect the diversity of experiences and opinions of all the individual cases of the refugee women they worked with. Having worked so closely with refugees and in territories close to where conflict had or was taking place, I considered each of the practitioners to have unique insights into the range of transitional justice initiatives that are being explored in the field, the ways in which they are being implemented and the extent to which refugee women were being included within them.

Causes of displacement

Each field practitioner outlined a complex interrelationship between the refugees they worked with and the conflict situation they had fled from. This interrelationship included refugees from minority groups or groups who had been discriminated against prior to the outbreak of conflict and then further targeted once conflict erupted (Darfur, Mauritania, Sudan), refugees who were members of a social, ethnic or political group who were targeted as part of a conflict (Sierra Leone, Sudan), refugees whose territory was under dispute so they could not live there in safety (Eritrea and Sudan) and refugees who faced statelessness issues during and after a conflict (Palestine, Sudan and South Sudan).

FP1 stated that the Eritrean refugees she worked with had fled Eritrea due to military conflict between 1998 and 2000 with Ethiopia over the ill-defined border, but the individual experiences of the refugees were not linked to the underlying causes of the conflict, but rather to their experience of the conflict itself. She said the refugee men she worked with from Eritrea had predominantly evaded national military service and were afraid of being punished without any form of trial or legal recourse. Punishment could consist of torture or arbitrary detention for an indefinite period. Penalties for

---

9 The aim of FP3's work was to identify patterns among reported rights incidents and then to support and advise on change in the pursuit of justice and accountability, at the local working level with civil society, traditional authorities, law enforcement, legal administration, judiciary, and also to affect high government policy and legislative action.

those who evaded national service also extended to family members. These refugees she worked with sought asylum in Italy on the basis of belonging to a social group of "military evaders".

FP1 stated that the Iraqi refugees she worked with had usually fled persecution in Iraq due to their political opinion or imputed political opinion. She said that some of the refugees had themselves been politically active whereas others had not been but were related to or had other associations with political activists. The Iraqi refugees she assisted had fled prior to the US-led invasion and occupation of Iraq in 2003, however the security situation in the country was deteriorating, including repression of political opponents and other human rights violations, and civil unrest exacerbated by the impact on the population of the economic sanctions placed on Iraq by the United Nations (UN) following the Gulf War.[10]

FP1 stated that the majority of refugees she worked with from Sierra Leone had fled the civil war and atrocities committed by the Revolutionary United Front (RUF). She stated that in almost all instances the refugees had suffered either directly or indirectly from brutalities committed by RUF members, which included the murder of family members, physical mutilation and torture. There was a direct link between the underlying causes of the conflict and the individual experiences of the refugees, in that they were predominantly persecuted on the basis of a political opinion or imputed political opinion that was in opposition to that of the RUF.

FP2 stated that in each of the refugee situations she worked, there was always a link between the underlying causes of conflict and the causes of displacement among the refugee population.

In relation to Mauritania, she stated the refugees she worked with were part of a minority group of African ethnicity who had been living in Mauritania at a time when it was asserting an Arab identity. The Mauritanians of African ethnicity previously lived on the southern border with Senegal and had a nomadic way of life, which meant that families and forms of land ownership often straddled the Senegalese border. The land there was fertile and sought after. Mauritania had a tense relationship with Senegal and Mauritanians of Arab ethnicity accused Mauritanians of African ethnicity of not being "real" Mauritanians and rather of being Senegalese, and these people were deported by the thousands.

FP2 stated that the Darfurian refugees she worked with had been persecuted by the central Sudanese Government for ethnic and economic reasons. She stated that the refugees were not necessarily from ethnic minorities but were from non-Arab ethnic groups. Sudanese of non-Arab ethnicity were discriminated against by the Arab central Sudanese Government. Refugees had also been displaced for economic reasons, relating to land ownership. Their villages had been burned and they were forced to flee into towns or cities and live in IDP camps.

---

10 United Nations Security Council Resolution 688, 5 April 1991.

FP2 stated that the Palestinian refugees in Syria that she worked with were displaced directly as a result of the conflict between Israel and Palestine. Questions of nationality and loss of land due to the creation of the Israeli state had caused significant displacement.

FP3 worked with several categories of refugees while in Sudan and South Sudan. She stated the complexity of the situation faced by each group illustrated the interwoven issues that hinder current and future development and security in the region. These interwoven issues in turn reflect the complexity of the causes and outcomes of the fighting that is still occurring in some parts of Sudan and South Sudan. The first group of refugees she worked with were "returnees". These were southerners who had been living in the north during the civil war but began returning south from the time of the Comprehensive Peace Agreement (CPA) in 2005, and in vastly increasing numbers after the referendum of January 2011 and the Declaration of Independence of South Sudan in July 2011. The large numbers of returnees was exacerbated by the Khartoum Government's announcement that dual citizenship would not be granted, creating issues for southerners living in the north and northerners living in the south. The lack of infrastructure to cope with the numbers of returnees in itself caused outbreaks of violence between the existing community and the returnees. The returnees sought plots of land on which to set up temporary housing as the South Sudan government did not have the resources to accommodate them. The second group of refugees FP3 worked with were members of ethnic groups who had been targeted as part of the conflict in particular areas and fled to Sudan, South Sudan or Ethiopia, including the Dinka Ngok from the Abyei area, ethnic Nubans from the eastern area of the Southern Kordofan State (SKS) and members of the Uduk, Funj and Maban ethnic groups from the Blue Nile State. FP3 stated that the Dinka Ngok and the Nuban had been marginalised and racially targeted by the Government of Sudan over a long period, whereas attacks against the Uduk, Funj and Maban ethnic groups from eastern SKS had been sudden and unexpected among those groups and caused a deep sense of bewilderment and betrayal among their members against the Government. The last group of Sudanese refugees she worked with were members of communities from a number of areas who were displaced interstate and intrastate due to the insecurity that had existed since 2009 in their homelands caused by fighting between rebel militia groups and the Sudan People's Liberation Army (SPLA).

While the interrelationships between the conflicts and the causes of displacement of the groups outlined above are inevitably as varied as the unique and complex situations they emerged from, where they reveal that refugees were also members of particular social, ethnic, political or other groups who were subjected to violence or discrimination prior to or during a conflict, those refugees are in a unique position to describe to transitional justice practitioners fractures in civil and political society that may have contributed to the outbreak of violence.

Referring back to the Secretary-General's 2004 *Rule of Law* report, he considered that a comprehensive transitional justice strategy should consider the nature of the underlying conflict, any history of widespread abuse and the condition and nature of the country's legal system, traditions and institutions. Anecdotal evidence of pervasive violence against minorities explicitly or tacitly supported by authority groups, an imbalance in power or wealth exacerbating tensions among social groups, or an overall rule of law vacuum, such as that reported by the field practitioners and outlined above, could be of significant value to transitional justice practitioners in understanding the underlying nature of any conflict and developing comprehensive strategies for transition.

Demographic characteristics of refugee women and their experiences of conflict

The field practitioners each reported that women made up a large percentage of the refugees they worked with, that women faced greater structural inequalities than men in their countries of origin prior to the eruption of conflict, such as a lack of education and empowerment, and that women had different experiences of conflict in comparison to the men from their communities, such as sexual or gender-based violence (SGBV) directed against them during the conflict and in some instances continuing after they reached refugee camps or other "safe" areas, reinforcing that refugee women are among those most affected by conflict.

As outlined above, currently, women make up 50 per cent of refugees worldwide. The field practitioners who worked with refugees in camps reported that the number of women they worked with was consistent with this or higher, whereas FP1 who worked with refugees seeking asylum in Italy reported a much lower rate of refugee women.

FP1 reported that the proportion of refugee women she worked with differed according to their country of origin. Refugees from Eritrea usually arrived in family groups, however each family had usually lost one or more family member in the conflict. The refugees from Iraq and Sierra Leone that she assisted were predominantly single men and she stated that this was probably due to it being physically easier for men to leave the country. The greater difficulties faced by women in leaving a conflict country include less access to the resources needed to leave, such as secure transport and cash, their responsibilities in the home and the potential of being subjected to violence whilst in transit when unaccompanied by a male.

The experience of FP2 was that 50 per cent of the Palestinian refugees in the Syrian camps were women, 60–70 per cent of the Mauritanian refugees returning to Senegal were women and 60 per cent of the Darfurian IDPs in West Darfur were women.

The experience of FP3 was that the rate of Sudanese refugee women varied among the refugee groups she worked with, however overall between 50 and

60 per cent were women. She also estimated that 80 to 85 per cent of those refugee women were supporting children and elderly or wounded family members.

Each of the field practitioners provided similar demographic character-istics of the refugee women they worked with, in terms of their level of edu-cation, employment history and the position of women in their societies prior to conflict.

Both FP1 and FP2 stated that the refugee women they worked with usually had very low levels of education. FP3 stated that among women in Sudan generally, there is an illiteracy rate of approximately 98 per cent, however the groups of refugee women she worked with varied in their edu-cation levels. She said refugee women who were older than 35 years of age generally had no education or education that was limited to primary school, ending at age 12 or 13. If these women had any further training beyond school it was predominantly midwifery, nursing or teaching. She advised that the situation was markedly different for refugee women who had left Sudan during the civil war and lived in Uganda: these women had received greater access to education and a higher level of education. She reported that the refugee women who had fled to northern Sudan during the civil war could be broken into two categories in relation to level of education. One group had better access to education than they would have received if they had stayed in South Sudan, however others, particularly if they came from a marginalised group, received no education at all.

FP1 and FP2 both reported that in the countries of origin of the refugees they worked with, women had limited to no involvement in government, military, religion or civil society and were extremely unlikely to hold posi-tions of authority. Both FP1 and FP2 reported that the refugee women they worked with were decision-makers in their countries only in relation to daily household matters, such as the care of children, cooking and cleaning. FP2 stated that the heavy household burden of women and cultural norms were contributors to the lack of participation of women in public forums. FP2 stated that the refugee women she worked with were less politicised than their male counterparts from the same country, in that lower levels of educa-tion usually meant they were less politically aware, but also that their house-hold responsibilities meant they were more interested in day-to-day practicalities than the mechanisms of abstract politics.

FP1 who worked with refugee women during resettlement stated that gender inequalities that existed in their countries of origin could continue in the protection country and hinder the successful integration of these women into their new country. She referred to increased freedoms given to some refugee women in relation to dress, attitude and employment in their pro-tection country whilst being embraced by the women could also generate conflict and tension within their family unit. She cited an example of Eri-trean refugee women who embraced European hair, make-up and clothing styles both because they enjoyed these new freedoms and also because they believed this would assist their and their children's integration, however some men from the Eritrean refugee community opposed these greater freedoms given to women, causing tension within individual families and the Eritrean refugee community as a whole.

FP3 stated that although capacity-building and democratisation efforts of international partners, UN programmes and NGOs in Sudan have resulted in women's civil society groups growing on a grassroots level, at higher levels within government and other authorities, men hold the power. She stated that while the parliament of South Sudan has a quota requiring 25 per cent female representation and that women do hold positions as governors and ministers, men still control the pillars of government. FP3 reported that male parliamentarians and party chiefs have interpreted the female quota as a maximum rather than a minimum and some have even argued that women cleaners working in the parliamentary building can be counted towards meeting the quota. She stated that women who have made it into positions of power often then struggle to have their views carry the same weight as their male counterparts. She also stated that women who hold positions of authority in South Sudan largely come from the returning Sudanese diaspora, from (northern) Sudan, Uganda and Kenya and a very small percentage from South Africa. She stated that while there are many women working in police and corrections in South Sudan, they are rarely given the same training or opportunities as men and are often reduced to being administrative assistants or maintenance workers. She reported that while women were instrumental during the north/south civil war for intelligence gathering and other "soft" skills, there were no longer as many women active in the military. Of particular relevance in the Sudanese context is that the church, a powerful humanitarian actor both before and after the civil war and trusted by both sides, is very male dominated and that this gender imbalance is highly unlikely to change. Women are only allowed to operate within the church at local levels such as acting as counsellors for communities.

The field practitioners also reported that the refugee women they worked with had commonly suffered from one or more types of violence, including SGBV, and that this violence occurred prior to the conflict, during the conflict, in transit and even after arrival in refugee camps or safe areas, making the experience of conflict by refugee women vastly different from that of refugee men and of other women.

FP1 reported that refugee women who had fled conflict in Eritrea often had violence perpetrated against them in transit in Libya rather than during the conflict itself. She reported that this violence had occurred at the hands both of civilians and of the military in Libya and was commonly experienced by women who had been placed in detention whilst in transit for having no documentation, such as identity papers.

FP2 reported that the refugee women from Palestine she worked with had experienced violence at the hands of Israeli forces at the time of expulsion from Palestine and also by Syrian forces if these women had been active in politics. FP2 also reported that most of the Darfurian refugee women she had worked with had experienced SGBV, usually by the Janjaweed (a militia group predominantly made up of Sudanese of Arab ethnicity) both during the conflict and during their flight from it. She also stated in relation to Darfurian women that on occasion this violence continued after displacement even though the refugee camps offered some security.

FP2 stated that SGBV including early and forced marriage, female genital mutilation and marital rape was reported by refugee women she worked with from Palestine, Senegal and Darfur. She also stated that many of the women who had experienced such violence considered it a common experience for women in the countries they were from.

FP3 estimated that 90 per cent of the refugee women she worked with had suffered direct physical violence to their person, during the fighting or during their flight from it. She stated that this violence had been perpetrated against women by members of the Sudanese Armed Forces (SAF) and the SPLA during the fighting and then by pursuit forces, protective forces/ security personnel or other civilians after women reached refugee camps or "safe" areas. She advised that members of the Dinka Ngok and Nuban ethnic groups reported racial slurs directed against them individually or as part of a targeted community during acts of violence. She also reported that there was evidence that only parts of regions or towns that had communities of Dinka Ngok or Nubans were bombed or targeted as part of the conflict. The Government of Sudan also engaged in rhetoric about the eradication of non-Arab persons. FP3 stated that it was very difficult to generalise about the numbers of women who had experienced SGBV during the conflict or after their arrival in refugee camps, as there was a large number of second-hand reports but very few confirmed cases. She stated that SGBV had been reported among the southern Sudanese women returnees in receipt transit areas. She also stated that where the military were on the ground for longer periods during fighting and the civil population had no means of escape, there were reports of SBGV against women by uniformed members of the SAF or proxy militia as part of a military strategy to terrorise the civilian population. She stated that this SGBV was part of a strategy that was approved of, or that at least tacitly consented to, by military commanders.

What is unsurprising is that the reports of the field practitioners consistently noted that refugee women had faced greater structural inequalities in their countries of origin prior to the outbreak of conflict than their male counterparts. Each of the field practitioners reported that the refugee women they worked with had low levels of education. They also reported that the refugee women and other women from their countries usually did not hold positions of authority or governance in their countries. These structural inequalities arguably made these women more vulnerable to violence during a conflict and less likely that violence would be reported after. This vulnerability was particularly demonstrated by reports of refugee women who were also a member of a political, social, ethnic or other group that had been discriminated against or persecuted prior to or during the conflict being subjected to SGBV (non-Arab Darfurian women) and for women who experienced SGBV as part of a military strategy to terrorise civilian populations (by the SAF and proxy militia in Sudan). The field practitioners also reported the incidence of SGBV from refugee women not only prior to and during the conflict, but also after reaching "safe" areas or refugee camps.[11] While this is unfortunately not new news for transitional justice practitioners, it is worth emphasising the extent to which refugee women have experienced conflict differently from refugee men and from other women from their communities, and in many cases more violently.

What can be confirmed from the reports outlined above is that women make up a large proportion of the refugee population, their experiences of conflict are often more violent than those of other civilians, they are regularly required to become the head of a household of other vulnerable family members such as children and the elderly[12] after a conflict and they face increased difficulties in doing so through the situation of displacement itself, such as difficulties accessing resources, security issues,[13] language and other cultural[14] barriers. Each of these circumstances faced by refugee women during conflict demonstrates why their inclusion in transitional justice initiatives should be among the highest of priorities.

Extent of and obstacles to participation of refugee women in transitional justice initiatives

Extent of participation

The field practitioners reported different levels of participation of refugee women in the various transitional justice contexts they worked in, however

---

11 FP2 reported that SGBV perpetrated by the Janjaweed against Darfurian refugee women continued even once they were in refugee camps. FP3 reported that southern Sudanese returnees experienced SGBV in refugee receipt areas. See also: International Committee of the Red Cross *supra*, note 4; Aolian, F. "Political Violence and Gender during Times of Transition" (2006) *Columbia Journal of Gender and Law* 15:3 831; Caprioli, Mary "Gender Equality and Civil Wars" (2003) *CPR Working Papers, Social Development Department, Environmentally and Socially Sustainable Development Network* 6.

12 This was reported by FP3. See also: Rubio-Marín, R. "Gender and Reparations: Setting the Agenda" (2006) *Reparations for Women Victims of Human Rights Violations: Case Studies*, Social Science Research Council, New York, 21–47.

13 As reported by FP2 in relation to Darfurian refugee women and FP3 in relation to Sudanese refugee women who suffered conflict violence of SGBV even once in refugee camps or safe areas.

14 As reported by all three field practitioners: women had lower levels of education and were less likely to hold positions of authority in their countries of origin. Also as cited by FP1 in relation to refugee women who faced problems successfully integrating due to different cultural norms existing in their displaced situations, such as increased freedom of dress.

in most cases refugee women were not consulted or informed about initiatives, or were not able to participate due to a number of obstacles.

FP1 reported that resettled refugees from Iraq and Eritrea would usually maintain strong connections with family members and friends from their home countries and would also engage with others from their community living in Italy. However, despite this she stated she was not aware of the refugees she worked with participating in transitional justice initiatives in their countries of origin.

FP2 stated that despite consultation with Palestinian refugees in peace processes and decision-making being high on the agenda of international and regional authorities, in practice it did not occur among the refugees she worked with. She noted that some of the authorities within Sudan have been responsible for the killing of internally displaced Darfurians and accordingly the views of the displaced population on peace and transition were definitely not sought. She further noted that as both the Palestinian and Darfurian conflicts are ongoing, none of the refugees she worked with in those contexts had received any justice or accountability for wrongs committed against them.

FP2 stated that the most successful inclusion of refugees within a transitional justice initiative that she had seen in her work, was the successful repatriation of Mauritanian refugees from Senegal coupled with reparations measures. She stated that this repatriation was seen as a crucial aspect of national reconciliation for Mauritania and therefore refugees had been consulted by the Mauritanian authorities and international agencies as part of the peace processes. However, she also stated that no special effort was made to include the views of Mauritanian refugee women in that consultation process.

Additionally, FP2 reported that some of the Mauritanian refugees repatriated from Senegal to Mauritania received reparations for land or cattle lost, however these reparations occurred on a one-size fits all basis, without a truth commission or trials. She stated that there was an attempt to establish a land commission to assess the claim of each individual returnee but it did not work in practice. She also stated that some reparation was made to victims of wrongdoing and that this and the other general compensation mechanisms definitely contributed to a peaceful repatriation. However, she also stated that whilst the repatriation and reparation scheme was very well received by the Mauritanian refugees she worked with, many felt that it was insufficient, as those responsible for their persecution and mistreatment remained in power.

FP3 stated that the participation of refugees in decision-making as to the future of Sudan and South Sudan, and in peace or transitional justice initiatives had been extremely limited. She stated that she was not aware of any of the refugees she worked with participating in any transitional justice initiatives. She noted that a number of transitional justice initiatives are occurring in South Sudan, such as the Southern Sudan Human Rights Commission (SSHRC), the Southern Sudan Recovery and Relief Commission

(SSRRC) and the Southern Sudan Peace Commission (SSPC), however the participation of refugees and the inclusion of refugee issues has not been a priority in any of them.

In relation to the CPA between the Sudan People's Liberation Movement (SPLM) and the Government of Sudan, FP3 stated she was not aware of any attempt to incorporate the views of refugees in its consultation or negotiation.

In relation to the referendum of January 2011 in South Sudan, FP3 stated there had been only a limited involvement of Sudanese IDPs, however the International Organisation for Migration (IOM) and the Government of South Sudan facilitated participation by refugees located outside the border in Uganda, Kenya and other areas. The IOM assisted refugees outside the borders to register for the referendum and the Government of South Sudan went above and beyond to coordinate transport for refugees to travel to South Sudan to vote or for them to report to proxy referendum centres in other countries. The Southern Sudan Referendum Bureau or Commission attempted to locate people who were registered in certain areas and who had been displaced or moved to other areas to participate in the referendum of January 2011 in South Sudan, however the emphasis was more on locating members of pastoral communities who had moved due to cattle grazing rather than refugees or IDPs.

Obstacles to participation

FP1 believes the lack of participation of the refugee women she worked with in transitional justice initiatives in their countries of origin was predominantly due to a lack of awareness by the refugees that those initiatives were taking place. She noted that during the period she was working with refugees, no one had the same access to information as they do today, as the internet and mobile phones were not nearly as prevalent and were even less accessible to refugees. She stated that refugees faced enormous obstacles accessing information about their home countries and used the resources they had at their disposal to maintain contact with family and friends. She believes that today the internet is vital in distributing information about transitional justice initiatives. FP1 also noted that whilst the refugees she worked with did not engage with peace initiatives, political activity or NGOs working in their home countries once resettled, the children of refugees were much more likely to do so. In particular she mentioned the children of Ethiopian refugees she worked with, whose family members were still in Ethiopia and were considered to be opponents of the government. She stated that these children became very active in the Ethiopian community in Rome and she believes that the children of refugees generally, through greater access to education in their protection countries, are better able to become pro-active, engaged and informed about their origin countries than their parents were.

FP2 stated that even if the views of Palestinian refugees were sought in transitional justice and peace initiatives, they suffer from an inability to see a long-term future for themselves that in itself would be an obstacle to their participation in such initiatives. FP2 reported that the resignation felt by the Palestinian refugees is due to the length of their exile, the protracted and seemingly unending nature of the conflict and a perception that due to support by Western countries and in particular the United States that the balance of power is held by the Israeli state. Therefore substantial preliminary work would need to be undertaken by any transitional justice practitioners working with these refugees to develop a belief in the value of their contribution before even attempting to tackle the underlying issues these refugees face.

FP2 stated that she believes the greatest obstacle faced by refugee women generally in participating in transitional justice initiatives is that it is against the cultural norms in many transitioning countries for women to participate in public life or political affairs. She said some refugee women she had worked with said they felt their participation in such initiatives had been imposed upon them by international aid workers and that they had not been comfortable with it. She also stated that refugee women were often too busy with the daily household work to be able to dedicate any time to other activities such as transitional justice initiatives. A further obstacle to the participation of refugee women in such initiatives was the low education level of women generally and that women themselves often viewed their lack of participation in public affairs as normal rather than something to be rectified. FP2 stated that she wasn't aware of any difference in what men and women wanted in terms of transitional justice or accountability for wrongs committed against them, but believed that men were more vocal about seeking justice because they were better educated and more politicised than the women. She also noted however, that the situations of transition she had worked in were conservative and hierarchical and often men were also absent from participation in decision-making as it was only a small stronghold of leaders that controlled the majority.

FP3 stated that there were a number of obstacles faced by refugee women in South Sudan to participating in transitional justice initiatives. In relation to the SSHRC, she stated that due to a lack of organisation, credibility, independence, corruption and capacity, the SSHRC has struggled to even address the issues of the general populace, let alone refugee issues. She stated that while refugee and returnee issues should be a priority of both the SSRRC and SSPC, particularly in relation to the disputes over the reclamation of land that regularly spiral into violence, tribal, local and national allegiances that exist within the commissions have frustrated the commissions' processes.

In relation to the obstacles faced by refugees in participating in the implementation of the CPA in Sudan and South Sudan, FP3 stated that the refugees she worked with only had a very limited understanding of the CPA and predominantly thought that it was just a mechanism that put an end to the civil war and that it gave people the opportunity to vote on whether South Sudan should be a separate country. She stated that refugees were not kept informed during the CPA negotiation process and did not know who the players were in making the agreement, the timeline or the other issues that were negotiated within it, such as wealth-sharing. She stated that how the CPA was to be implemented was completely beyond the comprehension of most refugees.

In relation to the January 2011 referendum in South Sudan, FP3 stated that many southern Sudanese who were residing in the north at the time of the referendum were not able to vote as they were fearful that they would not be able to re-cross the border after voting, that they would be tagged and then targeted by national security forces, or that they would face retribution by the Khartoum Government if they exercised their right to vote.

FP3 outlined a number of obstacles for the participation of refugee women in transitional justice initiatives more generally. She stated that even if the views of refugee women were actively sought, they often have a fundamental lack of awareness of what their rights are, what action can be taken to assert those rights and the ability and confidence to take that action. FP3 stated that the loss of land and property in Sudan has and will impact women differently from men, as women do not have the same access to or awareness of their rights to land or property. In the event that the refugee women are able to return home most women would have no idea how to ask for what was rightfully theirs in order to rebuild their and their family's lives.

Form of transitional justice initiatives sought by refugees

FP1 stated that she believed accountability of the perpetrators for crimes committed against the refugees she worked with or against their family members may have contributed to healing and reconciliation but she believes that this would only be the case once these refugees had gained economic and social stability. She stated that the refugees she worked with were always focused on their immediate needs rather than accountability or justice, at least initially. She stated that many who were focused on integrating into new communities only confronted the atrocities committed in the past, years later once they were resettled and stable.

FP1 stated that for the majority of refugees who maintained close connections with family members and friends in their countries of origin, that political reform, truth commissions and trials in their home countries would have eased the pain and losses they had suffered. However, she also stated she believed many refugees who had sought asylum in a protection country predominantly sought to move on with their lives, not necessarily to forget the past, but to focus on their future and that of their family. This corresponds to transitional justice studies that have showed reparations awarded to refugees to compensate them for harm experienced during conflict were regularly viewed by those refugees less as redress for that harm and more as providing a basis for their future.[15]

FP2 stated that in her opinion from her work with refugees, some form of justice, accountability or reconciliation mechanism would definitely help refugees to move on with their lives. FP2 stated that what was sought most by the refugees she worked with was reparations for their losses.

FP3 stated that among the refugees she worked with, justice both for men and women meant security for the immediate future of themselves and their family in terms of safety, food and shelter, wherever or however it could be provided. She stated that they sought the prevention of further humiliation through the provision of basic necessities and that they felt that this would hold together what remained of their dignity.

Field practitioners' views on transitional justice initiatives

The field practitioners provided their views as to transitional justice initiatives they believed would be most beneficial to refugees in the various situations they had worked in and also more general views about the interaction between transitional justice and refugees.

In relation to the Mauritanian context, FP2 stated that many of the refugees she worked with felt that the reparation and repatriation scheme was insufficient as many perpetrators of wrongdoing remained in power. However, she does not believe a process in which individual cases were aired, such as a trial or a truth commission, would have contributed to ongoing peace and stability for Mauritania.

On a broader level, FP2 stated that international aid agencies and NGOs were in a unique position to facilitate the participation of refugees and in particular refugee women in transitional justice initiatives. She noted that in many refugee populations, refugees had become politically organised and had representatives who consulted or negotiated with their government,[16] or if relations had broken down completely an international agency such as the UNHCR would act on their behalf.[17] She stated that international agencies or NGOs were well placed to also facilitate the participation of refugees in

---

15 Laplante, L. 'On the Indivisibility of Rights: Truth Commissions, Reparations and the Right to Development' (2007) *Yale Human Rights and Development Journal* 10 141; and Rubio-Marín *supra*, note 12.

16 FP2 stated that this was particularly the case with the Palestinian refugees and also, to a lesser extent, the Mauritanian refugees she had worked with.

17 FP2 stated that this was the case in Darfur in a town called Zalingei, close to Jabal Marra area which is a stronghold of the Sudan Liberation Army rebels where the situation was extremely tense. She stated people belonging to a government body could not even enter a Furawi IDP camp and that there were reports that the last government people to enter the camps (with the exception of some groups such as nurses and teachers) was two to three years ago: two members of the National Hydraulic Service entered and they were killed as camp residents suspected they came to poison the water.

transitional justice initiatives or advocate for initiatives that would be beneficial for those they worked with. She stated that this was particularly important for refugee women as often refugee representatives did not adequately represent the needs of an entire refugee community and that an independent third party was more likely to represent the needs of a greater proportion of that community, including the needs of women and young people.

In relation to the current refugee situation in Sudan and South Sudan, FP3 believes some sort of intervention is required to ensure the credibility and effectiveness of the SSHRC, the SSRRC and the SSPC to ensure refugee and returnee issues are made a priority. She stated that at a state and international level, although the current political climate and make-up of the UN Security Council meant that the International Criminal Court (ICC) and international sanctions would not be effective in addressing or preventing wrongs that have and will continue to occur in Sudan and South Sudan, a formal ICC investigation should be launched so that evidence can be gathered to place increasing pressure on ICC member states and the international community as a whole to take action. She stated that the faith of the people of both Sudan and South Sudan in the accountability and justice provided by the ICC has waned after watching the ICC's investigation of the situation in Darfur, and that on the whole the population believes the court to be impotent. She stated that the blatant and repeated breach of international standards by the Government of Sudan against members of its own population and citizens of neighbouring countries means that any higher level transitional justice initiatives would need to incorporate state or state-actor accountability, that it would need to occur on an international level or platform and it would have to provide for punitive measures either judicially or politically. She stated anything less than that would be harmful rather than beneficial to stabilising the security situation in Sudan and South Sudan. She noted that while transitional justice initiatives such as the SSHRC were necessary for the future of South Sudan, those initiatives needed to be sufficiently resourced and have the ongoing support of those in power to be effective.

On a more general level, in FP3's opinion, what is fundamental for transitional justice for women in Sudan is exposure to the behaviour of strong women, to enable other women to develop the critical thought processes necessary to assess whether something is just or unjust outside the traditional systems they are accustomed to. She believes that although Sudanese women intrinsically feel what is unfair or harmful to them, they do not have the modalities to communicate this unfairness and that examples given by other women would provide these women with a structure within which to assert their grievances or concerns.

FP3 stated that while in the long term the need for recognition of past wrongs or access to a mechanism to right those wrongs may be sought by refugees in Sudan, she believes the success of those mechanisms will fundamentally depend on who the perpetrator of the wrong-doing was. She noted that where there had been state involvement in the perpetration of wrong-doing, the question to be asked by transitional justice practitioners was not whether such justice modalities could be useful but rather what they could realistically be expected to achieve.

Lessons to be learned

Each of the field practitioners reported that the majority of refugees and in particular refugee women they had worked with had not participated in transitional justice initiatives that had or were occurring in their countries of origin. Each of the field practitioners reported that one obstacle faced by refugee women in participating in initiatives was simply a lack of awareness of such initiatives or the opportunity to participate in them, due to a lack of education, access to information or empowerment. This suggests that the participation of refugee women should be higher on the agenda of transitional justice initiatives, increased resources should be allocated to facilitate their participation and greater thought given as to how to communicate the existence of these initiatives to women, given the structural inequalities they face on an ongoing basis. For example, the internet or posters may be ineffective in communicating the existence of these initiatives to refugee women if the women are unable to read them, but oral presentations or word-of-mouth may be more successful. Further, if a presentation about the existence of such initiatives is given in a refugee camp, women may be more comfortable attending a women's only presentation and may greater understand that their participation, as much as that of refugee men, is sought in those initiatives than if a presentation was just given to the camp as a whole.

Each of the field practitioners reported that the immediate needs of refugee women, such as security, economic and social stability, were the priorities of the women they worked with. While some form of accountability or justice mechanism was recognised by each field practitioner as likely to contribute to individual healing and reconciliation among the refugee populations they worked with and, more generally, they each saw this type of initiative as more of a long-term goal and one that was subject to the effectiveness it would have in practice. Reports from the field practitioners that what was most sought after by refugee women for "justice" was reparations, is a further indication that refugee women look for transitional justice initiatives that will further their prospects for the future, not just provide some accountability for past wrongs done to them. While bringing perpetrators to justice and the installation of democratic systems of government are often perceived by members of the international community as fundamental in establishing stability in a society transitioning from conflict, such initiatives, at least at the outset, do not address the priorities of many of those most affected by that conflict, such as refugee women. This suggests that the focus of early transitional justice initiatives should be on ensuring stability, on consultation and reporting, on education and other capacity-building initiatives. It also indicates that more formal, higher-level justice and accountability initiatives such as trials and truth commissions, whilst beneficial, should only be considered if there is a genuine desire to progress transition and they possess the authority to implement it, rather than paying lip service to the goals of transition. Even then, such initiatives would be better considered only in the longer term. As succinctly put by Laurel Fletcher and Harvey Weinstein "Reconciliation – which requires empathy, forgiveness and altruism – draws on higher order manifestations of need that cannot be addressed until the more basic needs are satisfied".[18]

As outlined above, FP2 reported that some of the refugee women she worked with felt that their participation in transitional justice initiatives was against cultural norms in their countries of origin and was perceived by the women as imposed upon them by international workers. FP3 reported that the refugee women she worked with required education and sensitisation as to what rights they have and how those rights can be asserted through examples of the behaviour of strong women, particularly women from their own communities. Both of these reports suggest that consultation with refugee women as to their immediate needs, as to accountability for past wrongs and as to their hopes for the future requires a much longer process of education and empowerment by transitional justice initiatives, than merely asking those questions of refugee women or providing a quota for their participation in such initiatives. Arthur argues that:[19] "A holistic approach to [transitional justice] is of vital importance – not in achieving the desired transformation, which is too high a goal for [transitional justice], but rather in empowering key actors who may make such transformation possible". Both the success of transitional justice initiatives and the prevention of those initiatives reinforcing pre-existing structural inequities or re-victimising women, depends upon such an extended process.

Last, what was clearly reported by all the field practitioners was that refugee women, whether they were living in camps or in a protection country, maintained strong connections with their countries of origin, through contact with family and friends back home, sending money when they could and engaging with other refugees from their communities while abroad. As outlined above, FP1 reported that some of the refugees she worked with had passed this strong connection on to their children, who after being educated in a protection country, were more likely than their parents to engage politically with their parents' country of origin. FP3 also reported that women who held positions of power in South Sudan had predominantly come from the diaspora rather than from within South Sudan itself. She stated that these women brought more progressive sensibilities

18 Fletcher, L. and Weinstein, H. "Violence and Social Repair: Rethinking the Contribution of Justice to Reconciliation" (2002) *Human Rights Quarterly* 24:3 573–639.
19 Arthur, P. 'Identities in Transition: Developing Better Transitional Justice Initiatives in Divided Societies' (2009) *International Centre for Transitional Justice* http://ictj.org/sites/default/files/ICTJ-Global-Divided-Societies-2009-English.pdf.

back to South Sudan with them and therefore were protected from some of the political intimidation that came from the more established and conservative men in government. The maintenance by refugee women of a strong connection with their countries of origin as reported above, suggests transitional justice practitioners should consider, as a long-term transition strategy, a greater engagement with refugee communities and women in the diaspora in protection countries and not just with the often larger refugee population in refugee camps. Access to education, information, employment and other resources afforded to refugees in protection countries and women in the diaspora could greatly assist with many aspects of the transition of many countries. A return "home" by refugees of the diaspora also means bringing back with them the experience, resources and knowledge afforded to them through their time abroad, in addition to their intimate knowledge of their homeland and its conflict/s and therefore the opportunity to become extremely valuable members of a transitioning society. Even if members of the refugee community or diaspora did not desire to return home, their opinions and contribution to transitional justice initiatives nonetheless could be enormously valuable.

What refugee women and women field practitioners can offer to transitional justice initiatives

FP1 stated that she believes a greater participation of refugee women in transitional justice initiatives would be likely to result in the greater inclusiveness of the insights and experiences of women in the historical record of the relevant conflict, in particular the inclusion of SGBV in those records. She also stated that a greater participation of refugee women would help recognise the broad roles women play in societies that have suffered conflict beyond that of being victims. FP1 stated that greater inclusiveness of refugee women in peace and transitional justice initiatives could result in enabling more displaced women to return home in the future. She also believes that without the participation of refugee women in transitional justice initiatives that reconciliation in transitioning countries will be hampered as refugee women are key stakeholders in those initiatives. Her views as to the inclusiveness of women strengthening reconciliation in this regard are supported by studies outlined in transitional justice literature. A study conducted by the Brookings Bern Institute in 2007 on Internal Displacement[20] found:

> [T]here is a close relationship between finding solutions for displaced persons and peacebuilding ... If IDP concerns in [the areas of re-establishing security and law and order, reconstruction and economic

20 Ferris, E. "Internal Displacement, Transitional Justice and Peacebuilding: Lessons Learned" (2008) Summary Report of the Internal Displacement and the Construction of Peace Seminar, Bogota, Colombia, 42, www.brookings.edu/speeches/2008/1111_internal_displacement_ferris.aspx.

rehabilitation, reconciliation and social rehabilitation, and political transition to create more accountable governance structures and institutions] are not taken seriously, it may jeopardize the sustainability of peace in the country ... On the other hand, resolution of such [IDP] issues can be a positive force for political reconciliation, social development and economic stability.

FP1 stated that she believes that women transitional justice workers are better able to approach their work without seeing women only as victims of conflict and that they possess a greater ability to see what role women can play more broadly in peace initiatives and transitioning societies than their male colleagues.

FP2 stated that she believes a greater participation of refugee women in transitional justice processes and peace initiatives could lead to more pragmatic solutions and strategies being brought to the discussion table during conflict resolution. She stated the refugee women she worked with had a less politicised view than men from the same community and that they would be more likely to reach compromises.

FP3 referred to the increased participation of strong women from both the older and younger generation in South Sudan in the various levels of government had resulted in an increase in women's issues making it on to the political agenda, such as SGBV and education for girls. She stated that women in conflict communities need examples of the behaviour of strong women to enable them to recognise and assert their own rights and provide a modality within which to do so. She stated that international women working in transitional justice initiatives, such as the implementation of sensitisation and capacity-building programmes can also act as role models in that regard. The contribution of and example set by strong refugee women who have often faced even greater obstacles than other women from their communities, is also likely to be enormously beneficial to women in a transitioning society.

The views of the field practitioners reinforce that in addition to the benefits individual refugee women would receive through their participation in transitional justice initiatives, a wide range of benefits would also be seen by the transitioning country, such as a greater awareness of the experiences of women during conflict, both as victims and more generally as part of a conflict society; a greater reporting and awareness of SGBV that is perpetrated against women prior to, during and after conflict; and increasing the likelihood of the success of repatriation, reconciliation and peace initiatives.

The women field practitioners recognised that they and other women working in their field are in a unique position, not only to understand the broad role women play in a society undergoing and transitioning from conflict, but also to play a fundamental role in the successful development and implementation of transitional justice initiatives.

While it cannot be denied that equality for women has progressed significantly over the past century and continues to do so, there isn't one country in the world that could claim there isn't still work to be done. Consequently women transitional justice practitioners wherever they have studied, worked or lived, will have experienced some form of gender-based inequity within their lifetime. For this reason I believe that women working in this field can offer transitional justice insights that their male counterparts cannot, purely through their experience of their gender. This includes an ability to perceive inequities where their male counterparts cannot, to understand the potential outcomes of those inequities, empathise with those who have experienced them and the experience necessary to chart a way beyond them.

From interviews with the field workers, an emphasis on their belief in the power of collectivity, of the community of women could be sensed. There was distrust in politicised, higher-level and top-down approaches, even when those approaches were inclusive of women. This was particularly emphasised by the criticism of transitional justice initiatives that forced women to participate when they did not feel comfortable in doing so. This reiterates the importance of women transitional justice practitioners having a strong presence in the field and for greater periods of time.

The presence of such women will enable a better assessment of the most effective initiatives, for refugee women and women in post-conflict societies more generally, to be made, provide these women with a female role model who does participate in community healing and decision-making giving them a greater sense of ownership over the processes, and assist in developing trust between transitional justice structures and women in these communities that will encourage the engagement of women with transitional justice initiatives.

5 The adjudication of sex crimes under international criminal law

What does gender have to do with it?

Caroline Fournet[1]

Introduction

Generating a 'destruction of the spirit, of the will to live, and of life itself',[2] sexual violence is a very specific form of criminal behaviour, one that assaults the dignity, physical integrity and intimacy of the victim. Unlike other forms of violence, sexual violence is generally seen as one perpetrated mainly against women and girls and this gender consideration has undoubtedly penetrated the legal debate. International criminal law and justice have indeed found themselves affected by sub-legal considerations of gender and feminism over sexual violence, to the point that there appears to be a regrettable divide between male and female scholars, at times not deprived of high emotions and even a certain form of aggressivity, obviously harmful to the adequate implementation of the law and to the legal discourse in general.

Yet, this genderisation[3] of the law of sex crimes seems itself to be slightly taboo and the fact that certain arguments seem to find their sole legitimacy in the – female – gender of their author or in their feminist inspiration and source appears to have been overlooked. This is of course not to suggest that the law regulating crimes of a sexual nature is deprived of any defect or that cases systematically find a satisfactory outcome but rather that gender considerations might actually not be that relevant to the legal debate and issues. Put bluntly, sexual violence and gender issues should definitely not become the monopoly of female lawyers and scholars. In this respect, the attempt at appropriation of gender crimes and crimes of a sexual nature by certain feminist scholars is to an extent problematic – precisely because such crimes transcend gender and sexuality: not only is the outrage provoked by such crimes not shared exclusively by feminists, but the victims of these acts include both men and women.

---

1 Rosalind Franklin Fellow, Department of Criminal Law and Criminology, University of Groningen (the Netherlands). The author wishes to thank the editor of this book. The views expressed in this chapter are the author's own.
2 *Prosecutor* v. *Akayesu*, ICTR, Case No. ICTR-96-4-T, Trial Chamber I, Judgment, 2 September 1998, para. 731.
3 The term 'genderisation' is here used to refer to the impact of gender considerations on the law and case law.

Furthermore, and notwithstanding their seriousness and atrocious nature, one should refrain from establishing a hierarchy between crimes and arguments brought forward by some '[f]eminist academics and activists [who] have [urged] that sex crimes should be selected for prosecution even at the expense of prosecuting other serious crimes, including crimes resulting in deaths'[4] should, in this author's opinion, be resisted. Crimes of a sexual nature should be prosecuted, just like other international crimes should be.

The genderisation of the law seems to be a one-way path and is further reflected in a feminisation of the claims made. One author has criticised international law for laying 'claim to rationality, objectiveness, and abstraction, characteristics traditionally associated with Western masculinity, and it is defined in contrast to emotion, subjectivity, and contextualized thinking',[5] a finding which a lawyer should concur with: a strong and robust adjudication of the most serious crimes, including of course sexual crimes, requires 'rationality, objectiveness and abstraction'. It is the opinion of this author that genderisation of the law must be resisted as such claims can be counter-productive and lead to a multiplication of legal notions with approximate definitions which can only harm the effective prosecution of the crimes. For instance, there have been proposals in the legal doctrine that new categories of crimes should be created so as to specifically designate crimes against women: in particular, the term 'gendercide'[6] has been suggested for the qualification of the targeting of gender – which arguably would also include men – while 'feminicide' would characterise the specific destruction of women. Interestingly, the term 'manicide' has yet to emerge in scholarly works.

Not only have new words been coined but abbreviations and sets of initials are also being used throughout some works, GBV for gender-based violence and SGBC for sexual gender-based violence[7] – a shortening of the real words which undoubtedly diminishes the seriousness of the relevant issues and the gravity of the crimes. While it could be objected that the use of acronyms is rather widespread throughout Public International Law – one could think of the UN to designate the United Nations or the ICC to designate the International Criminal Court, to cite but two of an extensive list – and that such acronyms still hold a certain gravitas, it is here maintained that the reference to an institution by a set of initials is less problematic than their use to qualify

---

4 DeGuzman, M.M. 'Giving Priority to Sex Crime Prosecutions: The Philosophical Foundations of a Feminist Agenda', (2011) *International Criminal Law Review* 11, 515–528 at 516.

5 Charlesworth, H. 'The Women Question in International Law', (2010) *Asian Journal of International Law* 1, 1–6 at 2.

6 See e.g. Jones, A. *Genocide: A Comprehensive Introduction*, Oxford: Routledge, 2006, 325–341.

7 See e.g. Green, L. 'First-Class Crimes, Second-Class Justice: Cumulative Charges for Gender-Based Crimes at the International Criminal Court', (2011) *International Criminal Law Review* 11, 529–541; Amnéus, D. 'Insufficient Legal Protection and Access to Justice for Post-conflict Sexual Violence', (2011) *Development Dialogue* 3, 67–89.

a particular crime. It would indeed be highly problematic to refer to 'genocide' as G – with a possible confusion with 'gender' – or to 'crimes against humanity' as CAH in documents other than notes or drafts. Furthermore, victims and survivors also fight against the impunity of their tormentors and accept to testify at trials precisely to see the crimes perpetrated against them legally qualify, to put a name on their sufferings, to see their pain recognised by a judicial instance: reducing such pain and suffering to mere acronyms is nothing but yet another assault on the victims' dignity. Let's just take the time to write down the crimes perpetrated against them in full.

It is in this context that the following research proposes to assess the legal and judicial apprehension of crimes of a sexual nature within the international criminal law forum so as to clearly differentiate this apprehension of sex crimes from the gender discourse. Attempting to offer a dispassionate reflection on crimes of a sexual nature, this chapter will first review the international criminal law dispositions on sex crimes while analysing the input and impact of the relevant case law of the ad hoc International Criminal Tribunals[8] and of the International Criminal Court.[9] This chapter will also consider the procedural norms and rules of evidence regulating these institutions as well as, in the case of the ICC, the statutory dispositions aimed at ensuring gender equality within the Court itself.

Sex crimes, the law and judges

While the Nuremberg Charter fails to mention crimes of a sexual nature, the drafters of the ICTY and ICTR Statutes chose to expressly include them – albeit in a rather basic fashion – within the crimes over which the Tribunals would be able to exercise their jurisdiction. Articles 5(g) of the ICTY Statute and 3(g) of the ICTR Statute thus specifically list rape among crimes against humanity while Article 4(e) of the ICTR Statute also qualifies rape and enforced prostitution as a violation of Common Article 3 of the 1949 Geneva Conventions and Additional Protocol II. As the following development will show, this basic textual approach notwithstanding, the ad hoc International Criminal Tribunals have been able to prosecute crimes of a sexual nature in a progressive and firm fashion.[10]

---

8 International Criminal Tribunal for the Former Yugoslavia (hereafter referred to as the ICTY) and the International Criminal Tribunal for Rwanda (hereafter referred to as the ICTR).
9 Hereafter referred to as the ICC.
10 For excellent research on the case law of the International Criminal Tribunals, see: Askin, K.D. 'Women's Issues in International Criminal Law: Recent Developments and the Potential Contribution of the ICC', in Dinah Shelton (ed.), *International Crimes, Peace, and Human Rights: The Role of the International Criminal Court*, Ardsley: Transnational Publishers, 2000, 47–63; Askin, K.D. 'Gender Crimes Jurisprudence in the ICTR', (2005) *Journal of International Criminal Justice* 3, 1007–1018. See also Oosterveld, V. 'Gender-based Crimes against Humanity', in L.N. Sadat (ed.), *Forging a Convention for Crimes against Humanity*, Cambridge: Cambridge University Press, 2011, 78–101.

This is all the more interesting considering that this strong adjudication of sex crimes thus occurred in an arena regularly criticised for being predominantly male and where women still constitute an 'inadequate number' compared to the number of men.[11] Put differently, it does seem that gender representation on the bench – with a strong male representation – has not prevented robust prosecution of crimes of a sexual nature. While it is true that '[a]ll three of [the] organs [comprising the International Criminal Tribunals: the Registry, the Judges' Chambers and the Office of the Prosecutor] have been headed by a woman, sometimes concurrently', the fact that 'the presence [of women] has made a remarkable difference in the jurisprudence coming out of the Tribunals, including, but not limited to, the jurisprudence concerning gender or sex based crimes'[12] probably remains difficult to assess. What is obvious is that the Tribunals – composed of qualified men and women – have greatly contributed to the prosecution of sex crimes in spite of a law 'deficient when it comes to addressing women's issues and crimes committed on the basis of sex or gender'.[13]

It is therefore against a weak textual background that the Prosecutors of the Tribunals and the judges sitting on the bench, regardless of their gender, have had to address crimes of a sexual nature and have enabled the law to dramatically evolve. As observed by Askin:

> it is significant that the Office of the Prosecutor (OTP) has moved beyond the explicit language of these provisions to find other bases on which to prosecute sex crimes. The OTP has charged, and the judges have accepted by confirming the indictments, various forms of sexual violence as grave breaches, violations of the laws or customs of war, genocide, crimes against humanity, and violations of Common Article 3 and Additional Protocol II.[14]

Sex crimes and the law of genocide

Article II of the Genocide Convention provides that:

> in the present Convention, genocide means any of the following acts committed with intent to destroy, in whole or in part, a national, ethnical, racial or religious group, as such:
>
> Killing members of the group;
> Causing serious bodily or mental harm to members of the group;
> Deliberately inflicting on the group conditions of life calculated to bring about its physical destruction in whole or in part;

11 See Askin (2000) *supra*, note 10, 48.
12 Ibid., footnote omitted.
13 Ibid., 49, footnote omitted.
14 Ibid., footnote omitted.

Imposing measures intended to prevent births within the group;
Forcibly transferring children of the group to another group.

This definition of the crime of genocide has been reproduced verbatim in the respective Statutes of the ICTY, of the ICTR and of the ICC. As unequivocally explained by the different Chambers of the ICTR, '[t]he *actus reus* of genocide is found in each of the five acts enumerated in Article 2(2) of the Statute'[15] and, thus, 'for a crime of genocide to have been committed, it is necessary that one of the acts listed under Article 2(2) of the Statute be committed'.[16] The narrow selection of potential genocidal acts in the Convention – which remains silent on sex crimes – has been considered, according to a constant case law, to mean that 'the act must have been committed against one or several individuals, because such individual or individuals were members of a specific group, and specifically because they belonged to this group'.[17] It can be safely asserted that this jurisprudential position is respectful of the spirit of the conventional text, which leaves little doubt as to the necessarily restrictive understanding of the crime of genocide, generally seen as a safeguard against extensive interpretations, potentially leading to abuses and holding the risk of trivialising one of the most heinous international crimes. Where the conventional text is arguably more problematic is in its lack of definition, leaving the ICTY and ICTR judges with no other choice but to clarify the exact scope of application of the crime of genocide.

Thus crimes of a sexual nature, despite being notoriously absent from the definition of the crime of genocide, made their entrance into the definitional scope of genocide through the judicial door. In its progressive consideration of the act of 'causing serious bodily or mental harm to members of the group', the ICTR indeed specified that this 'phrase could be construed to mean harm that seriously injures the health, causes disfigurement or causes

---

15 *Prosecutor* v. *Gacumbtsi*, Case No. ICTR-2001-64-T, Trial Chamber III, Judgment, 17 June 2004, para. 251. See also *Prosecutor* v. *Kayishema and Ruzindana*, Case No. ICTR-95-1-T, Judgment, 21 May 1999, para. 100; *Prosecutor* v. *Semanza*, Case No. ICTR-97-20-T, Judgment and Sentence, 15 May 2003, para. 318; *Prosecutor* v. *Kajelijeli*, Case No. ICTR-98-44A-T, Trial Chamber II, 1 December 2003, Judgment and Sentence, para. 812; *Prosecutor* v. *Kamuhanda*, Case No. ICTR-95-54A-T, Trial Chamber II, Judgment, 22 January 2004, para. 631.

16 *Prosecutor* v. *Akayesu*, Case No. ICTR-96-4-T, Judgment, Trial Chamber I, 2 September 1998, para. 499.

17 Ibid., at para. 521. See also *Prosecutor* v. *Rutaganda*, Judgment and Sentence, 6 December 1999, ICTR-96-3, para. 60; *Prosecutor* v. *Musema*, Case No. ICTR-96-13-A, Trial Chamber I, Judgment and Sentence, 27 January 2000, paras 153–154 and 165; *Prosecutor* v. *Bagilishema*, Case No. ICTR-95-1A-T, Judgment, Trial Chamber I, 7 June 2001, para. 61; *Prosecutor* v. *Semanza*, Case No. ICTR-97-20-T, Judgment and Sentence, 15 May 2003, para. 312; *Prosecutor* v. *Niyitegeka*, Case No. ICTR-96-14-A, Appeals Chamber, Judgment, 9 July 2004, para. 50.

any serious injury to the external, internal organs or senses'[18] and found that it had to be 'determined on a case-by-case basis, using a common sense approach'.[19] Similarly, Trial Chamber I of the ICTY held that:

> the gravity of the suffering must be assessed on a case by case basis and with due regard for the particular circumstances.... serious harm need not cause permanent and irremediable harm, but it must involve harm that goes beyond temporary unhappiness, embarrassment or humiliation. It must be harm that results in a grave and long-term disadvantage to a person's ability to lead a normal and constructive life.[20]

Such findings enabled the Tribunals to include within the realm of 'causing serious bodily or mental harm' acts which are not conventionally enumerated, including crimes of a sexual nature. In *Seromba*, the ICTR Appeals Chamber, referred to the *'quintessential examples* of serious bodily harm' namely, 'torture, *rape*, and non-fatal physical violence that causes disfigurement or serious injury to the external or internal organs'.[21] On several occasions, it was judicially found that serious bodily and mental harm includes 'acts of sexual violence, rape,[22] mutilations and interrogations combined with beatings, and/or threats of death',[23] acts of bodily or mental torture,

18 *Prosecutor* v. *Kayishema and Ruzindana*, Case No. ICTR-95-1-T, Judgment, 21 May 1999, para. 109. See also *Prosecutor* v. *Krstić*, Case No. IT-98-33, Judgment, Trial Chamber I, 2 August 2001, para. 483; *Prosecutor* v. *Semanza*, Case No. ICTR-97-20-T, Judgment and Sentence, 15 May 2003, para. 320 and 322; *Prosecutor* v. *Stakić*, Case No. IT-97-24-T, Judgment, Trial Chamber II, 31 July 2003, para. 516; *Prosecutor* v. *Ntagerura*, Bagambiki, Imanishimwe, Case No. ICTR-99-46-T, Judgment and Sentence, Trial Chamber III, 25 February 2004, para. 664; *Prosecutor* v. *Seromba*, Case No. ICTR-2001-66-I, Judgment, Trial Chamber, 13 December 2006, para. 317.

19 *Prosecutor* v. *Kayishema and Ruzindana*, Case No. ICTR-95-1-T, Judgment, 21 May 1999, para. 108. For the case-by-case assessment of mental harm, see ibid., paras 110 and 113.

20 *Prosecutor* v. *Krstić*, Case No. IT-98-33, Judgment, Trial Chamber I, 2 August 2001, para. 486, footnote omitted.

21 *Prosecutor* v. *Seromba*, Case No. ICTR-2001-66-A, Appeals Chamber, Judgment, 12 March 2008, para. 46, emphasis added.

22 See e.g. *Prosecutor* v. *Akayesu*, Case No. ICTR-96-4-T, Judgment, Trial Chamber I, 2 September 1998, para. 502; *Prosecutor* v. *Kayishema and Ruzindana*, Case No. ICTR-95-1-T, Judgment, 21 May 1999, para. 110; *Prosecutor* v. *Rutaganda*, Judgment and Sentence, 6 December 1999, ICTR-96-3, para. 51; *Prosecutor* v. *Musema*, Case No. ICTR-96-13-A, Trial Chamber I, Judgment and Sentence, 27 January 2000, para. 156; *Prosecutor* v. *Semanza*, Case No. ICTR-97-20-T, Judgment and Sentence, 15 May 2003, paras 320–321.

23 *Prosecutor* v. *Kayishema and Ruzindana*, Case No. ICTR-95-1-T, Judgment, 21 May 1999, para. 108, footnotes omitted. See also *Prosecutor* v. *Akayesu*, Case No. ICTR-96-4-T, Judgment, Trial Chamber I, 2 September 1998, para. 502; *Prosecutor* v. *Rutaganda*, Judgement and Sentence, 6 December 1999, ICTR-96-3, para. 51; *Prosecutor* v. *Musema*, Case No. ICTR-96-13-A, Trial Chamber I, Judgment and Sentence, 27 January 2000, para. 156; *Prosecutor* v. *Semanza*, Case No. ICTR-97-20-T, Judgment and Sentence, 15 May 2003, paras 320–321.

inhumane or degrading treatment, persecution,[24] 'cruel treatment, torture, rape and deportation'.[25]

In other words, the ad hoc International Criminal Tribunals have – on their own initiative and using 'common sense' – interpreted the definition of genocide so as to include within its scope of application acts which are nowhere to be seen in the conventional definition of genocide, including crimes of a sexual nature. Perhaps even further, the act of 'imposing measures intended to prevent births within the group' was also judicially clarified and extended to cover acts of a sexual nature, as exemplified by the following finding of the *Akayesu* Trial Chamber:

> the measures intended to prevent births within the group, should be construed as sexual mutilation, the practice of sterilization, forced birth control, separation of the sexes and prohibition of marriages. In patriarchal societies, where membership of a group is determined by the identity of the father, an example of a measure intended to prevent births within a group is the case where, during rape, a woman of the said group is deliberately impregnated by a man of another group, with the intent to have her give birth to a child who will consequently not belong to its mother's group. [...] Furthermore, the Chamber notes that measures intended to prevent births within the group may be physical, but can also be mental. For instance, *rape can be a measure intended to prevent births* when the person raped refuses subsequently to procreate, in the same way that members of a group can be led, through threats or trauma, not to procreate.[26]

Arguably more radically, the *Akayesu* Trial Chamber emancipated crimes of a sexual nature from the pre-existing categories of genocidal acts to find that rape and sexual violence could constitute self-standing acts of genocide:

> with regard, particularly, to the acts described in paragraphs 12(A) and 12(B) of the Indictment, that is, rape and sexual violence, the Chamber

24 *Prosecutor* v. *Akayesu*, Case No. ICTR-96-4-T, Judgment, Trial Chamber I, 2 September 1998, para. 504; *Prosecutor* v. *Rutaganda*, Judgment and Sentence, 6 December 1999, ICTR-96-3, para. 51.
25 *Prosecutor* v. *Krstić*, Case No. IT-98-33, Judgment, Trial Chamber I, 2 August 2001, paras 482–486, footnotes omitted. It is also interesting to note that the Preparatory Commission for the ICC indicated that serious bodily and mental harm 'may include, but is not necessarily restricted to, acts of torture, rape, sexual violence or inhuman or degrading treatment'. Cited in ibid., emphasis added.
26 *Prosecutor* v. *Akayesu*, Case No. ICTR-96-4-T, Judgment, Trial Chamber I, 2 September 1998, paras 507–508, emphasis added. See also *Prosecutor* v. *Kayishema and Ruzindana*, Case No. ICTR-95-1-T, Judgment, 21 May 1999, para. 117; *Prosecutor* v. *Rutaganda*, Judgment and Sentence, 6 December 1999, ICTR-96-3, para. 53; *Prosecutor* v. *Musema*, Case No. ICTR-96-13-A, Trial Chamber I, Judgment and Sentence, 27 January 2000, para. 158.

wishes to underscore the fact that in its opinion, *they constitute genocide in the same way as any other act* as long as they were committed with the specific intent to destroy, in whole or in part, a particular group, targeted as such. Indeed, rape and sexual violence certainly constitute infliction of serious bodily and mental harm on the victims and are even, according to the Chamber, one of the worst ways of inflicting harm on the victim as he or she suffers both bodily and mental harm. In light of all the evidence before it, the Chamber is satisfied that the acts of rape and sexual violence described above, were committed solely against Tutsi women, many of whom were subjected to the worst public humiliation, mutilated, and raped several times, often in public, in the Bureau Communal premises or in other public places, and often by more than one assailant. These rapes resulted in physical and psychological destruction of Tutsi women, their families and their communities. Sexual violence was an integral part of the process of destruction, specifically targeting Tutsi women and specifically contributing to their destruction and to the destruction of the Tutsi group as a whole.[27]

Showing a clear understanding of the very specific nature of crimes of a sexual nature, the *Akayesu* Trial Chamber further added that '[s]exual violence was a step in *the process of destruction* of the Tutsi group'.[28] This finding was all the more fundamental insofar as the *Akayesu* trial was the first ever trial for genocide: put differently, the very first international judicial interpretation of the law of genocide explicitly included within the ambit of the crime crimes of a sexual nature. This groundbreaking aspect notwithstanding, some commentators have regretted that:

despite its historical significance in furthering progress in the prosecution of gender-related crimes committed in the context of war or mass violence, the ICTR has failed to capitalize on the *Akayesu* legacy, and consequently gender jurisprudence is relatively meager outside that achieved in *Akayesu*. Although rape and other forms of sexual violence were exceedingly common during the genocide, many indictments fail to bring rape charges, primarily because there has been very little genuine and rigorous investigation of the crime by the Prosecutor's Office. This has resulted in rape acquittals, dropped charges and other missed opportunities and debacles.[29]

Perhaps more regrettable is the fact that Article 6 of the ICC Statute merely reproduced Article II of the Genocide Convention and failed to expressly add

---

27 *Prosecutor* v. *Akayesu*, Case No. ICTR-96-4-T, Trial Chamber I, Judgment, 2 September 1998, para. 731, footnote omitted, emphasis added.
28 Ibid., para. 732, emphasis added.
29 Askin (2005) *supra*, note 10, at 1007–1008, footnotes omitted.

rape and acts of sexual violence to the list of prohibited genocidal acts. If it is of course to be hoped that this will remain without prejudice to the *acquis jurisprudentiel*, the drafters of the ICC Statute still missed an opportunity to explicitly integrate sex crimes within the definitional scope of genocide.

Sex crimes and international humanitarian law

While a review of humanitarian law instruments pre-dating the ICTY and ICTR Statutes reveals that crimes of a sexual nature are only very discreetly addressed,[30] the ICTY was nonetheless able to find that

> rape in time of war is specifically prohibited by treaty law: the Geneva Conventions of 1949, Additional Protocol I of 1977 and Additional Protocol II of 1977. Other serious sexual assaults are expressly or implicitly prohibited in various provisions of the same treaties.[31]

Proceeding to an extensive reading of the text, in particular with respect to Article 6(c) of the Nuremberg Charter, the *Mucić* Trial Chamber also held that:

> there can be no doubt that rape and other forms of sexual assault are expressly prohibited under international humanitarian law. The terms of Article 27 of the Fourth Geneva Convention specifically prohibit rape, any form of indecent assault and the enforced prostitution of women. A prohibition on rape, enforced prostitution and any form of indecent assault is further found in article 4(2) of Additional Protocol 11, concerning internal armed conflicts. This Protocol also implicitly prohibits rape and sexual assault in article 4(1) which states that all persons are entitled to respect for their person and honour. Moreover, article 76(1) of Additional Protocol I expressly requires that women be protected from rape, forced prostitution and any other form of indecent assault. An implicit prohibition on rape and sexual assault can also be found in article 46 of the 1907 Hague Convention (IV) that provides for the protection of family honour and rights. Finally, rape is prohibited as a crime

---

30 See Geneva Convention Relative to the Protection of Civilian Persons in Time of War, 75 U.N.T.S. 287, art. 27; Protocol Additional to the Geneva Conventions of 12 August 1949, and Relating to the Protection of Victims of International Armed Conflicts (Protocol I), 1125 U.N.T.S. 3, art. 75; Protocol Additional to the Geneva Conventions of 12 August 1949, and Relating to the Protection of Victims of Non-International Armed Conflicts (Protocol II), 1125 U.N.T.S. 609, art. 4(2)(e). See O'Byrne, K. 'Beyond Consent: Conceptualising Sexual Assault in International Criminal Law', (2011) *International Criminal Law Review* 11, 495–514 at 498.

31 *Prosecutor* v. *Furundžija*, Case No. IT-95-17/1, Judgment, Trial Chamber II, 10 December 1998, para. 165, footnotes omitted.

against humanity under article 6(c) of the Nuremberg Charter and expressed as such in Article 5 of the Statute.[32]

In this particular case, rape was recognised by Trial Chamber II of the ICTY as a form of torture, violating the Geneva Conventions and the laws and customs of war. A reading of the case reveals the willingness of the Trial Chamber to firmly establish its jurisdiction over crimes of a sexual nature in a legal and credible fashion. It is particularly remarkable that the Trial Chamber here proceeded to a careful review of the major decisions handed out by the various international and regional judicial bodies.[33] Furthermore, the language used by the Trial Chamber clearly demonstrates the seriousness with which such crimes are being considered:

> the Trial Chamber considers the rape of any person to be a *despicable act* which strikes at the very core of human dignity and physical integrity. The *condemnation and punishment of rape becomes all the more urgent* where it is committed by, or at the instigation of, a public official, or with the consent or acquiescence of such an official. Rape causes severe pain and suffering, both physical and psychological. The psychological suffering of persons upon whom rape is inflicted may be exacerbated by social and cultural conditions and can be particularly acute and long lasting. Furthermore, it is difficult to envisage circumstances in which rape, by, or at the instigation of a public official, or with the consent or acquiescence of an official, could be considered as occurring for a purpose that does not, in some way, involve punishment, coercion, discrimination or intimidation. In the view of this Trial Chamber this is inherent in situations of armed conflict.[34]

It is thus in unequivocal terms that the Trial Chamber found that: 'whenever rape and other forms of sexual violence meet the aforementioned criteria, then they shall constitute torture, in the same manner as any other acts that meet this criteria'.[35]

Interestingly for the purposes of the present research, the Trial Chamber also expressly held that gender could be a discriminatory ground in the perpetration of crimes of a sexual nature as it found that the violence had been inflicted on the two victims because they were women. Thus in the case of Ms Cecez, the Chamber held that: 'the violence suffered by Ms. Cecez in the form of rape, was inflicted upon her by Delic *because she is a woman*. [...] this represents a form of discrimination which constitutes a prohibited purpose

---

32 *Prosecutor* v. *Mucić* et al., Case No. IT-96-21-T, Judgment, Trial Chamber II quater, 16 November 1998, para. 476.

33 Ibid., paras 480–493.

34 Ibid., para. 495, emphasis added.

35 Ibid., para. 496.

for the offence of torture'.[36] Likewise, in the case of Ms Antic: 'the violence suffered by Ms. Antic in the form of rape, was inflicted upon her by Delic *because she is a woman*. [...] this represents a form of discrimination which constitutes a prohibited purpose for the offence of torture'.[37]

This recognition of gender as a ground for commission of international crimes and of sexual violence in particular is to be welcomed. There is no doubt that in some instances individuals are being victimised precisely because of their gender – male or female. As Leila Nadya Sadat recalls, '[o]bviously, women are not the only victims of sexual and gender-based crimes; and man and boys are also vulnerable to sexual violence, particularly if detained'.[38,39] As Solange Mouthaan further explains,

> until now the inclusion of a gender perspective has worked to the detriment of men, as these types of gender crimes have rarely been addressed within the same category of crimes when committed against women [rape in the case of female victims, but torture in the case of male victims].[40]

As stated at the very beginning of this chapter, crimes of a sexual nature constitute assaults on the very dignity and intimacy of the victim and do carry with them a stigma paradoxically – and obviously unfairly – attached to the victim, and arguably even more so if the victim is a man. This could partly explain the ill-qualification of sexual violence against men: in such cases the victims themselves might prefer to be recognised as victims of torture rather than stigmatised as victims of rape. Yet, '[g]ender covers a broader and thus more appropriate social context of gender inequality, which includes crimes committed against men and playing on gender norms to break victims down'.[41] Sexual violence perpetrated against men is as much a sign of the willingness to destroy the victim in his dignity and masculinity – and thus humanity – than similar violence perpetrated against women.

Already in its very first case, the ICTY had to deal with charges of sexual assault committed against men.[42] More recently, Pre-Trial Chamber II of the ICC in the *Bemba Gombo* case also recognised the perpetration of sexual

---

36 Ibid., para. 941, emphasis added.
37 Ibid., para. 963, emphasis added.
38 The Trust Fund for Victims, Learning from the TVF's Second Mandate: From Implementing Rehabilitation Assistance to Reparations, Fall 2010 Programme Progress Report, 25, footnote in original.
39 Sadat, L.N. 'Avoiding the Creation of a Gender Ghetto in International Criminal Law', (2011) *International Criminal Law Review* 11, 655–662 at 659.
40 Mouthaan, S. 'The Prosecution of Gender-based Crimes at the ICC: Challenges and Opportunities', (2011) *International Criminal Law Review* 11, 775–802 at 798.
41 Ibid., at 799.
42 See *Prosecutor* v. *Tadić*, Case No. IT-94-1-T, Opinion and Judgment including Separate and Dissenting Opinion of Judge McDonald, Trial Chamber II, 7 May 1997.

violence against men.[43] In some instances, men can also be targeted precisely because they are men, as was acknowledged in the *Krstić* case,[44] in which the Trial Chamber found that the exclusive targeting for destruction of military-aged men could constitute genocide:

> the Bosnian Serb forces could not have failed to know, by the time they decided to kill all the men, that this selective destruction of the group would have a lasting impact upon the entire group.... By killing all the military aged men, the Bosnian Serb forces effectively destroyed the community of the Bosnian Muslims in Srebrenica as such and eliminated all likelihood that it could ever re-establish itself on that territory.[45]

Sex crimes and the law of crimes against humanity

Sexual violence came to the forefront of the ICTY agenda in the *Furundžija* case where the Trial Chamber had to deal exclusively with crimes of a sexual nature and, in so doing, confirmed both the terms of its founding Statute according to which rape can be constitutive of a crime against humanity[46] and the *Akayesu* finding that rape can amount to genocide.[47] In reaching its decision, the *Furundžija* Trial Chamber further upheld the *Mucić* precedent, which had established that rape can also qualify as a grave breach of the Geneva Conventions and as a violation of the laws and customs of war, thereby addressing 'what is likely the most common form of wartime rape: random, isolated rape, crimes sometimes committed simply because the atmosphere of war, its hatred and violence and the breakdown of law and order, creates the opportunity'.[48]

It was not until the *Kunarac* case, which also exclusively focused on sexual violence, that Trial Chamber II of the ICTY considered rape not only as

---

43 See *Prosecutor* v. *Bemba Gombo*, ICC-01/05-01/08, Decision Pursuant to Article 61(7)(a) and (b) of the Rome Statute on the Charges of the *Prosecutor* against Jean-Pierre Bemba Gombo, Pre-Trial Chamber II, 15 June 2009, para. 177: 'Witness 80's husband tried to intervene but was beaten and threatened with rape himself' and para. 178: 'witness 23 was raped in the presence of his wife; his wife was also raped on the same day'.

44 *Prosecutor* v. *Krstić*, Case No. IT-98-33, Judgment, Trial Chamber I, 2 August 2001. See also *Prosecutor* v. *Krstić*, IT-98-33-A, Appeals Chamber, Judgment, 19 April 2004, paras 18–23.

45 *Prosecutor* v. *Krstić*, Case No. IT-98-33, Judgment, Trial Chamber I, 2 August 2001, paras 595–597.

46 Article 5(g) ICTY Statute.

47 See *Prosecutor* v. *Furundžija*, Case No. IT-95-17/1, Judgment, Trial Chamber II, 10 December 1998, notably at paras 174–188. See also *Prosecutor* v. *Krstić*, Case No. IT-98-33, Judgment, Trial Chamber I, 2 August 2001. See also *Prosecutor* v. *Krstić*, IT-98-33-A, Appeals Chamber, Judgment, 19 April 2004, paras 18–23.

48 Askin (2000) *supra*, note 10, 56.

isolated and random acts of violence but as a strategy of war[49] 'used by members of the Bosnian Serb armed forces as an instrument of terror'[50] and thus as crimes against humanity perpetrated in a systematic and/or widespread manner. Proceeding to a progressive reading of the text of the law, the *Kunarac* Trial Chamber also specified that enslavement as a crime against humanity included sexual servitude. According to Mertus:

> this case represents a significant advance in the international law pertaining to the treatment of sexual violence in wartime. [...] The decision demonstrates that rape will not be accepted as an intrinsic part of war. Rather, it is a crime against humanity and may constitute torture. The Tribunal sent a message that it would prosecute cases of sexual violence vigorously. That the accused were low-level soldiers was of no consequence.[51]

The work and findings of the ICTY with respect to sexual violence and rape have not gone unnoticed and were in fact expressly cited by the European Court of Human Rights. As indeed recalled by Pitea, the Strasbourg Court

> paid tribute [...] in an unprecedented exercise of cross-fertilization on the jurisprudence of international tribunals in the field of human rights, to the definition of the crime of rape given by another international judicial institution: The International Criminal Tribunal for the Former Yugoslavia (ICTY):[52]

> > In international criminal law, it has recently been recognised that force is not an element of rape and that taking advantage of coercive circumstances to proceed with sexual acts is also punishable. The International Criminal Tribunal for the former Yugoslavia has found that, in international criminal law, any sexual penetration without the victim's consent constitutes rape and that consent must be given voluntarily, as a result of the person's free will, assessed in the context of the surrounding circumstances (see paragraphs 102–107 above). While the above definition was formulated in the particular context of rapes committed against the population in the conditions of an armed conflict, it also reflects a universal trend

---

49 See Sharlach, L. 'State Rape: Sexual Violence as Genocide', in Samuel Totten and Paul R. Bartrop (eds), *The Genocide Studies Reader*, Oxford: Routledge, 2009, 180–192.
50 *Prosecutor* v. *Kunarac et al.*, Case No. IT-96-23 and IT-96-23/1, Judgment, Trial Chamber II, 22 February 2001.
51 Mertus, J. 'Judgment of Trial Chamber II in the Kunarac, Kovac and Vukovic Case', ASIL insights. Available at www.asil.org/insigh65.cfm, accessed on 28 February 2012.
52 Pitea, C. 'Rape as a Human Rights Violation and a Criminal Offence: The European Court's Judgment in *M.C.* v. *Bulgaria*', (2005) *Journal of International Criminal Justice* 3, 447–462 at 448, footnote omitted.

towards regarding lack of consent as the essential element of rape and sexual abuse.[53]

Not only has the case law emanating from The Hague and Arusha influenced the case law of the Strasbourg Court, it has also directly impacted upon the drafting of the Rome Statute of the International Criminal Court itself in which gender considerations and crimes of a sexual nature are expressly and unequivocally addressed.

Sex crimes, gender equality and the international criminal court

Although, and as has just been shown, the ad hoc International Criminal Tribunals have proved progressive in advancing the understanding and repression of sexual violence, irrespective of the gender of who was sitting on the bench, the drafters of the ICC Statute nonetheless chose to include therein express provisions aimed at ensuring gender balance among the judges sitting at the Court, thereby arguably responding to the criticism made regarding gender (in)balance at the Tribunals. In an unprecedented fashion, Article 36(8)(a)(iii) of the Statute provides that '[t]he States Parties shall, in the selection of judges, take into account the need, within the membership of the Court, for [...] [a] fair representation of female and male judges'. With respect to sex crimes, Article 36(8)(b) further provides that 'States Parties shall also take into account the need to include judges with legal expertise on specific issues, including, but not limited to, violence against women or children'.[54] While this does not necessarily imply that a greater proportion of women should sit on the bench, the emphasis on expertise relative to violence against women or children nonetheless shows the growing interest in the issue. The statutory concern for crimes of a sexual nature is also reflected in the dispositions relating to the duties and powers of the Prosecutor with respect to investigations, as reflected in the language of Article 54(1)(b):

> The Prosecutor shall [...] [t]ake appropriate measures to ensure the effective investigation and prosecution of crimes within the jurisdiction of the Court, and in doing so, respect the interests and personal circumstances of victims and witnesses, including age, *gender* as defined in Article 7, paragraph 3, and health, and take into account the nature of

---

53 *M.C.* v. *Bulgaria*, Application no. 39272/98, European Court of Human Rights, Judgment, 4 December 2003, para. 163. See also ibid., paras 102–107.
54 Rome Statute of the International Criminal Court, adopted by the United Nations Diplomatic Conference of Plenipotentiaries on the Establishment of an International Criminal Court on 17 July 1998, UN Doc. A/Conf.183/9, 1998.

the crime, in particular where it involves *sexual violence, gender violence* or violence against children.[55]

The ICC Statute – notably Article 7 – and the unprecedented inclusion of a whole range of crimes of a sexual nature within the ambit of crimes against humanity marks a stepping stone in the evolution of the apprehension of sex crimes in international criminal law. Where Article 7 is admittedly more problematic is in the – much commented upon – third paragraph which defines gender as 'the two sexes, male and female, *within the context of society*',[56] thereby creating unnecessary confusion and holding the risk of generating misunderstanding. Put simply, one can really wonder what gender 'within the context of society' actually means. A look at the *travaux préparatoires* reveals that this definition in paragraph 3 'represents an indication of the compromise that was achieved during the negotiations'.[57] As further explained by Solange Mouthaan:

> the adopted definition remains a lost opportunity to adopt a clear and complete definition of gender in international criminal law and puts another heavy burden upon the ICC to clarify the concept of gender for the purposes of the ICC. If anything, the ICC Statute could have more accurately reflected recent progress in this area. As it stands, the ICC will be under scrutiny when determining its understanding of gender, because gender is a recurrent theme not only in the possible investigations and prosecutions it may undertake, but also in the duties and powers of the Prosecutor[58] and the Office of the Prosecutor[59] as well as the protection and participation of victims and witnesses.[60,61]

Furthermore, the unsatisfactory definition embodied in paragraph 3 does not solely characterise gender in relation to crimes against humanity but applies to the whole Statute as evidenced by the use of the terms 'for the purposes of this Statute'. As clarified by William Schabas, paragraph 3 'was added at the Rome Conference so as to respond to concerns that the term might appear to endorse homosexuality. It was derived from a similar formulation negotiated at the 1995 Beijing Conference'.[62] Yet, Article 7(3) does not constitute the only reference to 'gender' in the Rome Statute and it is also to be found in Article 21 (3) as one of the prohibited grounds of discrimination. If this disposition gives no definition of the term 'gender' it is however interesting to

---

55 Article 54(1)(b), ICC Statute, emphasis added.
56 Emphasis added.
57 Mouthaan supra, note 40, 799, footnote omitted.
58 ICC Statute, Article 54(1)(b), footnote in original.
59 ICC Statute, Article 42(9), footnote in original.
60 ICC Statute, Article 68(1), footnote in original.
61 Mouthaan supra, note 40, 799.
62 Schabas, W. The International Criminal Court: *A Commentary on the Rome Statute*, Oxford: Oxford University Press, 2010, 186, emphasis in original, footnotes omitted.

note that the order of the list of prohibited grounds is 'curious, provocatively placing "gender" at the beginning, and following it with "age", a category that does not even appear in the classic human rights instruments. The more traditional grounds of discrimination – race, colour, religion, etc. – trail behind.'[63] This is arguably all the more curious insofar as the use of the term 'gender' proved highly controversial during the drafting, when '[o]stensibly, the debate focused on use of the word "gender" instead of "sex" as a prohibited ground for discrimination'[64] and when '[s]everal States, led by the Holy See, were opposed to such contemporary terminology.... There was a proposal to truncate the provision after the words "human rights", thereby eliminating the troublesome term "gender"'.[65,66] It thus appears that the divide here was created by religious considerations rather than by the gender of the State representatives.

While this definitional issue is far from being purely theoretical as the Court will ultimately have to define what is actually meant by 'gender' for the purposes of its founding Statute, it remains remarkable that gender has been included as a prohibited ground of discrimination in what could arguably be seen as one of the Statute's most fundamental provisions namely, Article 21(3). As rightly observed by William Schabas:

> no other provision of the *Rome Statute* governs the application and interpretation of all its provisions, as well as all of the other sources of applicable law. It is analogous to constitutional provisions in national law that authorize courts to interpret and even disallow legislated texts to the extent they are incompatible with fundamental human rights standards or that they are discriminatory. The provision has been repeatedly cited in the Court's early case law, signaling its great potential and its fundamental role.[67]

The constitutional status of this disposition coupled with 'gender' being placed first in the enumeration of prohibited grounds of discrimination are thus further indicators for the ICC that the opacity of Article 7(3) notwithstanding, gender considerations are to be taken seriously.

In this regard, the trial of Jean-Pierre Bemba Gombo, currently pending before the ICC, will prove a great test for the Court in its adjudication of rape and sexual violence.[68] It is the first case before the Court with such an extensive

---

63 Ibid., at 400, footnote omitted.
64 Ibid., at 398.
65 UN Doc. A/CONF.183/C.1/WGAL/L.1, 2, fn. 4. Also: UN Doc. A/CONF.183/C.1/WGAL/L.4, footnote in original.
66 Schabas supra, note 62, 398.
67 Ibid., at 398, emphasis in original, footnote omitted.
68 See *Prosecutor* v. *Bemba Gombo*, ICC-01/05-01/08, Decision Pursuant to Article 61(7)(a) and (b) of the Rome Statute on the Charges of the Prosecutor against Jean-Pierre Bemba Gombo, Pre-Trial Chamber II, 15 June 2009.

focus on crimes of a sexual nature namely, rape as a war crime and rape as a crime against humanity.[69] In its review of the crime of rape so far, it seems clear that the ICC intends to attach to sexual violence the consideration it deserves. The language used by Pre-Trial Chamber II in this instance is unequivocal and calls for no contradiction. Not only did the Chamber here proceed to a careful review of the facts, it also unequivocally rejected the arguments of the Defence based on the alleged consent to the victims, qualifying such claims as 'untenable'.[70]

With respect to admissible evidence, Pre-Trial Chamber II showed an understanding of the specific sufferings generated by sexual violence, even going as far as to admit that testimonies of victims of sexual violence could be imprecise – an obvious bending of evidentiary rules which could potentially be in contradiction with the right to a fair trial: according to the Chamber, 'due to the traumatic events the witnesses suffered and the time that has elapsed since the rapes and the collection of their testimonies (approximately six years), imprecision in dates may occur'.[71] In a similar vein, the Chamber also declared admissible indirect evidence, including hearsay evidence, insofar as it is

> of a corroborating nature and reflects the large number of acts of rape which occurred in the same locations referred to by direct witnesses during the same period, namely from on or about 26 October 2002 to 15 March 2003.[72]

If this judicial understanding of the law of evidence clearly stands in favour of victims of sexual violence, it may be asserted that such findings are hardly surprising considering the actual rules of procedure and evidence of the ICTY, ICTR and ICC, which also reveal a specific consideration of crimes of a sexual nature.

Sex crimes, procedural law and evidence

If the judicial interpretation of the different Statutes of the International Criminal Tribunals and of the ICC undoubtedly marked a great step forward in the punishment of crimes of a sexual nature, while both men and women were adjudicating the different cases, it is also striking to note that their respective rules of procedure and evidence further reveal a clear concern for the effective and adequate prosecution of such acts.

Most noticeably, Rule 96 of the International Criminal Tribunals' Rules of Procedure and Evidence relates to 'Evidence in Cases of Sexual Assault' and reads:

---

69 See also *Prosecutor* v. *Katanga and Ngudjolo Chui*, ICC-01/04-01/07 'Decision on the Confirmation of Charge', Pre-Trial Chamber I, 30 September 2008.
70 *Prosecutor* v. *Bemba Gombo supra*, note 68.
71 Ibid., para. 184.
72 Ibid., para. 186.

In cases of sexual assault:

(i)   no corroboration of the victim's testimony shall be required;
(ii) consent shall not be allowed as a defence if the victim
    (a)   has been subjected to or threatened with or has had reason to fear violence, duress, detention or psychological oppression, or
    (b)   reasonably believed that if the victim did not submit, another might be so subjected, threatened or put in fear;
(iii) before evidence of the victim's consent is admitted, the accused shall satisfy the Trial Chamber in camera that the evidence is relevant and credible;
(iv) prior sexual conduct of the victim shall not be admitted in evidence.[73]

This Rule calls for a number of remarks insofar as it lays down an innovative procedure specifically aimed at responding to the needs of victims of acts of sexual violence. First, the express non-corroboration rule alleviates the usual evidentiary standards applicable to other international crimes, thereby facilitating the admissibility of the evidence constituted by the victim's testimony. Second, Rule 96 explicitly lists the circumstances under which evidence of consent will be inadmissible, thereby reflecting the idea that '[i]t's just not foreseeable that consent could be a defence when a woman is in such a coercive and life threatening situation as a war'.[74] Third, Rule 96 (iii) protects the victims of sexual violence from an unnecessary public outpouring of highly private, sensitive and distressing details, which are thus not discussed in open court and which can only be pursued by the Defence if there is a valid basis. Fourth, it is recalled – and this is of course to be acclaimed – that 'prior sexual conduct of the victim shall not be admitted in evidence'.

The principles enunciated in Rule 96 have been reproduced both in the ICC Statute[75] and in its Rules of Procedure and Evidence. And indeed, Rule 70 on 'Principles of evidence in cases of sexual violence' reads:

---

73 ICTY, Rules of Procedure and Evidence, IT/32/Rev. 46, version as of 20 October 2011 and ICTR, Rules of Procedure and Evidence, adopted on 29 June 1995; as amended on 1 October 2009. Hereafter referred to in the footnotes as ICTY RPE and ICTR RPE respectively.
74 Judge Gabrielle Kirk McDonald, Former ICTY President, quoted on the ICTY website, available at www.icty.org/sid/3013, accessed on 28 February 2012. Incidentally, it is worth noting here that the ICTY devotes a whole part of its website to crimes of sexual violence.
75 See Article 68(2) of the ICC Statute:
    As an exception to the principle of public hearings provided for in article 67, the Chambers of the Court may, to protect victims and witnesses or an accused, conduct any part of the proceedings in camera or allow the presentation of evidence by electronic or other special means. In particular, such measures shall be implemented in the case of a victim of sexual violence or a child who is a victim or a witness, unless otherwise ordered by the Court, having regard to all the circumstances, particularly the views of the victim or witness.

In cases of sexual violence, the Court shall be guided by and, where appropriate, apply the following principles:

(a) Consent cannot be inferred by reason of any words or conduct of a victim where force, threat of force, coercion or taking advantage of a coercive environment undermined the victim's ability to give voluntary and genuine consent;

(b) Consent cannot be inferred by reason of any words or conduct of a victim where the victim is incapable of giving genuine consent;

(c) Consent cannot be inferred by reason of the silence of, or lack of resistance by, a victim to the alleged sexual violence;

(d) Credibility, character or predisposition to sexual availability of a victim or witness cannot be inferred by reason of the sexual nature of the prior or subsequent conduct of a victim or witness.

Although very similar to Rule 96, Rule 70 uses slightly different language. Not only does it cover both victims and witnesses but it also specifically addresses the issue of 'sexual availability' as non-inferable from the sexual conduct of a victim or witness. Furthermore, the terms 'prior sexual conduct' have been replaced with nature of the prior and subsequent conduct of a victim or witness, which is in fact the object of an additional rule of procedure and evidence:

In the light of the definition and nature of the crimes within the jurisdiction of the Court, and subject to Article 69, paragraph 4, a Chamber shall not admit evidence of the prior or subsequent sexual conduct of a victim or witness.[76]

The Rules of Procedure and Evidence of these institutions also set up special Victims and Witnesses Sections or Units, with the clear aim of responding to the specific needs of victims of, and witnesses to, sexual violence while promoting positive discrimination in favour of women for employment in such sections or units. Rule 37 of the ICTY's Rules of Procedure and Evidence thus reads:

(A) There shall be set up under the authority of the Registrar a Victims and Witnesses Section consisting of qualified staff to:
 (i) recommend protective measures for victims and witnesses in accordance with Article 22 of the Statute; and
 (ii) provide counselling and support for them, in particular in cases of rape and sexual assault.

(B) Due consideration shall be given, in the appointment of staff, to the *employment of qualified women*.[77]

---

76 Rule 71, ICC RPE.
77 ICTY RPE, emphasis added.

Using a very similar language, Rule 34 of the ICTR's Rules of Procedure and Evidence also adds that:

> (B) A *gender sensitive approach to victims and witnesses* protective and support measures should be adopted and due consideration given, in the appointment of staff within this Unit, to the *employment of qualified women*.[78]

The ICC Rules of Procedure and Evidence show similar concerns, specifying that it is the duty of the Registrar to take 'gender-sensitive measures to facilitate the participation of victims of sexual violence at all stages of the proceedings'[79] while it is the Victims and Witnesses Unit's functions to make 'available to the Court and the parties training in issues of trauma, sexual violence, security and confidentiality'[80] and to take 'gender-sensitive measures to facilitate the testimony of victims of sexual violence at all stages of the proceedings'.[81]

In its enumeration of the responsibilities of the Victims and Witnesses Unit, Rule 18 – thereby echoing Article 43 (6) of the ICC Statute – explicitly provides that it shall '[e]nsure training of its staff with respect to victims' and witnesses' security, integrity and dignity, including matters related to gender and cultural sensitivity'[82] while Rule 19 lists among the the areas over which the Unit should have expertise 'gender and cultural diversity'.[83]

Last but certainly not least, as a general principle relating to victims, Rule 86 unequivocally requires Chambers to take into account the specific needs of victims of sexual or gender violence:

> A Chamber in making any direction or order, and other organs of the Court in performing their functions under the Statute or the Rules, shall take into account the needs of all victims and witnesses in accordance with Article 68, in particular, children, elderly persons, persons with disabilities and victims of sexual or gender violence.

Reinforcing the terms of Article 68(1) of the ICC Statute,[84] Rule 88 specifically acknowledges and addresses the particularities of the potential needs of

---

78 ICTR RPE, emphasis added.
79 Rule 16, ICC RPE.
80 Rule 17(2)(a)(iv), ICC RPE.
81 Rule 17(2)(b)(iii), ICC RPE.
82 Rule 18(d), ICC RPE.
83 Rule 19(e), ICC RPE.
84 Article 68 of the ICC Statute deals with the protection of the victims and witnesses and their participation in the Proceedings. Its first paragraph reads:
    The Court shall take appropriate measures to protect the safety, physical and psychological well-being, dignity and privacy of victims and witnesses. In so doing, the Court shall have regard to all relevant factors, including age, gender as defined in article 7, paragraph 3, and health, and the nature of the crime, in particular, but not limited to, where the crime involves sexual or gender violence or violence against children. The Prosecutor shall take such measures particularly during the investigation and prosecution of such crimes. These measures shall not be prejudicial to or inconsistent with the rights of the accused and a fair and impartial trial.

victims of sexual violence when called to testify,[85] here also guiding the Chamber into adopting appropriate attitude and measures.

Concluding remarks

As noted by O'Byrne:

> recent armed conflicts, both regional and international, have highlighted the horrors of sexual assault committed during times of war. Largely in response to those conflicts, international law relating to sexual crimes has developed with increasing momentum. The statutes and jurisprudence of the United Nations (UN) ad hoc tribunals and the statute of the International Criminal Court (ICC) have made significant inroads towards the recognition of individual criminal responsibility for campaigns of sexual violence targeted at civilians during armed conflict. The separate international crimes of rape, sexual assault, sexual slavery, enforced prostitution, forced pregnancy and enforced sterilisation have been debated and defined, and their elements enunciated, to varying degrees.[86]

If there is no doubt that '[i]nternational criminal law has been slow to include a gender perspective in its prevention and punishment of crime',[87] there is equally no doubt that, as this chapter has attempted to demonstrate, the judicial input of the ad hoc International Criminal Tribunals in the strengthening of the adjudication of sex crimes has been invaluable. This is of course not to say that the law governing sex crimes is fully satisfactory or that the case law is without fault but it does seem that crimes of a sexual nature have now been emancipated and are not confined any longer to being 'secondary offences, which do not seem to merit the same institutional

---

85 See Rule 88(1), ICC RPE:
> Upon the motion of the Prosecutor or the defence, or upon the request of a witness or a victim or his or her legal representative, if any, or on its own motion, and after having consulted with the Victims and Witnesses Unit, as appropriate, a Chamber may, taking into account the views of the victim or witness, order special measures such as, but not limited to, measures to facilitate the testimony of a traumatized victim or witness, a child, an elderly person or a victim of sexual violence, pursuant to article 68, paragraphs 1 and 2. The Chamber shall seek to obtain, whenever possible, the consent of the person in respect of whom the special measure is sought prior to ordering that measure.

And Rule 88(5):
> Taking into consideration that violations of the privacy of a witness or victim may create risk to his or her security, a Chamber shall be vigilant in controlling the manner of questioning a witness or victim so as to avoid any harassment or intimidation, paying particular attention to attacks on victims of crimes of sexual violence.

86 O'Byrne *supra*, note 30, 496, footnotes omitted.
87 Mouthaan *supra*, note 40, 777.

response as other war crimes and crimes against humanity'.[88] In this respect, the warning issued by the former ICC Prosecutor to sexual offenders is worth reproducing here: 'Mr. Bemba's arrest is a warning to all those who commit, who encourage, or who tolerate sexual crimes. There is a new law called the Rome Statute. Under this new law, they will be prosecuted.'[89] While such a warning is to be applauded, one must also ensure that sex crimes remain – just like all the other international crimes – at the forefront of the ICC's agenda, notably through continuous research and analysis of the relevant law and case law. In so doing, however, the genderisation of the law and of the legal discourse must be resisted. As rightly stressed by Leila Nadya Sadat

> it must become standard practice not only for women, but also for men, to address the gendered nature of atrocity crimes and crimes of sexual violence. Rather than dismissed as second class 'women's work', attention to this phenomenon must be paid seriously by all those working in or writing about international criminal justice.[90]

Gender must be considered as a ground for the commission of some of the most heinous acts, not as a divide between legal scholars.

The following quote from Major Brent Beardsley, testifying in the course of the *Bagasora et al.* trial before the ICTR, serves as a clear reminder – which astonishingly sometimes appears to be needed – that women *and* men find themselves equal before the horror generated by sex crimes:

> Rape was one of the hardest things to deal with in Rwanda on our part. It deeply affected every one of us. We had a habit at night of coming back to the headquarters and, after the activities had slowed down for the night, before we went to bed, sitting around talking about what had happened that day, drink coffee, have a chat, and amongst all of us the hardest thing we had to deal with was not so much the bodies of the people, the murder of people – I know that can sound bad, but that wasn't as bad to us as the rape and especially the systematic rape and gang rape of children.[91]

---

88 Ibid., 776.
89 Prosecutor Luis Moreno-Ocampo, quoted in 'ICC Arrest Jean-Pierre Bemba – Massive Sexual Crimes in Central African Republic Will Not Go Unpunished', ICC-OTP-20080524-PR316 (2008).
90 Sadat *supra*, note 39, 661.
91 Quoted in Askin (2005) *supra*, note 10, 1008.

6 Denial, impunity and transitional justice

The fate of female rape victims in Bosnia and Herzegovina

Clotilde Pégorier[1]

Transitional justice: gender and international crimes

Since the late 1980s and early 1990s, the study of transitional justice has emerged as one of the most rapidly expanding and highly debated fields of international law. In the wake of the revolutions in the former Eastern Bloc and the democratisation of a number of countries in Africa and Latin America, legal scholars and lawyers, together with political scientists and theorists, have expended much critical energy in analysing the dynamics of regime change in post-authoritarian and post-conflict contexts. Parallel to this, they have also examined the mechanisms of transitional justice – including truth commissions, criminal prosecutions, security system reform and memorialisation effects – which have been implemented as favoured means of redressing the past wrongs of an oppressive violent order and advancing new forms of justice. At the present time, discussions regarding transitional justice have, in at least one regard, moved towards a point of seeming paradox. On the one hand, there is an emerging view that the purview of such initiatives has been expanding – and should continue to do so – from an initial focus on reparation, restitution and reconciliation towards broader concerns with development and social justice issues. On the other hand, however, a substantial part of the newest literature has concentrated attention on the weaknesses and shortcomings of transitional justice, on the 'frictions'[2] between global mechanisms and local exigencies, and on those areas where the overarching goal of securing justice for victims remains to be dealt with.

One key aspect of this discourse which has recently shifted towards the centre of debate has been the question of 'gender justice'. In part, this

---

1 Dr Clotilde Pégorier is Senior Research Fellow at the University of Luzern. Having previously studied at the universities of Paris Ouest, Hamburg and Artois, she obtained her PhD from the University of Exeter in 2011. Her primary research interests lie in the fields of international criminal law, international humanitarian law and human rights. She is currently working on a monograph study on the legal qualification of ethnic cleansing.

2 See Tsing, A., *Friction: An Ethnography of Global Connection* (Princeton, NJ: Princeton University Press, 2005).

mirrors and stems from the growing trend in legal scholarship towards the adoption of gender-oriented perspectives on mass violence, to which the increasingly frequent appearance of terms such as 'femicide', 'gynocide' and 'gendercide' – as referents for gender-specific policies of violence – provide testimony. With increasing attention being placed on the intersections between gender, power and violence in conflict situations, and on the fate of women in particular, it follows that such issues should also assume a prominent position in discussions of the problems of justice and trauma that arise in the aftermath of such instances. For while claims such as those made by a recent scholar that it is women who 'pay the disproportionate cost of war'[3] must be made with due caution for fear of entrenching discourses of (female) victimhood and (male) agency, and although we must be ever mindful of the realities of male rape in such contexts,[4] it is doubtless true that the aim of genocidal and ethnic cleansing policies, for example, does make women – as procreators of the next generation – an important target for violence.

The question of how to secure reparative justice and restitution for the suffering of victims in such situations thus acquires considerable significance. A key issue in this regard is that of rape and sexual violence, both of which remain acutely notable constants amidst the range of strategic crimes committed in conflict situations across the international stage. In the Democratic Republic of Congo, for instance, the eastern part of the country has frequently been referred to as the 'rape capital of the world',[5] while during the civil war in Burundi between 1993 and 2006, sexual violence was widely reported as an instrument of war employed by government and rebel forces.[6] In Bosnia and Herzegovina, meanwhile, during the remorseless ethnic wars of the 1990s, Bosnian women were systematically targeted by Serbian aggressors as part of a planned political programme of terror.[7] This pattern can be traced out across countless other arenas of con-

3 Valji, N. 'Gender Justice and Reconciliation', in Ambos, K., Large, J. and Wierda, M. (eds), *Building a Future on Peace and Justice: Studies on Transitional Justice, Peace and Development* (Berlin: Springer, 2009) 217–236, 218.

4 The report of the commission of experts relates how men were forced to rape women and to perform sexual acts on each other or on guards. They were also subjected to castration and other sexual mutilation (United Nations, Security Council, 'Final Report of the Commission of Experts established Pursuant to Security Council Resolution 780' (1992), 27 May 1994, UN Doc. S/1994/674 (1994), p. 56, para. 235). The focus in the present chapter on female victims is in no way intended to dismiss the occurrence and grave relevance of sexual violence against males, but rather reflects the overarching remit of the volume.

5 This expression was coined by UN Special Representative Margot Wallstrom.

6 See, for example, UNHCR, Internal Displacement Monitoring Centre, 'Burundi: Still No End to Displacement, Despite Political Progress', 11 April 2006.

7 It ought to be noted that Serbian women were also targeted and raped by Bosnian aggressors – instances which are, of course, equally worthy of judicial attention. The nature of the issues explored in this chapter lends itself, however, to a particular focus on the fate of Bosnian victims. For more on the rape of Serbian women, see Nikolić-Ristanović, V. 'Sexual Violence', in Nikolić-Ristanović, V. (ed.), *Women, Violence and War: Wartime Victimization of Refugees in the Balkans* (Central European University Press: Budapest, 1999), 41–79, 44.

flict, as can the fact that victims of such violence seldom find justice through the judicial system. As Dorean Marguerite Koenig remarks, 'history has shown that rape, even aggravated rape, in the context of wars has been little prosecuted or punished'.[8] Forced to endure both the physical and the psychological trauma of the act, and then denied the satisfaction of seeing their violators brought to justice, it is little wonder that those affected have been described as 'double victims', or that the issue of wartime rape and sexual violence has emerged as an important lens through which to spotlight the limitations and/or failings of transitional justice mechanisms.

The present chapter is written with the above perspectives in mind. Its aim is to shed new light on an aspect of the discourse of gender and transitional justice via an analysis of how the International Criminal Tribunal for the former Yugoslavia (ICTY)[9] has induced accountability for sexual violence against women in armed conflict. The ICTY recommends itself for a study of this kind on two principal grounds: first, on account of its concerted efforts to develop a jurisprudential framework for recognising sexual violence in armed conflict, and second, in view of the notable number of prosecutions in this area to date. Despite the latter accomplishment, however, there nonetheless remains a startling discrepancy between the number of instances of sexual violence committed against women during the conflict and the number of prosecutions. If, as Sarah Wagner points out, Bosnia's recent history serves as a referent for notions of 'return, reconstruction, recognition and reparation'[10] that aim to bring justice to the past – and secure it for the future – then the success of such mechanisms has, in this regard, been at best partial. Here, the intention is to consider and explore the factors that explain this occurrence by way both of a detailed analysis of legal norms and practice, and of a wider discussion of the possibilities and limitations of international criminal and humanitarian law as a vehicle for rendering justice in transitional societies.

War and rape in Bosnia and Herzegovina

The conflicts that raged through the countries of the former Yugoslavia in the early 1990s were, as is well known and documented, especially brutal, and left a wide trail of violence, destruction and suffering. In early 1992, Bosnia and Herzegovina entered into a devastating war that would last

8 Koenig, D. 'Women and Rape in Ethnic Conflict and War', (1994) *Hastings Women's Law Journal* 5, 129–142, 131.
9 Statute of the International Criminal Tribunal for the Former Yugoslavia, adopted on 25 May 1993 by Resolution 827 of the Security Council, UN Doc. S/RES/827 (1993).
10 Wagner, S. 'Identifying Srebrenica's Missing: The "Shaky Balance" of Universalism and Particularism', in Hinton, A. (ed.), *Transitional Justice: Global Mechanisms and Local Realities after Genocide and Mass Violence* (New Brunswick, NJ: Rutgers University Press, 2010), 25–48, 25.

for almost four years, and which would inflict enormous damage on its population, infrastructure and cultural heritage. Estimates suggest a death toll of approximately 100,000, with a further 2.2 million displaced persons.[11] The list of atrocities committed during the war is long and appalling: instances of mass murder, extrajudicial executions, torture, forced displacement, illegal detention and destruction of cultural sites – to name some of the acts[12] – all contributed to the awful paroxysm of violence. Alerted to the crisis by media reports that graphically captured both the wanton destruction and the brutalisation of victims, the international community began, even prior to the end of the war, to mobilise for intervention both in resolving the conflict and in transitional justice issues, to which end the ICTY was established in 1993. When the war officially ended in 1995, agreements were closed for a wide-reaching programme of measures intended to restore justice to the past and to safeguard it within the newly emergent political context. The complexity of the socio-political situation, however – together with both the unresolved (and virulently debated) question of the attribution of responsibility and the involvement of several internal and external agencies – has meant that the implementation of transitional justice has been complicated and drawn out. Even now, some 16 years after the end of the war, the country is, unfortunately, still struggling to find the best way to come to terms with and move beyond an immediate past permeated with violence.

It was during the war in the former Yugoslavia, meanwhile, that the issue of wartime rape and sexual violence also encroached, for the first time, on the popular consciousness. That rape is an abiding accompaniment to war and conquest is an all-too regrettable reality, recognised as such throughout history. Instances of rape during and after conflicts arise from different motivations; what is usually common is that they have little to do with sexuality and more to do with domination – as Ruth Seifert notes, 'the rapist's sexuality is not at the centre of his act; it is placed instrumentally at the service of the violent act'.[13] In Bosnia and Herzegovina, rape was used as an instrument of ethnic cleansing – the act was central to the overriding aim of Serbian

---

11 See Parmentier, S. and Weitekamp, E., 'Dealing with War Crimes in Bosnia: Retributive and Restorative Options through the Eyes of the Population', in Crawford, A. (ed.), *International and Comparative Criminal Justice and Urban Governance* (Cambridge: Cambridge University Press, 2011), 140–167, 146. Parmentier and Weitekamp quote here from figures provided by the Demographic Unit of the Office of the Prosecutor of the ICTY and the United Nations High Commissioner for Refugees.

12 For a complete list of acts see: United Nations, Security Council, 'Final Report of the Commission of Experts Established Pursuant to Security Council Resolution 780 (1992)', 27 May 1994, UN Doc. S/1994/674 (1994).

13 See Seifert, R., 'War and Rape: A Preliminary Analysis', in Stiglmayer, A. (ed.), *Mass Rape: The War against Women in Bosnia-Herzegovina* (Lincoln, NE: University of Nebraska Press, 1994), 54–72, 56.

conquest and the elimination of the Bosnian Muslim and non-Serb populations.[14]

Establishing the precise number of rape cases against women in this context is inevitably difficult, if not impossible. The very nature of the act, and the circumstances under which it is perpetrated, make it unlikely that an entirely reliable count shall ever emerge. In its report of 4 August 1995, the UN Human Rights Commission indicated the difficulties in assessing the number of victims, not least on account of a reluctance to report such traumatic experience due to social stigma and/or fear of reprisals.[15] In terms of numbers, the Commission has been able to produce evidence of approximately 12,000 cases of rape. This is considerably lower than earlier – and largely unsubstantiated – claims of there having been upwards of 20,000 instances. It points, nonetheless, towards the grave reality of mass rape having been used by the Serbs as an instrument of war. From this it follows that the issue of rape and sexual violence, and the matter of securing restitution for victims, must be a particularly relevant concern and challenge for transitional justice efforts.

Rape and sexual violence at the ad hoc international criminal tribunals

The question of the status of rape and sexual violence within the framework of international criminal and humanitarian law has, as a consequence of legal developments in Bosnia (and Rwanda), emerged as a major point of legal debate and discussion over the past 15 years. From the outset, the Security Council placed specific emphasis on concerns with instances of mass rape of women in the context of the conflict in Bosnia, expressing, in Resolution 827:[16]

> its grave alarm at continuing reports of widespread and flagrant violations of international humanitarian law [...], including reports of mass killings, *massive, organized and systematic detention and rape of women,* and

14 See United Nations, Security Council, 'Final Report of the Commission of Experts Established Pursuant to Security Council Resolution 780' (1992), 27 May 1994, UN Doc. S/1994/674 (1994), p. 59, para. 250(a):

> Rape seems to occur in conjunction with efforts to displace the targeted ethnic group from the region. This may involve heightened shame and humiliation by raping victims in front of adult and minor family members, in front of other detainees or in public places, or by forcing family members to rape each other.

15 General Assembly Resolution A/50/329, 'Human Rights Questions: Human Rights Situations and Reports of Special Rapporteurs and Representatives – Rape and Abuse of Women in the Areas of Armed Conflict in the Former Yugoslavia', 4 August 1995, UN DOC. A/50/329, para. 63.

16 United Nations Security Council, Resolution 827 (1993), 25 May 1993, UN Doc. S/RES/827 (1993), emphasis added.

the continuance of the practice of 'ethnic cleansing', including for the acquisition and holding of territory.

Traditionally, rape has not been explicitly regarded as a grave breach, or treated as the *actus reus* of genocide. Instead, it has been regarded as a crime against honour and dignity.[17] The Geneva Convention, for instance, states that 'women shall be especially protected against any attack on their honour, in particular against rape, enforced prostitution, or any form of indecent assault'.[18] The omission of rape from the list of grave breaches has led critics to level charges against the inherent 'masculinity' of international humanitarian law that fails to appreciate how 'acts committed against women *because* they are women might amount to a violation of international humanitarian legal norms'.[19] Such claims are valid, even if rape is not, as noted earlier, solely committed against female victims.[20] In the period since the outbreak of the war, however, major steps have been taken to address this issue, and the approach to gendered violence under international law has been transformed by such developments as the adoption of the Vienna Declaration of Violence Against Women (1993),[21] the General Assembly Resolutions on the Elimination of Violence Against Women (1993)[22] the Rape and Abuse of Women in the Areas of Armed Conflicts in the former Yugoslavia (1994)[23] and Security Council Resolution 1325 on Women, Peace and Security (2000).[24] In its efforts to confront the issue of sexual violence, the ICTY has also invested considerable resources and energies in considering how to prosecute such instances, issuing a number of indictments and

17   *Prosecutor* v. *Anto Furundžija* ('*Lašva Valley*'), Case No. IT-95-17/1-T, Judgment, Trial Chamber II, 10 December 1998, para. 184, *Prosecutor* v. *Dragoljub Kunarac et al.* ('*Foča*'), Case No. IT-96-23-A and No. IT-96-23/1-A, Judgment, Appeals Chamber, 12 June 2002, para. 67.

18   Art. 27 of the Geneva Convention (IV) Relative to the Protection of Civilian Persons in Time of War, 12 August 1949, 6 U.S.T. 3516, 75 U.N.T.S. 287. See also Article 3(1)(c) common to the Geneva Conventions.

19   Franke, K. 'Gendered Subjects of Transitional Justice', (2006) *Columbia Journal of Gender and Law* 15(3), 813–828, 816, emphasis in the original.

20   See Bassiouni, C. M. Sexual Violence: An Invisible Weapon of War in the Former Yugoslavia (Chicago, IL: International Human Rights Institute, 1996), Sivakumaran, S., 'Sexual Violence against Men in Armed Conflict', (2007) *European Journal of International Law* 18(2), 253–276; Campbell, K., 'The Gender of Transitional Justice: Law, Sexual Violence and the International Criminal Tribunal for the Former Yugoslavia', (2007) *International Journal of Transitional Justice* 1, 411–432.

21   UN Assembly General, Vienna Declaration and Programme of Action, 12 July 1993, UN Doc. A/CONF.157/23.

22   Assembly General Resolution 48/104, 'Declaration on the Elimination of Violence Against Women', 20 December 1993, UN Doc. A/RES/48/104.

23   General Assembly Resolution 49/205, 'Rape and Abuse of Women in the Areas of Armed Conflicts in the former Yugoslavia', 23 December 1994, UN Doc. A/RES/49/205.

24   Security Council Resolution 1325, 31 October 2000, UN Doc. S/RES/1325(2000).

convictions which have reflected and represented a significant shift in the *How many convictions on rape?* understanding and treatment of gendered violence during conflict.

This re-focusing of attention on how to confront rape and sexual violence within the framework of international law has not been without its difficulties. For one, it raises the question of how a usually individualised act might become the proper subject for internationally sanctioned prosecution.[25] Until recently, rape was considered as an ancillary crime to war, heinous but not an act which, in itself, violated international peace and thus not appropriate for international intervention. Only in recent years, with the emergent recognition of how rape during conflict may be committed not only as an indiscriminate 'spoils of war' action but also as a deliberate strategy of warfare, has a consensus begun to emerge that international action against sexual violence is justified. The UN's Commission of Experts, in its Final Report, identified, in this regard, five 'patterns' of rape and sexual violence: *we can assume lack of significant progress given the amount of time in which change occurs @ Intl. level*

i   sexual assaults perpetrated by small groups of men, often prior to the outbreak of conflict and frequently 'in conjunction with looting and intimidation of the target group';

ii rapes committed in the aftermath of attacks on towns and villages. In many such instances, local inhabitants were rounded up and women raped publicly in front of their neighbours [...];

iii detention camp rapes, whereby 'soldiers, camp guards, paramilitaries and even civilians may be allowed to [...] pick out women, [...] rape them and then either kill them or return them to the site';

iv detention for the purpose of rape: women are held for the sole object of being raped and are systematically brutalised [...];

v   imprisonment of women in 'hotels or similar facilities' for the single purpose of sexually entertaining soldiers.[26]

The point that crystallises out of the Commission's analysis is that such instances of rape are seldom an individualised or solitary act. As Aryeh Neier remarks:

It [rape] was usually done before witnesses – other combatants or guards, other detainees, or other villagers. The rapists did not fear that they would be found out; they did what was tolerated, or expected of them, or what they were required to do. [...] The public nature of the rapes was no doubt intended to exacerbate the pain and humiliation

25 See May, L. *Crimes against Humanity: A Normative Account* (Cambridge: Cambridge University Press, 2005), 96.

26 United Nations Security Council, 'Final Report of the Commission of Experts Established Pursuant to Security Council Resolution 780' (1992), 27 May 1994, UN Doc. S/1994/674 (1994), paras 244–249.

suffered by the victims and to terrorise other villagers and detainees who witnessed them. It also demonstrated that the rapists had no cause to fear the wrath of their commanders.[27]

It was from this perspective that the Commission determined that rape was a matter of international concern, occurring as it seemed to 'in conjunction with efforts to displace the targeted ethnic group from the region' – i.e. as a means of expediting ethnic cleansing.[28] The recognition of a nexus between sexual violence and a broader policy of action thus became the vital aspect that opened the way to international involvement and intervention. Reference to rape as a constituent element to 'ethnic cleansing' did not, however, provide an immediate framework for prosecution through international criminal justice mechanisms, on account of the practice not yet having been precisely defined or legally qualified – the common tendency being to assimilate the act to genocide or to consider it to constitute crimes against humanity or war crimes.[29] Rape too has traditionally been placed within the definition both of crimes against humanity[30] and of war crimes,[31] as well as being more recently regarded as a genocidal act.[32] Customary international law prohibits rape and other forms of sexual violence within the context of armed conflict. There is not, however, a separate and distinct offence recognised as such. It is rather the case that if the constituent elements are found, then sexual violence can be regarded and prosecuted as a violation of international humanitarian law – either as a war crime or crime against humanity, or as an act of genocide.

The modern inclusion of rape under these categories owes much to developments brought forth by the jurisprudence of the ICTY and the ICTR.[33] Earlier conventions have established a normative basis in customary international law for trying rape as a war crime or grave breach – albeit one which is undermined by a lack of precision with regards a definition of rape and the identification of its elements.[34] In confronting the modern realities of wartime rape and sexual violence, the ICTY and ICTR have sought to

27   Neier, A. War Crimes: Brutality, Genocide, Terror and the Struggle for Justice (New York: Times Books, 1998), 189–190.

28   United Nations, Security Council, 'Final Report of the Commission of Experts Established Pursuant to Security Council Resolution 780' (1992), 27 May 1994, UN Doc. S/1994/674 (1994), p. 59, para. 250(a).

29   For a detailed discussion on this point, see Pégorier, C., 'Ethnic Cleansing: A Legal Qualification' (London: Routledge, 2013) [forthcoming]).

30   See Article 7(1)(g) of the Rome Statute.

31   See Article 8(2)(b)(xxii) and 8(2)(e)(vi) of the Rome Statute.

32   See Prosecutor v. Jean-Paul Akayesu, Case No ICTR-96-4-T, Judgment, Trial Chamber I, 2 September 1998, paras 731 and 733.

33   Statute of the International Criminal Tribunal for Rwanda (ICTR), adopted on 8 November 1994 by Resolution 955 of the Security Council, UN. Doc. S/RES/955 (1994).

34   See Bassiouni, C. M. Crimes Against Humanity in International Criminal Law (The Hague: Kluwer, 1994), 346–348.

redress this by providing greater clarity of understanding and definition. In the *Akayesu* case, the ICTR defined sexual violence – which includes rape – as:

> any act of a sexual nature which is committed on a person under circumstances which are coercive. Sexual violence is not limited to physical invasion of the human body and may include acts which do not involve penetration or even physical contact.[35]

The terms of this definition follow from the view that the 'essence of rape is the aggression that is expressed in a sexual manner under conditions of coercion', and that, as such, 'the central elements of the crime of rape cannot be captured in a mechanical description of objects or body parts'.[36] This approach, focusing on the 'essence' of rape, was subsequently upheld in both *Delalić* (ICTY)[37] and *Musema* (ICTR).[38] In the *Furundžija* case,[39] however, the ICTY took the opposite view that it was necessary 'to arrive at an accurate definition of rape based on the criminal law principle of specificity', and to this end developed a 'mechanical' definition which stated the objective elements of rape to be:

> (i) the sexual penetration, however slight: (a) of the vagina or anus of the victim by the penis of the perpetrator or any other object used by the perpetrator; or (b) of the mouth of the victim by the penis of the perpetrator; (ii) by coercion or force or threat of force against the victim or a third person.[40]

This definition was also followed in the *Kunarac* case,[41] in which it was further reiterated that the *mens rea* of rape is 'the intention to effect this sexual penetration, and the knowledge that it occurs without the consent of the victim'.[42] Force, in the form of coercion, is not, as such, considered a

---

35 *Prosecutor* v. *Jean-Paul Akayesu*, Case No. ICTR-96-4-T, Judgment, Trial Chamber I, 2 September 1998, para. 688.
36 *Prosecutor* v. *Jean-Paul Akayesu*, Case No. ICTR-96-4-T, Judgment, Trial Chamber I, 2 September 1998, paras 597–598.
37 *Prosecutor* v. *Zdravko Mucić et al.* ('*Čelebići Camp*'), Case No. IT-96-21-T, Judgment, Trial Chamber, 16 November 1998, paras 478–479.
38 *Prosecutor* v. *Alfred Musema*, Case No. ICTR-96-13-T, Judgment, Trial Chamber I, 27 January 2000, paras 222–223.
39 *Prosecutor* v. *Anto Furundžija* ('*Lašva Valley*'), Case No. IT-95-17/1-T, Judgment, Trial Chamber II, 10 December 1998, para. 177.
40 *Prosecutor* v. *Anto Furundžija* ('*Lašva Valley*'), Case No. IT-95-17/1-T, Judgment, Trial Chamber II, 10 December 1998, para. 185.
41 *Prosecutor* v. *Dragoljub Kunarac et al.* ('*Foča*'), Case No. IT-96-23-T and No. IT-96-23/1-T, Judgment, Trial Chamber II, 22 February 2001, paras 437–438.
42 *Prosecutor* v. *Dragoljub Kunarac et al.* ('*Foča*'), Case No. IT-96-23-T and No. IT-96-23/1-T, Judgment, Trial Chamber II, 22 February 2001, para. 460.

necessary element per se. With regard to the *actus reus* of the act, the definition provided in *Furundžija* may be viewed as something of a retrogressive step – one which, by restricting the crime to the notion of penetration, unduly limits the broader and more progressive definition supplied in *Akayesu*. It would certainly seem warranted, particularly under the conditions of war and conflict, to consider other methods of committing sexual violence as potentially constituting rape, and in this respect the practice of the ICTR appears to provide a more effective definitional framework for rape and sexual violence in international law.

At the same time, however, it ought to be borne in mind that even in the *Furundžija* case the ICTY did not merely focus on a narrowly defined concept of rape, while recent jurisprudence has, moreover, viewed the essential and mechanical definitions of rape not as necessarily contradictory but rather as potentially complementary: in *Muhimana*, for instance, it was concluded by the ICTR that they were 'not incompatible or substantially different',[43] and that the later definition provided in *Furundžija* and *Kuranac* augmented that offered in *Akayesu* by providing additional details on the constituent elements of rape.[44] The position outlined in the International Criminal Court's[45] Elements of Crimes concerning rape as a crime against humanity follows the mechanical definition supplied by the ICTY in terms of specificity, but also conveys a broader (and gender-neutral) understanding of the act:

> The perpetrator invade[s] the body of a person by conduct resulting in penetration, however slight, of any part of the body of the victim or of the perpetrator with a sexual organ, or of the anal or genital opening of the victim with any object or any other part of the body.[46]

The developments instantiated by the ICTY and ICTR have played a vital role in allowing for the emergence of a framework for prosecuting rape and sexual violence which is of foremost significance to international humanitarian law. Both tribunals have recognised rape and sexual violence to be not ancillary violations but rather among the most serious crimes over which

43 *Prosecutor* v. *Mikaeli Muhimana*, Case No. ICTR-95-1B-T, Judgment, Trial Chamber III, 28 April 2005, paras 549–551.

44 *Prosecutor* v. *Mikaeli Muhimana*, Case No. ICTR-95-1B-T, Judgment, Trial Chamber III, 28 April 2005, para. 550.

45 Rome Statute of the International Criminal Court (ICC) adopted by the United Nations Diplomatic Conference of Plenipotentiaries on the Establishment of an International Criminal Court on 17 July 1998 UN Doc. A/CONF.183/9 (1998).

46 Art. (7)(1)(g)–1(1) of the Elements of Crimes of the ICC, reproduced from the 'Official Records of the Assembly of States Parties to the Rome Statute of the International Criminal Court, First Session, New York, 3–10 September 2002' (United Nations Publication, Sales No. E.03.V.2 and corrigendum), Part II.B. The Elements of Crimes adopted at the 2010 Review Conference are replicated from the 'Official Records of the Review Conference of the Rome Statute of the International Criminal Court, Kampala, 31 May–11 June 2010' (International Criminal Court Publication, RC/11).

they have jurisdiction, and both – though particularly the ICTY – have issued a series of indictments and convictions which have essentially altered paradigmatic concepts. The practice of the ad hoc international criminal tribunals has, perhaps above all else in this context, established compelling precedent for the prosecution of individuals responsible for rape or other forms of sexual violence in situations of armed conflict, whether international or non-international.

The manner in which both the ICTY and ICTR have dealt with instances of mass rape, enforced prostitution, sexual enslavement and forced pregnancy in relation to wider-ranging violence and policy has set an important guideline that has made it possible to include such crimes in the ICC Statute, which explicitly recognises such violations as war crimes and crimes against humanity.[47] In particular, it is the readiness to accept a latitude of interpretation in line with modern exigencies which has allowed for such developments – as stated in the *Kunarac* case with regards traditional laws and customs of war, for instance:

> The determination of what constitutes a war crime is [...] dependent on the development of the laws and customs of war at the time when an act charged in an indictment was committed. As once noted, the laws of war 'are not static, but by continual adaptation follow the needs of a changing world'. There is no question that acts such as rape, torture and outrages upon personal dignity are prohibited and regarded as criminal under the laws of war and that they were already regarded as such at the time relevant to these indictments.[48]

In the Rwandan context, meanwhile, a similar approach has enabled the ICTR to find that rape and sexual violence, though not expressly included in the Genocide Convention, may also be considered to constitute genocide: in the *Akayesu* case, for instance, it was held that such could be the case 'as long as [such actions] were committed with the specific intent to destroy',[49] while in *Rutaganda*, the Trial Chamber further recognised that rape could fall

---

47 Article 7(g), Article and 8(2)(b)(xxii) and Article 8(2)(e)(vi) of the Rome Statute.
48 *Prosecutor* v. *Dragoljub Kunarac et al.* ('*Foča*'), Case No. IT-96-23-A and No. IT-96-23/1-A, Judgment, Appeals Chamber, 12 June 2002, para. 67 (footnote omitted). See also *Prosecutor* v. *Zejnil Delalić et al.* ('*Čelebići Camp*'), Case No. IT-96-21-I, Initial Indictment, 19 March 1996, Counts 29 and 22, *Prosecutor* v. *Anto Furundžija* ('*Lašva Valley*'), Case No. IT-95-17/1-PT, First Amended Indictment 2 June 1998, count 14, *Prosecutor* v. *Miroslav Kvočka et al.* ('*Omarska, Keraterm et Trnopolje Camps*'), Case No. IT-98-30/1-I, Amended Indictment, 9 November 1998, counts 16 and 17, *Prosecutor* v. *Dragan Zelenović et al.* ('*Foča*'), Case No. IT-96-23/2-I, Amended Indictment, 7 October 1999, counts 4, 8, 12, 16, 20, 24, 28, 31, 35, 39, 43, 47, 51, 55 and 59, and *Prosecutor* v. *Dragoljub Kunarac et al.* ('*Foča*'), Case No. IT-96-23-I and No. IT-96-23/1-I, First Amended Indictment, 13 July 1998, counts 3, 4, 7, 8, 10, 11, 12, 13, 16, 17, 20 and 21.
49 *Prosecutor* v. *Jean-Paul Akayesu*, Case No. ICTR-96-4-T, Judgment, Trial Chamber I, 2 September 1998, para. 731.

under the ambit of 'serious bodily and mental harm' prohibited by Article II(b) of the Convention.[50] Viewed in the full light of its context and relevance, the jurisprudence of the two ad hoc international criminal tribunals can thus be seen to have brought forth major substantive developments which promise both greater protection for victims, and accountability for perpetrators, of rape and sexual violence.

'Savoir ... et faire semblant'[51]: impunity, denial and prospects for justice

By expanding the classifications under which sexual violence can be tried – as grave breaches under Article 2 of the Tribunal's Statute, as violations of the laws and customs of war (Article 3) or crimes against humanity (Article 5) – the ICTY has made major strides towards authorising and inviting prosecutions for such acts. In relative terms – that is, set over and against other tribunals, and viewed in the light of the few international precedents – the number of instances brought before the Tribunal is notable. Over 70 cases have involved sexual violence, of which more than 20 have offered judgments containing relevant findings. As commendable as this is, however, it nonetheless points to the startling discrepancy between the number of instances of sexual violence and the number of perpetrators held to account, leading to the view that most offences are committed with 'complete impunity'.[52]

That there should be this variance between the number of instances and prosecutions is hardly surprising. International criminal tribunals cannot, as Katherine Franke puts it, secure 'perfect justice':[53] logistics alone mean that the Tribunals can only deal with a fraction of cases through which they might establish important precedent and/or identify the masterminds of the violence. In its Final Report, the Commission of Experts for the Former Yugoslavia recommended concentrating on rape and sexual violence as a means of ethnic cleansing and ignoring individual and opportunistic rapes – the implication being that any such individualised acts, as far as they might be considered as such, fall outside the remit of the Tribunal. As a consequence, thousands of victims have been dealt the double blow of not only being subjected to such violence, but also being denied the satisfaction of seeing their violators brought to justice – hence why it is they have been aptly referred to as 'double victims'.

A further factor which contributes to this impunity for perpetrators of sexual violence is the complex political structure of the peace process in

50 *Prosecutor* v. *George Rutaganda*, Case No. ICTR-96-3-T, Judgment, Trial Chamber I, 6 December 1999, para. 50.
51 Semelin, J. Purifier et détuire: Usages politiques des Massacres et génocides (Paris: Le Sevil, 2005).
52 Parliamentary Assembly of the Council of Europe, Resolution 1670 (2009), 'Sexual Violence Against Women in Armed Conflict', 29 May 2009.
53 Franke *supra*, note 19, 820.

Bosnia and Herzegovina. In the aftermath of the conflict, political and state actors of all allegiances officially subscribed to transitional justice and the need for justice, truth and reconciliation. However, their visions of how Bosnia should move forward were and remain at variance, and political uncertainties and mutually exclusive strategies checked the progress of transitional justice projects. With questions of culpability and identity so violently contested, such projects became less human rights oriented and ever more politicised in the service of appeasement and reconciliation, and so the disposition for pursuing perpetrators of past harm abated somewhat.[54] While understandable, such developments are scarcely defensible, and the dangers of such politicking are spotlighted by Israel W. Charny who, in his wide-ranging classification of genocide denial psychologies, lists both the inclination to put aside issues of justice for the sake of current economic and political interests, and the purpose of not wanting to antagonise perpetrator groups and their successors who might then abandon the peace process.[55] Gregory H. Stanton, meanwhile, has put the mechanisms of genocide denial and the issue of the need to pursue justice into sharp relief:

> Denial is the eighth stage that always follows a genocide. It is among the surest indicators of further genocidal massacres. The perpetrators of genocide dig up the evidence and intimidate the witnesses. They deny that they committed any crimes, and often blame what happened on the victims. They block investigations of the crimes, and continue to govern until driven from power by force, when they flee into exile. There they remain with impunity, like Pol Pot or Idi Amin, unless they are captured and a tribunal is established to try them.[56]

To view the fate of female victims of rape and sexual violence in Bosnia and Herzegovina as a form of genocide denial may be problematic – not because of the nature of the violation, which has, as we have seen, been recognised as a genocidal act, but rather in view of the fact that only the massacre at Srebrenica has been qualified as an act of genocide, with other crimes considered as crimes against humanity, war crimes and grave breaches of the Geneva Convention. That notwithstanding, many of the denial mechanisms listed in the above correlate with practices in the Bosnian context, and it is clear that the failure to confront such harm at the judicial level represents a denial of justice which goes against the ideas of recognition, reparation and redress which underpin the transitional justice process.

54 See Subotić, J., *Hijacked Justice: Dealing with the Past in the Balkans* (Ithaca, NY: Cornell University Press, 2009).
55 Charny, I. W. (ed.), *Encyclopedia of Genocide*, 2 vols (Santa Barbara, CA: ABC-Clio, 1999).
56 Stanton, G. H. 'The Eighth Stage of Genocide', Genocide Watch at: www.genocidewatch. org/aboutgenocide/8stagesofgenocide.html.

This issue of the apparent failing of legal process which allows for impunity is linked to a broader question of relevance – namely, that of the effectiveness of criminal prosecutions and truth commissions as a mechanism for transitional justice. In general terms, this debate is well rehearsed, with several commentators making the case that war crime tribunals do little to aid the processes of coming to terms with the past and securing justice for the future. In the case of rape and sexual violence, this issue can be well addressed in relation to the psychological trauma suffered by the victims. That such instances of violence leave terrible physical and mental scars is a point which needs here no elaboration. The ICTY has, indeed, prosecuted rape as a means of psychological terror. In the *Tadić* case, for instance, rape victims were called to bear witness to the psychological abuse to which prisoners were subjected.[57] At the Tribunal, legal experts have shown themselves alive to the particular psychological consequences for victims and efforts have been made to be sensitive to the peculiar considerations which inhere in the prosecution of sexual violence. Rule 34 of the Rules of Procedure and Evidence holds that:

(A) There shall be set up, under the authority of the Registrar, a 'Victims and Witnesses Section' consisting of qualified staff to:
(i) recommend protective measures for victims and witnesses in accordance with Article 22 of the Statute; and (ii) provide counselling and support for them, in particular in cases of rape and sexual assault.
(B) Due consideration shall be given, in the appointment of staff, to the employment of qualified women.[58]

Further efforts have also been made to ensure witness protection – Rule 69(A) of the Rules of Procedure and Evidence, for example, states that the prosecutor 'may apply to a Judge or Trial Chamber to order the non-disclosure of the identity of a victim or witness who may be in danger or at risk until such person is brought under the protection of the Tribunal'.[59] Following the lead of the Tribunals, Article 68 of the Rome Statute likewise sets down conditions for the protection of the physical and psychological welfare of witnesses:

The Court shall take appropriate measures to protect the safety, physical and psychological well-being, dignity and privacy of victims and

---

57 *Prosecutor* v. *Duško Tadić* ('Prijedor'), Case No. IT-94-1-T, Judgment, Trial Chamber II, 7 May 1997.
58 Rule 34 on Victims and Witnesses Session of the Rules of Procedure and Evidence of the ICTY, adopted on 11 February 1994.
59 Rule 69(A) on Protection of Victims and Witnesses of the Rules of Procedure and Evidence of the ICTY, adopted on 11 February 1994 and amended on 13 December 2001.

witnesses. In so doing, the Court shall have regard to all relevant factors, including age, gender as defined in article 7, paragraph 3, and health, and the nature of the crime, in particular, but not limited to, where the crime involves sexual or gender violence or violence against children. The Prosecutor shall take such measures particularly during the investigation and prosecution of such crimes.[60]

Despite such measures, however, many victims nonetheless refuse to come forward as witnesses. For some, it is a sense of shame and degradation which inhibits them, for others, it is the fear of brutal reprisals. Even for those who do testify, the experience can be unnerving, and many struggle to cope with the trauma of facing their attacker and reliving the reality of the rape. To compound this, several victim-witnesses have relayed that they found testifying at a judicial proceeding dehumanising on two principal grounds. The first is that of their testimony being publicly called into question – in the Appeals Chamber, for instance, Delić used this tactic as his main defence, arguing (in a manner which starkly recalls the mechanisms of denial noted earlier) that the victim's testimony:

> was so weak and contradicted, that the Trial Chamber's conclusions were clearly wrong. In particular, he refers to elements of her testimony which illustrate her unreliability because: (1) she failed to identify Delić properly; (2) her own evidence was weak and contradictory when given in relation to certain issues; (3) her evidence contradicted evidence given by other witnesses, in particular Milojka Antic; and (4) she was unable to recall certain events, illustrating what he describes as her 'selective memory'.[61]

The second ground for victims feeling degraded is the manner in which the rules of relevance and due legal process proscribe the personal retelling of their story. As Franke notes:

> Forced to testify to their experiences by answering prosecutors' questions in a 'yes' or 'no' manner, and interrupted by judges when their testimony veered beyond the immediate question of the culpability of the individual defendant, many victims who have testified before the ICTY have found their experiences as witnesses humiliating and disrespectful.[62]

For the victims of sexual violence, the securing of justice involves the public disclosure of their stories and the sense that the full extent of their trauma is

---

60 Article 68 of the Rome Statute.
61 *Prosecutor* v. *Zdravko Mucić* et al. ('Čelebići Camp'), Case No. IT-96-21-A, Judgment, Appeals Chamber, 20 February 2001, para. 489.
62 Franke *supra*, note 19, 818.

heard and understood. And yet the context of a criminal prosecution is not one which permits such an unburdening of personal experience – the limited demands of establishing culpability necessarily leads to both an externalisation and instrumentalisation of personal experience in the service of judicial process. This fundamental tension between the requirements of legal process and the claims of personal traumatic redress is irresolvable, and points to a significant limitation on the effectiveness of criminal prosecutions as a method of transitional justice. For where the demands of a personal reckoning with past harm and securing of justice entail an intimate retelling of physical and psychological experience, there are few settings less conducive to such truth-telling than a court of law, with its claims to strict relevance and more mechanical pursuit of truth and accountability. Thus while it is that witnessing their violators being brought to justice may alleviate the (misplaced) shame of the victim and provide a sense of reparation, it seems unlikely that legal proceedings can ever achieve full redress for the trauma of gender-related violence of the recent past, with even those who testify before the court often left with a disappointed feeling of truth untold and justice denied.

The role of international criminal law in facilitating transitional justice for women

With all this in mind it is clear to see how, in coming to terms with instances of sexual violence and assault, criminal prosecutions inevitably fall short of delivering 'perfect justice', both in terms of bringing all perpetrators to account and providing a full sense of personal redress for victims. Yet as much as we should be ever mindful of the limitations that attend such proceedings, there should be no doubting that they nonetheless play a significant role in the transitional justice process. Indeed, the contribution of criminal prosecutions is in several ways critical to the success of transitional justice. First, such prosecutions serve, by seeking accountability for abuses of law (especially amongst high-profile figures), as a means of rebuilding the rule of law and strengthening justice systems in post-conflict societies. As noted in the *Blaškić* case: 'Individual and affirmative prosecution aimed at influencing the legal awareness of the accused, the victims, the relatives, the witnesses, and the general public in order to reassure them that the legal system is being implemented and enforced.'[63]

Second, and related to the above, the prosecution of those responsible for gross human rights violations secures a sense of justice for victims that furthers the aims of redress, reparation and reconciliation amongst the population. Third, legal sanctions may also serve as an important and effective deterrent against future possible perpetrators. For these reasons, and

---

63 *Prosecutor* v. *Tihomir Blaškić* ('*Lašva Valley*'), Case No. IT-95-14-A, Judgment, Appeals Chamber, 29 July 2004, para. 678.

although they cannot on their own secure full justice in these areas, criminal prosecutions remain an integral part of any comprehensive programme of transitional justice aiming at redressing past wrongs and advancing new forms of law, justice and peace.

What, then, might this all mean for the fate of female victims of rape and sexual violence in Bosnia and Herzegovina (and beyond), and for the future development of international criminal law more generally? On the one hand, there exists the realisation that many such victims will not be granted the satisfaction of seeing their violators held to account, and that, in this regard, the overarching aims of transitional justice will go unmet. Yet despite the fact that criminal sanctions against the perpetrators of such acts will inevitably be incomplete, this ought not, on the other hand, be used as an excuse for a let up in the pursuit of accountability. The temptation to fudge the issue for the sake of appeasing actors and groups party to the peace process must be resisted as a flagrant denial of justice to the victims. Instead, continuing efforts should be made to bring further cases and to issue indictments for violations of international criminal law, and thereby close the gap, however slightly, between the number of instances and prosecutions. With the end of the ICTY mandate approaching, however, the onus for this will shortly pass on to the Bosnian domestic courts.

Taking a broader view with regards to the issues of rape and sexual violence in international criminal law, the existing case law of the ICTY and ICTR should provide a basis for further consideration of substantive developments which may aid in the pursuit of accountability. An exemplary issue here is that of the connection between rape and genocide, and whether, following the *Akayesu* judgment, the explicit inclusion of rape – committed with the requisite *mens rea* – in the Genocide Convention may reinforce and promote prosecutions, as it surely should.

In turn, this question also invites reflection on the gendered and sexual harms of rape and sexual violence. For it is, specifically, the rape of women that might be perpetrated so as to enforce pregnancies, prevent future births and inflict conditions 'calculated to bring about [the group's] physical destruction in whole or in part'.[64] As such, it warrants consideration whether it is necessary to distinguish between acts committed against the sexes, not in terms of the severity or gravity of the act in itself, but rather in terms of the overriding intention and effect. Of course, such questions must be approached with due care so as not to give rise to any kind of hierarchy or 'privileging' of female violence over male violence. Nor should the terrain of international criminal law be permitted to become a battleground for gender and feminist discourses. It is rather the case that efforts should be made to continue to consider and adapt legal conceptions of the harms of sexual violence in armed conflict, and to evaluate the practices that constitute 'sexual violence' and the *mens rea* both of rape and of sexual violence, including

---

64 Article II(c) of the Genocide Convention.

questions of intent, coercion and absence of consent. By way of an ongoing reassessment of such issues, and by actively seeking accountability, the instruments of international criminal law continue, and will continue, to play a vital role in furthering the aims of transitional justice neatly articulated by the ICTY in its mission statement: 'to bring to justice persons allegedly responsible for violations [...]; to render justice to the victims; to deter further crimes; [and] to contribute to the restitution of the peace by promoting reconciliation'.[65]

---

65 *Prosecutor* v. *Radoslav Brđanin* ('Krajina'), Case No. IT-99-36-T, Decision on the defence 'objection to intercept evidence', Trial Chamber II, 3 October 2003, para. 63(7).

7 A tool for reconciling gender and customary law

Lauren Fielder[1]

In periods of transitional justice, particularly in Africa where there is a history of colonization, a legal reorganization that incorporates African customary law is valuable. However, African customary law can have the effect of oppressing women. Constitutional Courts, another key player in times of transition, can serve as an important tool in the process of transforming African customary law into a body of law that reflects women's equal place in society. There is a deep connection between constitutional courts and a successful program of transitional justice.

This chapter will explain the role of constitutional courts in transitional societies. It will also examine the connection between African customary law and transitional justice. Most importantly, it will explain how the courts can become a tool for women to transform African customary law into a body of law that reflects women's equality. In doing so, the chapter will point out that women have a fundamental right to be part of the constitutional process as embodied by constitutional adjudication and explain how women can practically increase their participation in the process by becoming aware of their rights and demanding them.

At the outset, it is important to mention that Africa means sub-Saharan Africa. In addition, it is obvious that Africa is a continent with indescribable variation. However, there are some systemic failures and recurrent themes in Africa that make generalization valuable.

Transitional justice and the role of constitutional courts

Transitional justice centers around the place of law in political transitions.[2] One of the pillars of successful transitional justice is a constitutional process that fosters inclusion and participation.[3] Two components of inclusion and participation reflect the court's role as a place to give voice to the people.

---

1 Lauren Fielder, JD, LL.M, is Assistant Professor of Law and Assistant Director of the Transnational Legal Studies Program at the University of Luzern Faculty of Law, Switzerland.
2 Gross, A. "The Constitutional, Reconciliation, and Transitional Justice: Lessons from South Africa and Israel" (2004) 40 *Stanford Journal of International Law* 47, 50.
3 Gross ibid. 96.

Courts are the voice of the people because they belong to the people, and not just the political elite.[4] This is very pressing in transitional justice situations, as there is usually a considerable disparity in the political and social power of elite and non-elite citizens.[5] Writing about the role of the South African Constitutional Court, Aeyal Gross explains that the framers of the South African Constitutional Court found it fit to emphasize in the constitution, itself, that the constitution is the property of all its citizens:[6]

> We the people of South Africa ... believe that South Africa belongs to all who live in it, united in our diversity. We therefore ... adopt this Constitution as the supreme law of a society based on democratic values, social justice, and fundamental human rights.[7]

It is hard to define exactly what "the people" means, because the concept is complex.[8] "There are religious groups, ethnic groups, the disabled, women, youth, forest people, pastoralists, 'indigenous peoples,' farmers, peasants, capitalists and workers ... each pursuing his or her own agenda."[9] Each group contributes differing levels of awareness and sophistication to the process.[10] It is clear, however, that women are an important underrepresented group that must be given a voice in the constitutional process of transitional justice, since transitional justice rests on an expansive view of equality.[11] Women should be a part of this dialogue. Unfortunately, until the 1980s the plight of African women and the tensions created by the application of customary law were largely ignored by legal academics and the law reformers.[12] Women's issues were ignored by the judiciary, as well. Inclusiveness was not part of the constitutional process in many African states.[13] That can be remedied by constitutional jurisprudence that is the product of dialogue that is inclusive, diverse, participatory, autonomous and accountable.[14] Women should be involved in the negotiation of African values, which is

---

4 See section IV, B., *supra*.
5 Banks, A. "Expanding Participation in Constitution Making: Challenges and Opportunities" 49 *William and Mary Law Review* 1043, 1044 and 1055.
6 Gross, *supra* note 2.
7 Ibid., quoting South African Constitution (Constitution Act 108, 1996) pmbl.7.
8 "Introduction to Public Participation Issues," Constitution Making for Peace: Interpeace at 4: www.interpeace.org/constitutionmaking/part-2-tasks-constitution-making-process/22-public-participation/221-introduction-public. Indeed, it is easier to define that it does not mean – only the elite, political or otherwise.
9 Ibid., 4.
10 Ibid., 4.
11 Gross, *supra* note 2, 96, discussing factors important to transitional justice.
12 Graycar, R. "Book Review: Gender and the New South African Legal Order" (1996) 12 *South African Journal of Human Rights* 669, 670.
13 Udombana, N. "Interpreting Rights Globally: Courts and Constitutional Rights in Emerging Democracies" (2005) 5 *African Human Rights Law Journal* 47, 49.
14 Ibid.

important to maintain their dignity,[15] providing a foundation for all other rights.

Transitional justice has the potential to both empower and disempower women. They have often fought alongside men in struggles for national liberation,[16] and then they have been increasingly involved in the peace process.[17] While these conflicts are ongoing, there is a spike in women's equality and empowerment. When society is in flux, some women may benefit from greater liability and social mobility,[18] yet this period of increased empowerment is fleeting.[19] When the fighting ends and a state enters a period of transition, states often fall back on customary law that discriminates against women.[20] This is because customary law fills in the accountability (legal) gap left by the collapse of more formal justice "mechanisms."[21] Furthermore, there is the desire to "reestablish normality" by encouraging cultural practices.[22] The result is that "women's rights are generally the most ignored and under-enforced category of norms in a transitional context."[23]

African customary law and transitional justice

Despite the potential for disempowering women, it is important for transitional justice in Africa to reflect African culture. Culture is "an historic

---

15 Banda, F. "Global Standards: Local Values" (2010) 17 *International Journal of Law, Policy and Family* 1, 19.

16 Ibid., 4: examples include the struggles in Zimbabwe and Guinea-Bissau. However, "women had participated in armed struggles for national liberation, they have tended to be marginalized and few have attained formal positions of power or gained rights to land and resources in their own name."

17 Manuh, T. "Women in Africa's Development: Overcoming Obstacles, Pushing for Progress," African Recovery at 1: www.un.org/en/africarenewal/bpaper/maineng.htm.

18 Aolain, F.N. and Hamilton, M. "Gender and the Rule of Law in Transitional Societies" (2009) 18 *Minnesota Journal of International Law* 380, 389. There are periods in history when popular forces – workers, peasants and women's organizations – through their militation or struggles gain access to the state, which can act to facilitate their own control and authority within the political system. In other words, the state provides an opening such that the interests of the oppressed and that of the state can at least partially correspond, and the oppressed can draw advantages from the situation. Hassim, S. "Gender Location and Feminist Politics in South Africa" (1991) 15 *Transformation* 65, 87, quoting Boyd, R. "Empowerment of Women in Contemporary Uganda: Real or Symbolic?" (1989) 22 *Labour, Capital and Society* 1, 3.

19 Ibid., 87.

20 Oba, A. "The Future of Customary Law in Africa" in *The Future of African Customary Law* 58, 77 (Jeanmarie Fenrich, Paolo Galizzi and Tracy E. Higgins, eds., Cambridge: Cambridge University Press, 2011): "Traditional African legal concepts can be and are often invoked when state law proves inadequate."

21 Kasande, K.S. "Centring Women's Rights in Transitional Justice Processes in Northern Uganda: FIDA-Uganda's Experience," Restorative Justice Online at 9: www.restorative-justice.org/articlesdb/articles/10031.

22 Aolain and Hamilton, *supra* note 18, 389.

23 Aolain, F.N. "Political Violence and Gender during Times of Transition" (2006) 15 *Columbia Journal of Gender and Law* 829, 830.

transmitted pattern of meanings in symbols, a system of inherited conceptions expressed in symbolic form by means of which men [and women] communicate, perpetuate and develop their knowledge and attitudes toward
life."[24] It includes a specific African identity. This African identity is important to people because it "affirms their own dignity and worth as human
beings, satisfies their need to belong to a desirable group, and attracts solidarity of other members of that group."[25] Importantly, culture is an "irredu-
cible social good" that should be preserved wherever possible.[26] The loss of
culture can equate to the loss of collective power and responsibility.[27]
Culture can provide psychological and spiritual clarity and can be the catalyst for creativity, productivity and confidence.[28]

Loss of culture can equal disempowerment. One commentator argues that
disempowerment is possibly the largest unrecognized problem in Africa
today.[29] This is largely in part due to the African people's belief that they
cannot act on their own behalf.[30] It is a reaction to leaders' attitudes and policies over the past forty or fifty years.[31] What flows from this is the tendency

24 Bond, J. "Women's Rights, Customary Law, and the Promise of the Protocol on the
    Rights of Women in Africa" in *The Future of African Customary Law* 462, 472 (Jeanmarie
    Fenrich, Paolo Galizzi and Tracy E. Higgins, eds., Cambridge: Cambridge University
    Press, 2011), quoting An-Na'im, A.A. "Toward a Cross-Cultural Approach to Defining
    International Standards of Human Rights: The Meaning of Cruel, Inhuman, or Degrad-
    ing Treatment or Punishment" in *Human Rights in Cross-Cultural Perspectives: A Quest for
    Consensus* 19, 23 (Abdullahi Ahmed An-Na'im, ed., Philadelphia, PA: University of
    Pennsylvania Press, 1992).
25 An-Na'im, A.A. *African Constitutionalism and the Role of Islam* (Philadelphia, PA: Univer-
    sity of Pennsylvania Press, 2006) 130.
26 McKinley, M.A. "Cultural Culprits" (2009) 24 *Berkeley Journal of Gender Law and Justice*
    91, 94.
27 Maathai, W. *The Challenge for Africa* (London: Arrow Books, 2010) 165.
    Interestingly, in every seminar, participants point to the loss of traditional culture as
    one of the major causes of troubles such as the misuse of alcohol and drugs, irrespons-
    ible behavior toward women and girl children, high secondary school dropout rates
    (especially for girls), prostitution, theft, the breakup of family relationships, and the
    commercialization of religion. The express distress at the phenomenon of street chil-
    dren, and the spread of HIV/AIDS. As they analyze further the causes of their prob-
    lems, many people come to the conclusion that their society has lost its accepted
    values and taboos and has, therefore, become both vulnerable and susceptible to any
    leader who promises them the immediate satisfaction of their felt needs. (Ibid., 169)
28 Ibid., 171 and 183, stating that
    [t]here is enormous relief, as well as anger and sadness, when people realize that
    without a culture one not only is a slave, but also has in effect collaborated with the
    slave trader, and that the consequences have been long-lasting and devastating,
    extending back through generations. A new appreciation of culture gives traditional
    communities a chance, quite literally, to rediscover themselves, [and] reevaluate and
    reclaim who they are.
29 Ibid., 129.
30 Ibid.
31 Ibid.

to leave fate in the hands of third parties.[32] Wangari Maathai terms this helplessness "dependency syndrome."[33]

An important embodiment of culture that is specifically important to transitional justice in Africa is customary law.[34] "A customary law may be defined as a normative order observed by a population, having been formed by regular social behavior and the development of an accompanying sense of obligation."[35] It remains a highly relevant source of law in Africa, particularly in family law.[36] As mentioned above, customary law is important in post-conflict situations.

Despite the tremendous value of culture and custom, both cultural practices and customary law can be harmful to women. In fact, sometimes culture and tradition are "so closely linked with control of women that they are virtually equated."[37] Examples of customary law that are potentially harmful to women include laws regulating early marriage, female circumcision, *lobolo* (bride price), abductions, the inability to choose the number and spacing of children and inheritance laws that disadvantage women.[38] Cultural practice as a defense to crime (including domestic violence) is another way culture has been invoked to violate the rights of women.[39]

Customary law can be an obstacle to women's full participation in society.[40] Wangari Maathai explains:

> [C]ulture is a double edged sword that can be used as a weapon to strike a blow for empowerment or threaten those who would assert their own self-expression or self-identity. In many communities in Africa and other regions, women are discriminated against, exploited, and controlled through prevailing cultures, which demand that they act a certain way. They are denied power, access to wealth and services, and even control of their bodies through [cultural practices]. Some cultures demand that men be warriors and learn to kill, or to treat women a certain way, or to repress

32 Ibid. Reliance is not limited to the temporal. Many Africans also believe that "whatever happens is God's will, predetermined and inevitable."

33 Ibid.

34 Bond, *supra* note 24, 472. Customary law is conceptually distinct from culture, it is an expression of it.

35 Woodman, G. "A Survey of Customary Laws in Africa in Search of Lessons for the Future" in *The Future of African Customary Law* 9, 10 (Jeanmarie Fenrich et al. eds., Cambridge: Cambridge University Press, 2011), explaining that "a normative order is a body of interrelated norms, or of rules and principles."

36 Oba, *supra* note 20, 79.

37 Okin, S. *Is Multiculturalism Bad for Women* 16 (Princeton, NJ: Princeton University Press, 1999).

38 Tsanga, A. and Stewart, J. *Women and Law: Innovative Regional Approaches to Teaching, Research and Analysis* (Harare: Weaver Press, 2011), 19, and Kasande, *supra* note 21, 10.

39 McKinley, *supra* note 26, 94, and Kasande, *supra* note 21, 10.

40 Nyamu, C. "Constitutional Barriers to Challenging Women's Equality in Family Property Arrangements" (2000) 94 *American Society of International Law Proceedings* 289, 381.

emotions, such as affection, pain, and compassion. Those who break away from the norm are punished or ostracized. These are some of the negative aspects of culture. We cannot shy away from these.[41]

Cultural values that are the foundation of traditional justice systems employ mechanisms that marginalize women.[42] "Often when women seek to bring about change, culture becomes sacred and unchangeable."[43] Those in power seek to keep it.

The courts' role in balancing culture and equality in transitional justice situations

The above sections show clearly that there is a tension between preserving culture and supporting equality in the transitional processes. What is the solution for resolving this tension? How can culture and customary law be a part of transitional justice situations while not further entrenching the gross injustices women face in the name of cultural protection? This section will explore approaches taken by African Constitutional Courts. There are several possibilities.

Prioritize culture

When balancing competing values, courts can prioritize culture and customary law above other rights such as the right to gender equality. This was the approach taken by Zimbabwe's Supreme Court in *Magaya* v. *Magaya*.[44] The *Magaya* case concerned a dispute over an estate. In this case, a local court appointed Venia Magaya heir to her father's estate. Ms. Magaya's younger half-brother, Nakayi Magaya, appealed the case on the grounds that African customary law prohibits a woman from inheriting property when there is a man in the family entitled to claim it. The appellate court was persuaded by this agreement and reversed Ms. Magaya's heirship. Nakayi Magaya promptly removed Ms. Magaya from the home she had lived in for over twenty years and moved her into a one-room shack in a neighbor's yard. He sold the house and used the proceeds to buy himself a car. Ms. Magaya appealed to the Supreme Court of Zimbabwe claiming that her constitutional right to equality was

---

41 Maathai, *supra* note 27, 164.
42 Kasande, *supra* note 21, 9. "Cultural views of gender have created, facilitated, and perpetrated the schism between paper rights and the realities of women's lives," Hernandez-Truyol, B.E. "Women's Rights as Human Rights, Rules, Realities and the Role of Culture: A Formula for Reform" (1995–1996) 21 *Brooklyn Journal of International Law* 605, 650.
43 Kasande, *supra* note 21, 9.
44 *Magaya* v. *Magaya*, (1999) 3 L.R.C. 35 (Zimb. Sup. Ct.). This case was extensively discussed in Fielder, L. "Customary International Law and the Internationalization of African Constitutional Law: A Way Forward in the Protection of Human Rights?" in Zukunft und Recht (Mannhart, A. and Buergi, S., eds., Zurich: Schulthess, 2012) 243, 253.

breached.[45] The Supreme Court upheld the appellate court's decision on the grounds that violations of equality arising from the application of customary law are exempt from constitutional scrutiny.[46] The Court explained that in Zimbabwe's constitutional construction, there is a division between customary law and civil law, which prevented the court from deciding whether there had been a breach of the anti-discrimination provisions in the constitution.[47] In so holding, the court refused to consider case-specific concerns and international human rights law obligations, even though Ms. Magaya argued that "the case struck at the heart of her internationally recognized human rights, and that denying her heirship would run contrary to basic principles of gender equality and individual rights."[48] The Court's decision focused on the nature of African society and declined to consider comparative constitutional decisions and regional and international agreements which arguably would have outweighed these cultural considerations.[49] For example, Zimbabwe is party to numerous international human rights treaties, including CEDAW.[50]

This decision came despite the fact that the Chief Justice of Zimbabwe had stated in another case in close temporal proximity to the Magaya decision that

> judiciaries should make a greater conscious effort towards the protection and active enforcement of fundamental human rights and freedoms, and should always endeavor, wherever possible, to construe domestic legislation so that it conforms with the developing international jurisprudence of human rights.[51]

However, the approach taken by the court is because §111B of Zimbabwe's constitution explains that treaties do not have an effect as domestic law unless it has been incorporated into domestic law by an act of parliament.[52]

---

45 Zimbabwe Constitution, §23(2) (1996), prohibits discrimination on the basis of sex.
46 Zimbabwe Constitution, §23(3)(b) (1996), exempts customary laws from its anti-discriminatory provision, §23(2).
47 Bigge, D.M. and von Briesen, A. "Conflict in the Zimbabwean Courts: Women's Rights and Indigenous Self-Determination in Magaya v. Magaya" (2000) 13 *Harvard Human Rights Journal* 289, 294.
48 Knobelsdorf, V. "Zimbabwe's Magaya Decision Revisited: Women's Rights and Land Succession in the International Context" (2006) 15 *Columbia Journal of Gender and Law* 749, 752.
49 Ibid.
50 Ibid., 787.
51 Banda, *supra* note 15, 11, citing *Zimnat Insurance Co Ltd* v. *Chawanda* (1990) ZLR 143, 154.
52 Zimbabwe Constitution, §111B (1996), stating that:
   Effect of international conventions etc.
   (1) Except as otherwise provided by this Constitution or by or under an Act of Parliament, any convention, treaty or agreement acceded to, concluded or executed by or under the authority of the President with one or more foreign states or governments or international organizations –
   (a) shall be subject to approval by Parliament; and
   (b) shall not form part of the law of Zimbabwe unless it has been incorporated into the law by or under an Act of Parliament.

Prioritize equality – outright ban on harmful practices

Many proponents of women's human rights have called for an abolitionist approach to cultural practices that infringe on women's human rights.[53] This approach assumes that there is no possibility for the protection of women's human rights in traditional systems.[54] Therefore, the only tolerable solution is one that replaces the traditional system with a western style international human rights system,[55] or at the very least, voids customary laws that are found to be incompatible with human rights norms such as equality.

A recent case from the Constitutional Court of Benin took this approach. The *Review of Constitutionality of Family Legislation*,[56] was a constitutional challenge to Benin's Code of Individuals and Family, which permitted polygamy.[57] Article 143 of the law allowed a man to marry more than one woman but did not allow a woman to marry more than one man.[58] The article stated "[b]oth forms of marriage monogamic or polygamic are recognised. However, the future couple must choose one option before the marriage is celebrated."[59] Ms. H. Rosine Vieyra-Soglo, a member of the national assembly, claimed that the law was discriminatory against women in violation of article 26 of Benin's Constitution.[60] The Court found this provision of the family code to be unconstitutional, making polygamous marriage unconstitutional in Benin.[61] However, the Court made provisions for polygamous marriages contracted prior to the code, so that there would not be unjust transitory effects on women.[62]

Incremental approaches that balance culture and equality

Perhaps the best approach is a middle ground between an outright rejection of culture and an absolute preference for it. According to one commentator, "[w]e do not reject our culture when we find it replete with oppression and the violation of rights; we try to reform it."[63] Radical change can be accomplished

---

53 Nyamu, *supra* note 40, 392 citing Mutua, M.W. "The Politics of Human Rights: Beyond the Abolitionist Paradigm in Africa" (1996) 17 *Michigan Journal of International Law* 591.

54 Ibid., 393.

55 Ibid., citing Nhlapo, T. "Cultural Diversity, Human Rights and the Family in Contemporary Africa: Lessons from the South African Constitutional Debate" (1995) 9 *International Journal of Law and Family* 208, 216.

56 "Review of Constitutionality of Family Legislation" (2004) AHRLR 127 (BeCC 2002).

57 "Family Legislation," paras. 1 and 4.

58 "Family Legislation," para. 4.

59 "Family Legislation," para. 6.

60 "Family Legislation," paras. 3–4. Ms. Vieyra-Soglo also challenged parts of the law concerning division of property. "Family Legislation," para. 4.

61 "Family Legislation," para. 10.

62 "Family Legislation," para. 19.

63 Raz, J. "How Perfect Should One Be? And Whose Culture Is?" in *Is Multiculturalism Bad for Women?* 95, 97 (S. Okin ed., Princeton, NJ: Princeton University Press, 1999).

in an incremental manner.[64] One such incremental approach that can be taken by constitutional courts is to transform customary law through the judicial process to harmonize it with human rights protections.

Culture cannot just be dismissed; while culture can present obstacles for gender equality, it can also present opportunities for reform.[65] "Proponents of gender equality must appropriate positive openings presented by cultural and religious traditions, instead of dismissing culture as a negative influence."[66] It can be an "empowering framework" for women to use to confront prejudices.[67] Culture must be rediscovered and used to help people reconnect with the past and construct a future that promotes equality.[68]

What must be done by those who seek greater gender equality for women within traditional systems is to challenge the "ossified" idea of cultural law.[69] Codifications and scholarship that attempt to describe the content of cultural law are merely a snapshot of the state of law at any given time, but they can never capture the current situation because of the very fluid nature of African customary law.[70] This makes it very hard for judges to ascertain the exact contours of African customary law.[71] When judges are called on to interpret African customary law, they often look at a picture or codification of the law that does not accurately reflect the current status of the law or where the law has evolved since the codification.[72] This confusion over the content of customary law has caused it to be ignored by legal reformers, preventing it from developing into an advanced body of law that is "duly documented and acknowledged by the legal fraternity."[73] The result is often that out of date material is the only resource available.[74] Experts' opinions can be problematic

---

64 Fombad, C.M. "Constitutional Reforms and Constitutionalism in Africa: Reflections on Some Current Challenges and Future Prospects" (2011) 59 *Buffalo Law Review* 1007, 1100.

65 Nyamu, *supra* note 40, 382.

66 Ibid., 382.

67 Citing Maboreke, M. 'Understanding Law in Zimbabwe' in *Gender, Law and Social Justice* (A. Stewart, ed., Oxford: Oxford University Press, 2000), in Tsanga and Stewart, *supra* note 38.

68 Maathai, *supra* note 27, 171. How to harness religious and customary laws to effect a change in power relations. Tsanga and Stewart, *supra* note 38, 203.

69 Nyamu, *supra* note 40, 413; see also, McKinley, *supra* note 26, 96, explaining that many view culture as "fixed."

70 Nyamu, *supra* note 40, 413–414.

71 Himonga, C. 'The Future of Living Customary Law in African Legal Systems in the Twenty-First Century and Beyond, with Special Reference to South Africa' in *The Future of African Customary Law* 31, 50 (Jeanmarie Fenrich, Paolo Galizzi and Tracy E. Higgins, eds., Cambridge: Cambridge University Press, 2011).

72 Ibid.

73 Rautenbach, C. and Plessis, W. "Reform of the South African Customary Law of Succession: Final Nails in the Customary Law Coffin?" in *The Future of African Customary Law* 336, 358 (Jeanmarie Fenrich, Paolo Galizzi and Tracy E. Higgins, eds., Cambridge: Cambridge University Press, 2011).

74 Nyamu, *supra* note 40, 414, stating that new empirical evidence is needed.

as well.[75] It is usually only powerful elites that are called on to testify to what is the definitive interpretation of customary law.[76]

The connection between tradition and culture makes it harder to understand culture as something that can change, yet a "sophisticated and accurate understanding of culture requires us to recognize its fluidity."[77] Customary law is thought to be static, but it is constantly changing and modernizing. This idea of customary law as fixed harks back to the period of colonization, when colonial courts sought to apply customary law by looking at a snapshot of it at some point in time.[78] This was done in part because of a lack of understanding of African legal systems and a desire to conform African customary law into a written format to make it look similar to western law.[79] However, evidence overwhelmingly proves that customary law has undergone tremendous changes over the last century and continues to change today.[80] No society is "stable, timeless, ancient, lacking in internal conflict."[81] The assumption that it is, is largely made by outsiders looking at a culture they do not understand.[82]

Furthermore, culture evolving does not equate with culture disappearing. Indeed, the opposite is true. There is no need to freeze culture in order to preserve it.[83] Allowing culture to evolve keeps it alive. Wangari Maathai explains:

> Cultures are dynamic, changing with time and place, interacting with other cultures and evolving and adapting: people should not have to become walking museums. Progressive cultures help their peoples survive and pass their wisdom and a sense of destiny to the next generation.[84]

---

75 Ibid.
76 Bond, *supra* note 24, 473. These elites have an interest in keeping definitions of customary law that further entrench their power.
77 Volpp, L. "Blaming Culture for Bad Behavior" (2000) 12 *Yale Journal of Law and Humanities* 89, 98.
78 "Virtually all of Africa came under colonial rule" Menski, W. *Comparative Law in a Global Context: The Legal Systems of Asia and Africa* 448 (Cambridge: Cambridge University Press, 2nd ed. 2006).
79 Ibid., 452–453.
80 Woodman, *supra* note 35, 15.
81 Pollitt, K. 'Whose Culture?' in *Is Multiculturalism Bad for Women* (S. Okin ed., Princeton, NJ: Princeton University Press, 1999) 27, 29.
82 Volpp, *supra* note 77, 94: "We sometimes assume culture to be static and insular, a fixed property of groups rather than an entity constantly created through relationships. This assumption is made much more frequently for outsider communities such as communities of color."
83 Tamir, Y. "Siding with the Underdogs" in *Is Multiculturalism Bad for Women* (S. Okin ed., Princeton, NJ: Princeton University Press, 1999) 47, 51: "Trust the ability of individuals to withstand change and reform their traditions and lifestyle without surrendering completely their particular identity."
84 Maathai, *supra* note 27, 182.

Therefore, reformers can be viewed as much a part of the preservation of culture as strict adherents to traditional rules.[85] Cultures that are not hospitable to change are more likely to disintegrate, while those that are more flexible are more likely to flourish.[86]

The judicial process of the constitutional courts is an appropriate tool for revising African customary law in a way that achieves women's equality.[87] Transitional justice must ensure that structures that allowed abuses to occur must be dismantled.[88] As explained above, African customary law is one structure that has entrenched gender inequality.

Two cases of the South African Constitutional Court exemplify how the judicial process can be used to transform African customary law. The first case, *Bhe* v. *Magistrate*,[89] is actually a set of companion cases that concerned African customary inheritance laws that favored men. In its analysis of the issues presented in these cases, the South African Constitutional Court discussed the positive aspects of customary law as a dynamic system of law that is constantly evolving to meet the changing circumstances of the community.[90] In doing so, the Court emphasized its continuing commitment to the preservation and advancement of customary law in South Africa.[91] The Court made reference to Ubuntu, the dominant value in African traditional culture, which calls for communality, consensus building and the inter-dependence of members of the community.[92] The Court explained that the obligation to care for family members is "vital and fundamental" in the African social system.[93] However, the Court emphasized that despite culture's important role in society, customary law must always be consistent with the Constitution.[94] The Court then explained that African women and descendants who are not first-born males are a vulnerable group and that the application of the

---

85 Tamir, *supra* note 83, 50, stating that "[i]f, however, culture and tradition are seen in a less static light, then reformers could be seen as contributing to the preservation of the communal identity no less than conservatives."

86 Ibid.

87 Depending on the state, the Constitutional Court might not be the highest court. For example, in Anglophone Africa, the highest court may be the Appeal Court or the Supreme Court.

88 "Institutional Reform," International Center for Transitional Justice: http://ictj.org/our-work/transitional-justice-issues/institutional-reform.

89 Rautenbach and Plessis, *supra* note 73, 344, explaining that the term "transformative constitutionalism" is a theme explored in Klare, K.E. "Legal Culture and Transformative Constitutionalism" 14 *South African Journal on Human Rights* 146 (1998). It is a term that has grown in popularity with scholars and judges since that time. Ibid., note 58. This case was extensively discussed in Fielder, *supra* note 44, 251.

90 Rautenbach, C., et al. 'Is Primogeniture Extinct Like the Dodo, or is There Any Prospect of it Rising From the Ashes? Comments on the Evolution of Customary Succession Laws in South Africa' (2006) 22 *South African Journal on Human Rights* 99.

91 Bond, *supra* note 24 at 338 and *Bhe* at 24–25, para 41.

92 *Bhe*, 28, para. 45.

93 Rautenbach, *supra* note 90, 99.

94 *Bhe*, 24–25, para. 41.

customary law system of primogeniture violates their rights to equality and dignity.[95] This, reasoned the Court, is because primogeniture excludes women from inheritance, and is based on a system of patriarchy that kept women in a position of subservience and subordination.[96]

In deciding the case, the Court made reference to international and comparative law, stating that the South African Constitution is not alone in the emphasis it places on the right to equality:

> The right is cherished in the constitutions and the jurisprudence of many open and democratic societies. A number of international instruments, to which South Africa is a party, also underscore the right to protect the rights of women, and to abolish all laws that discriminate against them as well as to eliminate any racial discrimination in our society.[97]

In addition, the Court referred to provisions of the Convention on the Rights of the Child, the ICCPR and the African Charter on the Rights and Welfare of the Child in confirmation of the "best interests of the child principle" in the South African Constitution.[98] After carefully balancing the rights to equality and custom,[99] the Court held that the primogeniture rule applied in customary law is inconsistent with the South African Constitution's guarantee of equality.[100] In the end, the majority struck down the customary primogeniture rule to bring it in compliance with South Africa's Constitution.[101]

Bhe is an example of transformative constitutionalism because "the Court left a window for the development and evolvement of living customary law,"[102] when it allowed the African customary law of inheritance to evolve into a law that reflects South African Constitutional protection of equality.[103] In doing so, the Court pointed out that customary law was changing due to numerous factors including urbanization, individualization, the formation of nuclear families, poverty, unemployment and women's changing role in society.[104] The unanimous opinion recognized that it must "forge innovative remedies" to bring African customary law in harmony with the right to equality.[105]

---

95 *Bhe*, 56, paras. 91–92.
96 *Bhe*, 49, para. 78.
97 *Bhe*, 31.
98 Viljoen, F. *International Human Rights Law in Africa* (Oxford: Oxford University Press, 2007) 559, citing *Bhe*.
99 *Bhe*, 45, para. 70.
100 *Bhe*, 64, para. 109.
101 Rautenbach and Plessis, *supra* note 73, 343.
102 Himonga, *supra* note 71, 44.
103 Ibid.,44.
104 Rautenbach and Plessis, *supra* note 73, 344, citing *Bhe*, para. 78.
105 Ibid., 344, citing *Bhe*, para. 107.

Shilubana and Others v. *Nwamitwa and Other*,[106] is an even stronger example of the South African Constitutional Court directly transforming African customary law through its jurisprudence. Like *Bhe*, *Shilubana* was another case where there was a need to resolve the tension between African customary law and international human rights.[107] *Shilubana* was a case about succession of a tribal leadership position.[108] The issue in this case was whether a female could succeed as a leader of the Valoyi community of the Limpopo Province.[109] In this instance, the leader of the community, Hosi Fofoza, died without a male heir. Leadership passed to his younger brother, Hosi Richard, instead of to Ms. Shilubana, his eldest daughter.[110] Thirty-three years later, Hosi Richard died.[111] As had been decided by tribal leaders five years before the death of Hosi Richard, tribal chieftainship passed to Ms. Shilubana in line with South Africa's constitutional principle of gender equality.[112] The son of Hosi Richard, Mr. Nwamitwa, contested Ms. Shilubana's appointment, claiming that it violated customary law of succession.[113] Mr. Nwamitwa took his case to the Pretoria high court, which ruled in his favor.[114] Ms. Shilubana appealed, arguing that "customary law is dynamic and adaptable, and that the community acted within its power to amend its customs and traditions."[115]

The main issue before the South African Supreme Court in this case was the proper approach courts should take when dealing with an issue of African customary law.[116] The Court pointed out that importance of customary law is recognized by the South African Constitution.[117] Section 211 governs traditional leadership and states that customary law must be applied where it is relevant subject to the constitution.[118] The Court emphasized, just as it had in *Bhe*, that customary law must accord with the Constitution.[119] It then articulated guidelines to be used when courts in South Africa must decide how to handle customary law.[120] The Court suggested the courts consider:

---

106 *Shilubana and Others* v. *Nwamitwa and Other* 2009 (2) SA 66 (CC).
107 Himonga, *supra* note 71, 48.
108 *Shilubana*, *supra* note 106, para. 1.
109 Ibid., Para. 3.
110 Ibid., Para. 3.
111 Ibid., Para. 3.
112 Ibid., Para. 6. Note that a very complicated chain of events occurred (with Hosi Richard waivering on his support of Ms. Shilubana) between Ms. Shilubana's appointment and Hosi Richard's death.
113 Ibid., Para. 7.
114 Ibid., Para. 7.
115 Rautenbach and Plessis, *supra* note 73, 354.
116 *Shilubana*, *supra* note 106, para. 41.
117 Ibid., Para. 42.
118 Ibid., Para. 42.
119 Ibid., Para. 43.
120 Ibid., Para. 44.

- traditions of the community concerned, since customary law has developed over centuries;[121]
- respect for the right of communities to develop their own law including amending and repealing their own customs, stating that "the free development by communities of their own laws to meet the needs of a rapidly changing society must be respected and facilitated";[122]
- the reality that customary law regulates the lives of real people, so the flexibility of customary law must be balanced against the needs of people to have legal certainty, respect for vested rights and compliance with constitutional rights.[123]

The Court used this balancing approach on the facts of the case. In doing so, the Court explained, "[t]he legal status of customary law norms cannot depend simply on their having been consistently applied in the past ... [d]evelopment implies some departure from past practice."[124] The result would be courts applying customary law that communities no longer follow. The Court examined whether the traditional leaders had the authority to take the steps they did.[125] Voloyi authorities' intention was to bring an important custom in compliance with equality under the South African Constitution.[126] The Court stressed the importance of equality,[127] and reasoned that since this is a single community, the Court could leave the revision of the customary law to the community itself, since there was not such a high degree of legal certainty riding on the decision calling for interim measures, as was the case in *Bhe*.[128] Therefore, the Court found that the tribal leaders acted constitutionally in revising African customary law, and correspondingly, Ms. Shilubana was entitled to her position.[129]

Active development of customary law, the solution employed by the Court and advanced by some scholars, "facilitates the alignment of customary law with human rights while preserving, as far as possible, the values and fundamental features of customary law."[130] This approach corresponds with the minority approach in *Bhe*, which made a strong argument for adapting customary law instead of abolishing it.[131] It is expected that women

---

121 Ibid., Para. 44.
122 Ibid., Para. 45.
123 Ibid., Para. 47.
124 Ibid., Para. 55.
125 Ibid., Para. 60.
126 Ibid., Para. 68.
127 Ibid., Para. 69.
128 Ibid., Para. 77.
129 Ibid., Para. 91.
130 Himonga, *supra* note 71, 46, citing Lehnert, W. "The Role of the Courts in the Conflict Between African Customary Law and Human Rights" (2005) 21 *South African Journal on Human Rights* 241; Himonga, *supra* note 71 at 49, expressing the hope that scholars and judges will continue to develop the progression of African Customary Law.
131 Rautenbach and Plessis, *supra* note 73, 360.

in South Africa will use this decision to establish their rights to leadership positions.[132]

A rights based approach to women's involvement in the judicial process of revising African customary law

People, including women, have the right to be involved in their own development.[133] Women, especially young women, must be fully represented in negotiations about group rights, so that their interests can be protected rather than harmed.[134] In the transitional justice process, it is a part of the idea of inclusion. Inclusion guarantees that people are both physically present in decision-making forums and able to effectively influence the process.[135] The importance of inclusion has been recognized as central to the constitution-making process.[136] It follows that this holds true as constitutionalism is expanded through the constitutional adjudication process. In fact, legitimacy of the decision-making forums rests on inclusion and participation.[137] Participation in this process has also attained the status of international law through several treaties.[138]

International and regional law: the International Covenant of Civil and Political Rights (ICCPR)[139]

The ICCPR is one of the foundational multilateral human rights treaties to be created in the aftermath of the atrocities of World War II. It was adopted by the United Nations General Assembly on December 16, 1966, and entered into force March 23, 1976. It provides an important right of participation. Article 25 states that: "[e]very citizen shall have the right and the opportunity, without any of the distinctions mentioned in article 2 and without unreasonable restrictions: (a) to take part in the conduct of public affairs, directly or through freely chosen representatives."[140] General Comment 25 of the UN Human Rights

---

132 Ibid., 360.
133 Maathai, *supra* note 27, 130.
134 Okin, *supra* note 37, 24, explaining that "older women often are co-opted into reinforcing gender inequality."
135 Banks, *supra* note 5, 1044.
136 Banks emphasizes that "[s]cholars and policy makers concerned about democratization efforts in post-conflict states are beginning to focus on the process by which reforms are made, not just the substance of the reforms." Ibid., 1046.
137 Ibid., 1047.
138 Ibid., 1046.
139 *Opened for signature* December 16, 1966, art. 2(1), 999 U.N.T.S. 171, reprinted in 6 I.L.M. 368 (1967).
140 *Opened for signature* December 16, 1966, 999 U.N.T.S. 171, reprinted in 6 I.L.M. 368 (1967).

Committee extends the right of participation to the constitutional making processes.[141]

CEDAW, right to define cultural practices

The Convention on the Eradication of Discrimination Against Women (CEDAW)[142] is a treaty that is focused on the equality of women and has been a successful tool for the realization of women's rights around the world.[143] One very important feature of CEDAW is that it holds governments directly responsible for what happens in the private sector.[144] This is an important departure from earlier treaties that address discrimination against women. It is also noteworthy in that it incorporates affirmative action provisions.[145] A highly relevant provision that deals with women's right to participate is Article 7(b), which guarantees women the right: "[t]o participate in the formulation of government policy and the implementation thereof and to hold public office and perform all public functions at all levels of government."[146]

The protocol to the African Charter on human and peoples' rights on the rights of women in Africa (African Women's Protocol)

The African Women's Protocol is another treaty with enormously important provisions for gender equality.[147] This treaty, which was the result of a working group on African women's rights, "embodies a progressive vision of

---

141 Dann, P., Riegner, M., Vogel, J. and Wortmann, M. "Lessons Learned from Constitution Making: Processes with Broad Based Public Participation," Democracy Reporting International, Briefing Paper No. 20, November 2011: www.democracy-reporting.org, at 3, citing General Comment 25: www.unhchr.ch/tbs/doc.nsf/0/d0b7f023e8d-6d9898025651e004bc0eb; see also Banks, *supra* note 5, 1052.

142 *Opened for signature* March 1, 1980, 1249 U.N.T.S. 14, reprinted in 19 I.L.M. 33 (1980).

143 Bond, J. "Gender, Discourse, and Customary Law in Africa" (2010) 83 *Southern California Law Review* 509, 524.

144 Chinkin, C. "Gender Mainstreaming in Legal and Constitutional Affairs: A Reference Manual for Governments and Other Stakeholders," Commonwealth Secretariat 28–29 (2001): www.genderandtrade.org/shared_asp_files/uploadedfiles/%7B7712A695-36F7-4302-B422-B7AB9E05B843%7D_LegalConstitutionalAffairs.pdf. One major substantive problem with the enforcement of CEDAW is the fact that large numbers of states added reservations to their ratifications, even core provisions, often to shield family law, customary and/or religious law from their obligations. Bond, *supra* note 143, 527, noting that approximately forty states have made roughly 105 reservations to important treaty provisions.

145 Bond, *supra* note 143, 524, citing art. 4, calling for temporary measures aimed at achieving *de facto* equality. Ibid., note 83.

146 *Opened for signature* March 1, 1980, arts. 2, 2(e), 2(f), 1249 U.N.T.S. 14, reprinted in 19 I.L.M. 33 (1980).

147 July 11, 2003, OAU Doc. CAB/LEG/66.6.

women's rights on the continent, one which African women played a significant role in creating."[148] Article 2 calls for an end to discrimination and includes a requirement that states include provisions in their constitutions and legislation to give effect to this requirement. Similar to the provision found in CEDAW, Article 2(2) mandates that social and cultural practices that are harmful or discriminatory to women must be eliminated.[149] Other important provisions of the African Women's Protocol that guarantee women's participation include: Article 8, Access to Justice and Equal Protection before the Law; Article 9, Right to Participation in the Political and Decision-Making Process;[150] and Article 10, Right to Peace also includes a right of women to participate in the peace process.[151]

148 Bond, *supra* note 143, 540.
149 Article 2(2)
    States Parties shall commit themselves to modify the social and cultural patterns of conduct of women and men through public education, information, education and communication strategies, with a view to achieving the elimination of harmful cultural and traditional practices and all other practices which are based on the idea of the inferiority or the superiority of either of the sexes, or on stereotyped roles for women and men.
150 Article 9
    1. States Parties shall take specific positive action to promote participative governance and the equal participation of women in the political life of their countries through affirmative action, enabling national legislation and other measures to ensure that:
       a) women participate without any discrimination in all elections;
       b) women are represented equally at all levels with men in all electoral processes;
       c) women are equal partners with men at all levels of development and implementation of State policies and development programmes.
    2. States Parties shall ensure increased and effective representation and participation of women at all levels of decision-making.
151 Article 10 Right to Peace
    1. Women have the right to a peaceful existence and the right to participate in the promotion and maintenance of peace.
    2. States Parties shall take all appropriate measures to ensure the increased participation of women:
       a) in programmes of education for peace and a culture of peace;
       b) in the structures and processes for conflict prevention, management and resolution at local, national, regional, continental and international levels;
       c) in the local, national, regional, continental and international decision making structures to ensure physical, psychological, social and legal protection of asylum seekers, refugees, returnees and displaced persons, in particular women;
       d) in all levels of the structures established for the management of camps and settlements for asylum seekers, refugees, returnees and displaced persons, in particular, women;
       e) in all aspects of planning, formulation and implementation of post-conflict reconstruction and rehabilitation.
    3. States Parties shall take the necessary measures to reduce military expenditure significantly in favour of spending on social development in general, and the promotion of women in particular.

How women can increase participation in the process

Women as rights bearers have an important role in the process of changing African customary law. When their equality rights are violated, through the application of African customary law that is discriminatory (as mentioned above), one tool women have is constitutional adjudication. Women participate in the process of exercising their right to equality in transitional justice situations first by understanding that they have rights in the first place. Sadly, many women do not know what their rights are or that there is a possibility to enforce their rights in the courts. Therefore, one of the most vital solutions for having women avail themselves of their rights is educating women. This education must occur on many levels.

The first is socialization. In Africa, women are socialized to believe that they are inferior to men.[152] Education about rights begins at home. Young girls should be taught not that they are inferior, but that they have as much value as boys. This socialization within the family and close community should continue all the way until a woman prepares for her marriage.[153] In many cases, women are told what to expect in a marriage and what is expected of her and this teaching lets the woman know that equality is not something she should expect in her marriage. For example, a woman may be told that she will not like her husband taking a second wife, but that it is something she must endure.[154] Women's lack of formal education is another serious barrier to their understanding of and ability to profit from their constitutional rights. This lack of access to formal education and training has been identified as a key barrier to women's ability to women's work and advancement in society.[155] Much higher illiteracy rates of African females than African males show that access to education is a right, that itself, is gendered.[156] Particularly high percentages of illiteracy experienced in Africa are Burkina Faso at 86.6 percent, Sierra Leone at 88.7 percent, Chad at 82.1 percent and Guinea at 86.6 percent.[157] Even when a girl is lucky enough to attend school, her formal education is rife with gender biases, leading women into traditionally female jobs such as teaching, nursing and secretarial work.[158] With a system of socialization and formal education as deficient as it is, it is not surprising that women's access to higher education is severely limited.

152 Manuh, *supra* note 17, 14.
153 Note that there is so much resistance to socializing women about equality that in some areas, such as Nigeria, this can be considered subversive. Coleman, I. "The Payoff from Women's Rights" (May/June 2004) *Foreign Affairs* 80, 81.
154 A more severe example is female genital mutilation.
155 Manuh, *supra* note 17, 10.
156 Ibid., 10. In Africa, female illiteracy rates were over 60 percent in 1996, compared to 41 percent for men. Note other figures put illiteracy among adult females at 45 percent of sub-Saharan African females. Coleman, *supra* note 153, 84.
157 Manuh, *supra* note 17, 10.
158 Ibid., 11.

For the reasons discussed above, women are often ignorant about laws that give them rights and how these laws can be invoked to protect them.[159] Women need to strengthen their coalitions with the goal of educating other women about their rights so that they can participate in the process of revising discriminatory African customary law and claiming equality. How can women best organize grassroots efforts for rights education? "We must look for them in places such as kitchens, watering sites, kinship gatherings; women's political and commercial spaces where women speak in the absence of men."[160] Women-only mutual aid societies, benevolent groups, churches, cooperatives and women's market groups are additional places women gather.[161] Churches are a particularly important source of empowerment for women. Religion, a common source of disempowerment, can be both a sword and shield for empowering for women and provide women with a source of strength in their struggle for equality.

Women also need to be involved in the process directly, as lawyers and judges. Women need to see that they resemble those who represent them and the judges that decide their claim.

A judge's race or gender makes for a dramatic difference in the outcome of the cases they hear – at least for cases in which race and gender allegedly play a role in the conduct of the parties, according to two recent studies.[162]

Women in power make different policy choices.[163] For example, US Supreme Court Justice Sonia Santomayor said in a highly debated quote: "I would hope that a wise Latina woman with the richness of her experiences would more often than not reach a better conclusion than a white male who hasn't lived that life."[164] In Africa, there are far too few female judges but the percentages are growing.[165] For example, in 1992, women were 8.1 percent of high court judges, in 1993, women were 11 percent of the judiciary in Zambia and, in 1994, women were 17 percent of the judges in Uganda.[166]

159 Ibid., 13
160 Tsanga and Stewart, *supra* note 38, 19, quoting Ogundipe-Leslie, M. "Moving the Mountains: Making the Links" in *Oxford Readings in Feminism: Feminism and "Race"* (Kum-Kum Bhaunani, ed., Oxford: Oxford University Press, 2001).
161 Manuh, *supra* note 17, 3–4.
162 Chew, P.K. "Race & Gender of Judges make Enormous Differences in Rulings, Studies Find," *American Bar Association Journal*, February 6, 2010: www.abajournal.com/news/article/race_gender_of_judges_make_enormous_differences_in_rulings_studies_find_aba.
163 Coleman, *supra* note 153, 85. These choices have profound implications for development.
164 Chew, *supra* note 162.
165 Manuh, *supra* note 17, 14.
166 Ibid.

Conclusion

All customs are not negative; many things about them are beneficial to society.[167] Some are even beneficial to women. These need to be identified and preserved.[168] In post-conflict situations, Africans must claim what is good about their own culture and those cultures that have influenced Africa, decide what is not good and discard it.[169] This is a job that Africans must do for themselves.[170] But when looking to the past to reclaim lost culture, it is a mistake to try to replicate it exactly.[171] This would not help Africa move forward.[172] Culture as embodied by customary law that discriminates against women must be transformed. This is a hopeful task, since culture is dynamic.[173] It can and does respond to changes in society, which makes it an excellent vehicle for the protection of women's human rights.[174] Customary law cannot escape constitutional transformation.[175] The transitional state must change customary laws that are discriminatory in that they violate women's right to equality.[176] A tool for accomplishing this customary law transformation can be the constitutional courts with the input of women. "How ... should activists go about getting people to abandon practices that are clearly at variance with women's human rights, in a way that is non-defensive and non-offensive to the holders of such traditions?"[177] The perfect place to include women's voices is the constitutional process. Focusing on women's equality during periods of transition is one of the best ways to achieve far reaching political and social results.[178]

---

167 Twinomugisha, B.K. "African Customary Law and Women's Human Rights in Uganda" in *The Future of African Customary Law* 446, 466 (Jeanmarie Fenrich, Paolo Galizzi and Tracy E. Higgins, eds., Cambridge: Cambridge University Press, 2011).

168 Ibid.

169 Maathai, *supra* note 27, 179, citing Pope John Paul II.

170 Ibid.

171 Ibid., 182.

172 Ibid., 182.

173 Nyamu, *supra* note 40, 393.

174 See also, ibid., 393.

175 Rautenbach and Plessis, *supra* note 73, 358.

176 Twinomugisha, *supra* note 167, 466.

177 Tsanga and Stewart, *supra* note 38, 205.

178 Coleman, *supra* note 153, 80 explaining that
    women are critical to economic development, active civil society, and good governance, especially in developing countries. Focusing on women is often the best way to reduce birth rates and child mortality; improve health, nutrition, and education; stem the spread of HIV/AIDS; build robust and self-sustaining community organizations; and encourage grassroots democracy.

8 Reparations in Colombia

Advancing the women's rights agenda

Catalina Díaz with Iris Marin[1]

Introduction

There is a new wave of transitional justice in Latin America. Two countries that experienced authoritarian regimes during the 1970s and 1980s decided in the last five years to establish truth commissions in order to examine those periods of their history: Paraguay, Ecuador and Brazil. In its turn, Colombia has adopted a series of special mechanisms to address the gross crimes committed by demobilized prostate paramilitary groups in the course of its persisting internal armed conflict. All of these initiatives have – in various ways – resulted in recommendations and efforts towards the provision of reparations for the victims of gross human rights violations. At the same time, it is noteworthy how all of the initiatives have shown certain preoccupation – in varying degrees – for the explicit incorporation of the rights and needs of women. There seem to be signs of quite positive developments in both areas, reparations and the incorporation of a gender perspective, of the latest generation of transitional justice in Latin America. However, reparations recommendations and even legal frameworks do not necessarily translate into effective implementation.

The case of Colombia constitutes a rich research site with regard to both, reparations and the extent to which the women's justice agenda has been incorporated therein. In the last six years Colombia has seen the adoption and implementation of subsequent transitional justice and, particularly, reparations initiatives. In July 2005, the Colombian Congress approved Law 975/2005, widely referred to as the 'Peace and Justice Law' (hereinafter PJL).[2] The law established a special criminal justice procedure under which those demobilized combatants referred by the President of the Republic would be prosecuted and sentenced. According to the law, a series of reparations

---

1 Independent researcher and consultant and Reparations Director, Colombian Government Unit for the Integral Assistance and Reparations for Victims respectively.
2 For a detailed discussion of the parliamentary proceedings that led to the adoption of the Peace and Justice Law, see Diaz, C. 'Colombia's Bid for Justice and Peace' in Ambos, K., Large J. and Wierda, M. (eds.) *Building a Future on Peace and Justice* (Springer, Berlin, 2009).

measures would be ordered by the magistrates in the last phase of the proceedings.

In addition to PJL, the Government has adopted a series of administrative-based reparations programs. In April 2008, through executive decree 1290 the national Government created a so-called administrative individual reparations program, largely based on an already existing humanitarian assistance scheme.[3] A preliminary property restitution program was adopted in May 2011 and a month later the official National Commission for Reparations and Reconciliation (CNRR) – also established by PJL – publicly presented a proposal for a collective reparations program. After four years of intense public debate, in June 2011, the national congress adopted a very ambitious and comprehensive victims' rights statute addressing, among other issues, individual and collective reparations, including property restitution. All of these efforts are currently at various phases of implementation.

The purpose of this study is twofold. On the one hand, our aim is to examine to what extent the reparations components of the transitional justice arrangement in Colombia has developed a gendered approach to reparations, particularly regarding women's rights and needs. On the other hand, we explore whether progress in engendering reparations is, or is not, linked to the participation of women's rights organizations and networks in the processes of formulating and implementing reparations measures. As an alternative explanation we consider the penetration of the women's rights agenda into the reparations initiatives at the hand of high level expert advisors to official bodies recommending and implementing reparations. The general idea that lies behind our inquiry is that local ownership of transitional justice arrangements is a key variable in the effective implementation of reparations recommendations.

We map the reparations legal framework and we look into its implementation through official and non-official statistics and reports. We also use our own observation and first-hand experience as data. Both authors have been active within the human rights movement in Colombia from very early stages in our professional careers and have been first-hand witnesses and participants of the debates and initiatives that resulted in the formulation and implementation of the legal framework for the paramilitary demobilization. While this could be a source of bias, we have made a conscious effort to consider opposing views and alternative explanations.

The first section of the chapter provides a brief background on the Colombian armed conflict, the paramilitary demobilization process and the peace and justice arrangement examined from the perspective of women as victims and as agents of transformation. In the second section, we assess the reparations

3 See Lozano, C.H. 'Quince años de prestación de ayuda humanitaria por muerte en Colombia: un estudio normativo' in Díaz, C., Sánchez, N.C. and Uprimny, R. (eds.) *Reparar en Colombia: los dilemas en contextos de conflicto, pobreza y exclusión* (ICTJ and De Justicia, Bogotá, 2009).

component of the transitional justice arrangement in the country: we discuss first developments within the special peace and justice criminal proceedings and then those concerning the administrative-based reparations program; we also examine the recently adopted comprehensive victims' rights statute. Finally, we offer some conclusions.

Given the limited scope of this piece, our study does not address truth seeking and truth telling initiatives; neither do we fully examine prosecutions and criminal justice, beyond their reparations role. In both areas, judicial and non-judicial truth seeking, there has been substantive progress in Colombia and gender justice agendas have also permeated their development. Finally, our approach explicitly concentrates on the needs, rights and experiences of women. We do not examine those of the Lesbian, Gay, Bisexual and Transgender (LGBT) community, neither do we use a masculinity lens.

The armed conflict, the paramilitary demobilization process and the peace and justice arrangement: women as victims and as transformation agents

The Colombian armed conflict has now lasted almost 50 years and has left more than four million victims. It is often depicted as a war between the official government and the left-wing guerrillas of the Fuerzas Armadas Revolucionarias de Colombia (FARC) and the Ejército de Liberación Nacional (ELN), who have been trying (unsuccessfully) to take national power, but who have achieved control over some of the least accessible territories of the country.[4] The war between the guerrillas and the state was largely contained until the late 1980s, when right-wing paramilitaries began to spread in the countryside to provide peasant self-protection and to defend businesspeople and landowners from guerrilla kidnapping and extortion.[5] Drug trafficking has also played an important role in fueling the Colombian armed conflict.[6]

---

4 For comprehensive and detailed accounts of the origins of the internal armed conflict in Colombia, as well as the origins of the various armed groups, see United Nations Development Program (UNDP), *El conflicto, callejón con salida: Informe Nacional de Desarrollo Humano para Colombia – 2003* (UNDP, Bogotá, 2003) and Inter-American Commission of Human Rights, 'Third Report on The Human Rights Situation in Colombia', 1999. For a political economy analysis of the Colombian civil war, see Guaqueta, Alexandra 'The Colombian Conflict: Political and Economic Dimensions' in Ballantine, K. and Sherman J. (eds.) *The Political Economy of Armed Conflict* (Lynne Rienner Publishers, London, 2003).

5 For an influential account of the emergence of self-defense and paramilitary groups in Colombia, see Romero, M. *Paramilitares y Autodefensas 1982–2003* (Universidad Nacional, Instituto de Estudios Políticos y Relaciones Internacionales, IEPRI, and Editorial Planeta, Bogotá, 2003). For an account inspired by the ideas on 'warlordism', see Duncan, G. *Los señores de la guerra* (Editorial Planeta, Bogotá, 2006).

6 For a detailed account of the relationship between paramilitary groups and drug-trafficking see Cubides, F. 'Narcotráfico y paramilitarismo: matrimonio indisoluble?' in Rangel, A. (ed.) *El Poder Paramilitar* (Fundación Seguridad y Democracia and Editorial Planeta, Bogotá, 2005).

Despite the demobilization of the paramilitary federation Autodefensas Unidas de Colombia (AUC) between 2003 and 2006, new, transformed and never-demobilized paramilitary organizations remain active in various regions of the country.[7] The internal armed conflict continues and official peace negotiations with FARC and ELN guerrillas still seem uncertain.

As Colombian women's groups, the Colombian Constitutional Court and inter-governmental organizations have documented, the Colombian armed conflict has had a differentiated and disproportionate impact on women. Recent quantitative studies have confirmed these findings. According to survey data, by 2006, 12 percent of urban homes,[8] and by 2008, 20 percent of rural homes,[9] were affected by the action of an illegal armed group or by the official armed forces. While the majority of fatal victims (executed and/ or subjected to enforced disappearance) are men, most of the surviving victims who claim their rights before the different governmental institutions are women (68 percent).[10] Most of them head their households (54.9 percent) and are in charge of several children (around four children on average).[11] A total of 30.5 percent of the women who have registered before the Office of the Prosecutor General report that they have not gone to school at all and 44.9 percent report to have completed only primary school.[12]

As reported by the then national official register of displaced people (Registro Único de Población Desplazada, RUPD), by December 2010 there were 3,461,223 displaced persons in the country and around half of them were women. Recent survey data show that, while 29.9 percent of Colombian homes have a woman as the head of the household, in homes of displaced people the percentage rises to 45 percent.[13] The illiteracy rate among displaced people is also significantly higher (29.5 percent), compared to the general one in the country (6.9 percent of the population). The rate is also higher for displaced women (30.8 percent) than for displaced men (27.9 percent).

---

7 With regard to the re-armament of paramilitary groups, see Comisión Nacional de Reparación y Recoonciliación, La reintegración: Logros en medio de rearmes y dificultades no resueltas, II Informe de la Comisión Nacional de Reparación y Reconciliación (CNRR, Bogotá, 2010). See also Human Rights Watch, Paramilitaries' Heirs: The New Face of Violence in Colombia (Human Rights Watch, New York, February 2010).

8 Fundación Social, *Percepciones y opiniones de los colombianos sobre justicia, verdad, reparación* (Fundación Social, Centro Internacional para la Justicia Transicional, Bogotá, 2006).

9 Fundación Social, *Los retos de la justicia transicional en Colombia, Panorama cualitativo y cuantitativo nacional, con énfasis en cuatro regiones. Percepciones, opiniones y experiencias* (Fundación Social, Bogotá, 2009).

10 Comité Interinstitucional de Justicia y Paz, 'Informe Mensual. Matriz Comité Interinstitucional de Justicia y Paz', March 2011.

11 Rettberg, A. *Reparación en Colombia: Qué Quieren las Víctimas?* (GIZ, Fiscalía General de la Nación, Universidad de los Andes and Embassy of the Federal Republic of Germany, Bogotá, 2008).

12 Ibid.

13 Ibid.

Specific pre-existing forms of discrimination in the access to education by rural women were also documented by the Historical Memory Working Group of the Reparations and Reconciliation Commission (MH-CNRR) in its first report on the *Trujillo* Massacre.[14] MH-CNRR specifically reported that surviving female victims were not sent to school by their fathers, who thought that school was 'men's business'.[15] Many female victims expressed that in the households where they grew up, schooling was seen as something reserved for boys, as a 'non-necessary expenditure' in the case of girls. With regard to preexisting forms of violence, MH also offered various testimonies of surviving female victims explaining that the households where they grew up were very violent spaces. Several victims claimed that their fathers chose their husbands and forced them to marry when they were very young – 15 and 16 years old.

As in many other contexts, in the Colombian case, women have transcended their condition of victimization and have, on the one hand, organized in defense of their rights and become active in the broader struggle against impunity. On the other hand, women's groups and networks have played key roles within broader peace movements. In the first place, in certain events, women have been targeted precisely because of their political engagement. This has been the case, for example, of the leaders and members of the national association of peasant and indigenous women in Colombia (ANMUCIC), an organization established in the early 1980s to lead the agenda of the democratization of rural property and the rights of women therein.[16] On the other hand, existing women's organizations whose main objectives were around civic participation and feminine empowerment have become key platforms for the formation of victims' support groups and later on of formal victims' organizations. This has been the case, for example, of local associations of victims in rural areas of Eastern Antioquia.[17] Furthermore,

14 The Historical Memory Working Group is a research group established by the Reparations and Reconciliation Commission (CNRR) in 2007. MH-CNRR has adopted as its general objective to design, elaborate and disseminate an analytical and well-researched investigation into the reasons for the establishment and development of illegal armed groups, with an emphasis on the concerns of the victims and memories that were silenced or suppressed. To the date of writing, MH-CNRR has published 14 reports addressing some of the most emblematic massacres and other violent events in the course of the internal armed conflict, as well as experiences of civic mobilization and resistance. MH-CNRR has adopted an explicit gender approach: it counts with a specific group working on gender issues, it adopted a research agenda on 'gendered memories and war' and it has published a series of reports specifically addressing the experiences of women as victims and as political and community leaders. See www.memoriahistorica-cnrr.org.co.

15 Memoria Histórica de la Comisión Nacional de Reparación y Reconciliación, *Trujillo: Una tragedia que no cesa* (Editorial Planeta, Bogotá, 2008).

16 Meertens, D. 'Mujeres en la guerra y en la paz: cambios y pemanencia en los imaginario sociales' in Museo Nacional (ed.) *Mujer, nación, identidad y ciudadanía, siglos XIX y XX* (Museo Nacional, Bogotá, 2005).

17 Villa, J.D. *Nombrar lo innombrable: reconciliación desde la perspectiva de las víctimas* (CINEP, Bogotá, 2007).

new victims' organizations with female leadership have emerged and in many cases their leaders have gained national visibility.[18]

The paramilitary demobilization process and the enactment of the peace and justice law

In 2002 the government of the then President of the Republic, Alvaro Uribe Velez (2002–2010), entered into political negotiations with the leadership of the prostate paramilitary umbrella organization AUC. Apparently, the paramilitary leadership expected favorable political and legal conditions for their demobilization given certain ideological coincidences with the right-wing president and given significant national and international support to Uribe's 'Democratic Security' policy. In July 2003, government representatives and AUC paramilitary leaders signed the Santa Fé de Ralito Accord. Under the one-page agreement, the paramilitary leadership agreed to demobilize its troops gradually, by December 31, 2005, and the government committed itself to reintegrating the demobilized combatants into civilian life. According to official sources, between November 2003 and August 2006, 31,671 paramilitary combatants were demobilized in 38 public ceremonies throughout the country.[19] In addition, between August 2002 and September 2007, 9,800 guerrillas voluntarily deserted their organizations, to avail themselves of the demobilization program.[20]

Contrary to what had been the case of the peace talks with the FARC during the administration of President Andres Pastrana Arango (1998–2002), the 2002 negotiations with the AUC were held in secrecy and did involve only minimal civil society participation. Certainly, the women's movement that had been quite active in the peace talks with the FARC did not play a role in the peace negotiations with the paramilitary umbrella organization.[21] Women's groups' representatives were not included within the official Exploratory Peace Commission, a five-member body created by the President, whose mandate was to formulate recommendations to the Government in order to guarantee the ceasefire.[22] In fact, none of the

---

18 The Medellín-based victims' group Associación Caminos de Esperanza Madres de La Candelaria, for example, won the prestigious National Peace Award in 2006. The association has been led since its inception in 1999 by Teresita Gaviria, the mother of a boy subjected to enforced disappearance by paramilitary groups in Antioquia. See www.madresdelacandelaria.org/.

19 República de Colombia, Alto Comisionado para la Paz, 'Proceso de Paz con las Autodefensas: Informe Ejecutivo' (Bogotá, December 2006).

20 República de Colombia, Ministerio de Defensa, 'Logros de la Política de Consolidación de la Seguridad Democrática' (Bogotá, September 2007).

21 Velazquez, M. 'El papel de las mujeres en los procesos de construcción de paz' in UNIFEM *'Justicia Desigual': Género y derechos de las víctimas en Colombia* (UNIFEM, Bogotá, 2009).

22 'Comisión Exploratoria de Paz con las Auto defensas', created by Governmental Resolution 185/2002.

members of the Commission was a woman. The Commission did not make any recommendation about the protection of women in the course of the negotiation and demobilization process or about the inclusion of women within the decision-making bodies relevant for the peace negotiations. Neither did the mandate of the Organization of American States Mission to support the Peace Process in Colombia (MAPP/OEA)[23] include any express reference to the verification of attacks against women as part of its role of verifying the ceasefire. The MAPP/OEA only started to expressly report on incidents of violence against women in its ninth Report, in 2007.

The Santa Fé de Ralito Accord did not address any issue related to paramilitary accountability for the serious crimes committed throughout the conflict. Instead of being finalized between the negotiating parties, the accountability framework was debated and adopted by the National Congress. Apparently, the Government and the paramilitary leadership were aware of the domestic and international legal and political constraints to a generalized, blanket amnesty – prosecution for drug-trafficking related charges in the US and the shadow of the International Criminal Court (ICC) certainly played a role to that respect.

In July 2005, the Colombian Congress approved Law 975/2005, widely known as the 'Peace and Justice Law', establishing a special criminal justice procedure for demobilized combatants. PJL was the result of more than two years of intense public debate by the national Government, Colombian and international civil society organizations, intergovernmental agencies and the donor community. Language about the rights to truth, justice and the provision of reparations was widely used by different actors wanting to contest official proposals with high impunity doses.[24]

Colombian women's organizations were divided with respect to the decision whether to participate or not within the parliamentary debate. While several groups decided not to participate considering that the draft legislation proposed by the government was a covered impunity mechanism, others opted for submitting concrete proposals in order to correct the initial draft. The groups who preferred to abstain from the parliamentary debate considered that, on the pretext of implementing UN Resolution 1325, their participation could be used by the Government to legitimize impunity in Colombia, instead of empowering women. However, Congress adopted some of the specific proposals made by the women's groups who participated. As a result, the final PJL included a few specific provisions on gender aspects

---

23 In 2004, the MAPP/OEA was created through an agreement signed by the General Secretary of the Organizations of American States – OAS – and the Colombian Government. The agreement was then approved by the Permanent Council of the OAS by Resolution 859/2004.

24 For a detailed account of the Peace and Justice law parliamentary proceedings see Díaz, C. 'Colombia's bid for Justice and Peace' in Ambos, K., Large J. and Wierda, M. (eds) *Building a Future on Peace and Justice: Studies on Transitional Justice, Peace and Development* (Springer, Berlin, 2009).

within the peace and justice judicial proceedings and with respect to the participation of women in the newly created CNRR.

With respect to the special peace and justice criminal procedure, PJL established that judicial authorities should protect victims and witnesses taking into account gender factors, as well as the nature of the crime to be investigated, especially when it involved sexual violence, gender discrimination or violence against children, both girls and boys. To that end, the law mandated to train peace and justice officials on those topics (PJL, art. 38). Additionally, PJL stated that judicial authorities, as well as the office of the Procurator General ('Procuraduría Judicial') should consider the specific needs of women, girls and boys who participate in the proceedings. Regarding sexual violence specifically, PJL included some provisions aiming at protecting the privacy of the victim rendering testimony, even for historical memory purposes (PJL, art. 58.3).

Other proposals were rejected, however. For example, the 'Mesa de Mujer y Conflicto Armado', a broad and well-known women and human rights organizations alliance, had suggested incorporating ICC's rules on procedure and evidence on sexual violence. The incorporation of the rules was initially excluded. It had to wait six years, until their final incorporation into the victims' rights statute (Law 1448/2011).

In terms of women's participation within the newly established peace and justice institutions, PJL specifically provided for two seats at CNRR. CNRR was established by PJL as a temporary (eight years) mixed body composed of representatives of several governmental agencies and civil society sectors, with monitoring, advisory and executive functions. As provided for by PJL, among the five 'important figures' who should be appointed by the President of the Republic to CNRR, two must be women. In 2006 the President of the Republic designated two well-known women with long trajectories within the women's and the peace movements, respectively. Their acceptance of the appointment was harshly criticized by several organizations within both the women's and human rights movements, because it was perceived as a way to legitimize what was seen as an impunity operation. CNRR was ultimately closed down in 2011 by express provision of the victims' rights statute with hardly any opposition by civil society groups. Despite the efforts of the two women representing civil society sectors and others, being presided – as per express JPL disposition – by the Vice-President of the Republic CNRR was unavoidably tight to the controversial Uribe Velez's administration.

The women's movement was then neither particularly active within the political process and negotiation that led to the demobilization of the AUC paramilitary groups nor within the parliamentary debates that concluded with the adoption of PJL. But, as we will discuss in detail below, the two processes opened up important political, legal and institutional space for continuing in the search for accountability and justice. Women's organizations became an important player in all of them.

The reparations component of the transitional justice arrangement: women's justice agenda on paper and in practice

In its original version, the transitional justice arrangement in Colombia privileged the judicial scenario as the way for victims to claim reparations. PJL established the special peace and justice criminal process as the mechanism through which victims and family members should request reparations for the harm inflicted by those criminally responsible. PJL did not provide for the adoption of an administrative-based reparations scheme that would distribute individual benefits. It only envisaged the creation of a collective reparations program whereby,

> the Government, following the recommendations by the National Reparations and Reconciliation Commission, should implement an institutional program of collective reparations which includes actions oriented towards the recovery of the welfare state institutions and the rule of law, particularly, in the areas most affected by violence; [the program should also include actions aiming at] recovering and promoting the rights of those citizens affected by violence and to acknowledge and dignify the victims of violence.
>
> (PJL, art. 49)

In its original version, PJL assigned the duty to provide reparations to those declared as criminally responsible within peace and justice criminal proceedings. The demobilized combatants who benefited from alternative punishment benefits (five to eight years' imprisonment instead of ordinary 40 year sentences for the most serious crimes), were supposed to hand in illegally acquired assets to a victims' trust fund, which in its turn was supposed to pay for judicially ordered compensation. Under the original scheme, the role of the Government in providing reparations was minimal. The massive forced displacement and land and property dispossession to which peasants have been subjected in Colombia was also not adequately addressed by the original reparations provisions.

It was only with the historical decision by the Constitutional Court (C-370/2006) responding to a constitutional challenge to PJL advanced by a group of human rights and grass roots organizations that the Government was given a more central role in providing reparations to the victims. The Court assigned the Government the duty to provide for the reparations of victims when the assets turned in by the individual perpetrators and the front or bloc to which they belonged were not sufficient to cover the reparations orders by the Tribunal. This interpretation was essential in order to assure the actual fulfillment of the judicial reparations provisions. Moreover, the Court stated that ex-combatants who benefit from the provisions of PJL should provide for the financial compensation of victims not only with illegally acquired property, but also from their personal estates, including property that they have legally acquired. The Court affirmed that the state is not authorized to exempt those responsible for gross crimes from civil responsibility[25] and explained that under Colombian and international law, economic compensation is an element of the right to reparations of victims and a condition to promote the fight against impunity.[26]

Reparations within the peace and justice criminal proceedings

Up to January 2012, there have been 13 judgments sentencing demobilized combatants and ordering reparations. All the decisions have been pronounced by the Justice and Peace Chamber of the Bogotá Superior Tribunal. The first one was issued on March 19, 2009 in the case of the assassination of three persons, including that of Aida Cecilia Lasso, who was at the time running for local mayoral elections, and her 13 year old daughter Sindy Paola Rondón, who attempted to defend her mother from the attackers.[27] The decision was ultimately overturned by the Supreme Court of Justice.

The second decision was issued on June 29, 2010 concerning the case of a large massacre and the subsequent mass displacement of more than 1,000 people from the villages of Las Brisas, San Cayetano and Mampuján (Montes de María).[28] The decision was partially confirmed by the Supreme Court, substantively modifying the sections on economic compensation among others.[29] The fourth decision was issued on December 2, 2010 in the case of 170 targeted assassinations, torture and forced displacements in the northeastern city of Cúcuta and its surroundings. All the parties challenged the decision and to the date of writing, the Supreme Court has not yet resolved the appeal.

The last three decisions were rendered in December 2011 by two female Magistrates of the Peace and Justice Chamber of the Bogota Superior Tribunal. The first (December 1) of this group of sentences concerned a series of targeted killings, forced disappearances, forced displacement and two cases of rape committed by three paramilitaries of the Bloque Vencedores de Arauca operating in the eastern part of the country. The second decision (December 7) dealt with more than 150 targeted assassinations and the subsequent forced displacement of population, attributing command responsibility to one of the leaders (alias 'Don Antonio') of a paramilitary structure

25 Corte Constitucional de Colombia, Sentencia No. C-370/2006, Section 6.2.4.1.11.

26 Ibid., Section 6.2.4.1.12.

27 For a detailed discussion of the decision see Díaz, C. and Bernal, C. 'El diseño institucional de reparaciones en la ley de justicia y paz: unaevaluaciónpreliminar' in Díaz, C., Sánchez, N.C. and Uprimny, R. (eds.) *Reparar en Colombia: los dilemas en contextos de conflicto, pobreza y exclusión* (ICTJ and DeJusticia, Bogotá, 2009).

28 For a detailed discussion of the decision see Aponte-Cardona, A. *El Proceso Penal de Justicia y Paz* (Centro Internacional de Toledo para la Paz, Bogotá, 2011).

29 Corte Suprema de Justicia, Sala de Casación Penal, Sentencia del 27 de abril de 2011.

of the so-called Northern Bloc. Finally, the third one (December 16) concentrated on the illegal recruitment of more than 100 boys and girls by the paramilitary structure led by alias 'El Aleman' in a very poor province on the Colombian Pacific coast populated mostly by afro-descendants.

The comparison between the first decisions and the December 2011 group of three allows us to affirm that there has been notorious appropriation by prosecutors – especially female prosecutors – and magistrates of the women's needs and rights discourse. As we will discuss below, while the first (March 2009) decision was a lost opportunity to address the gender dimension of the purposeful killing of a woman who was running for local mayoral elections in a province dominated by patriarchy, in the December 2011 decisions conscious efforts were made to render visible the differentiated aspects of forced recruitment of girls and to address the crime of rape.

It is important to note, in the first place, that the provision of reparations has occupied a central place in all six decisions by the Justice and Peace Chamber of the Bogotá Superior Tribunal. It is evident that international human rights law on reparations is being used by all the parties to the peace and justice criminal proceedings. The reparations requests by the representatives of victims as well as the specific orders by the Tribunal show a clear understanding of the components of the right to obtain reparations, way beyond economic compensation. In addition to economic compensation, in all the cases the Tribunal ordered a series of rehabilitation measures, other restitution measures related to health and education and a wide range of symbolic reparations. Non-repetition guarantees and a series of initiatives to confront structural problems of resource availability for reparations were also included. However, the decisions clearly evidence a series of problems that have in great part to do with structural characteristics of criminal justice proceedings as a scenario for providing reparations in a context of massive victimization.

As we mentioned in the introduction to this chapter, a systematic and comprehensive analysis of the operation of the peace and justice criminal proceedings as truth seeking instances exceeds the purpose of this chapter. There is, however, a basic fact that clearly illustrates the acquiring of certain gender lenses by the peace and justice prosecutors and magistrates, which is the sharp contrast between the first and the last peace and justice sentences. The way in which the Peace and Justice Chamber of the Bogotá Superior Tribunal addressed the facts of the assassination of local female leader Aida Cecilia Lasso in its first sentence (March 2009), was a major sign of the lack of gender sensitivity of the magistrates in that case.

The Tribunal treated the case as an ordinary assassination and did not contextualize it within a pattern of victimization against community and political leaders from left-wing parties in that particular region. It did not construct the facts as an instance of systematic violence, constituting a war crime or a crime against humanity. Moreover, the Tribunal absolutely ignored the fact that the victim was a woman empowered enough to be politically active and running in the local elections in a social context dominated by patriarchy. The decision was a lost opportunity to have explored the gendered dimension of the violence against political opponents and community leaders in a region where peasant organization and the role of women therein were brutally oppressed by paramilitary action.

The treatment of the assassination of Aida Cecilia Lasso and her daughter sharply contrasts with the way in which the Chamber addressed the two cases of rape and the forced recruitment of girls in its December 2011 decisions. With regard to the cases of rape, using recent quantitative data, the Tribunal adopted the thesis that sexual crimes in Colombia are forms of generalized and systematic violence and thus, constructed them as crimes against humanity. It stated that the two instances of rape of the female partners of peasants accused by the paramilitaries of being guerrilla supporters are also part of a clear pattern of violence against civilians, confirmed by the fact that from the 2,113 victims of the particular paramilitary structure in question as registered by the Office of the Prosecutor General, only a very small percent (0.76) were killed in combat. The Tribunal emphasized the need to render visible sexual crimes committed in the context of the armed conflict, in order to combat impunity and contribute to non-recurrence.

The decision addressing the case of forced recruitment by the paramilitary structure Bloque Elmer Cardenas also constituted a major step with regard to the gender dimension of the crime. The Magistrate invited several expert witnesses to specifically address the question of the various forms of harm that children suffer as recruits and in the decision she contextualized the case of Colombia within the international literature and state of the art on forced recruitment. The decision includes a specific section describing in detail and through victims' deposition excerpts the experiences of girls (all of them are now over 18). The decision further identifies the various roles that girls played within the paramilitary group and how the life as child recruits differently impacted them as girls. Sexual crimes are also discussed – in fact, it is clear from the depositions that the girls were recruited at very young ages (12 and 13 in several cases) and that all of them became pregnant soon after. Some of them were forced into 'marriage' or sexual relations with paramilitary commanders and, at least one of them experienced an unwanted abortion due to stress and overexertion associated with military life. It is also noteworthy, how a preexisting context of vulnerability was identified in the decision linked to extreme poverty and domestic violence. The facts were also construed as crimes against humanity and war crimes.

Both cases also constitute significant efforts toward engendering reparation measures, specifically rehabilitation, satisfaction and guarantees of non-repetition. The effective provision of physical and psychological rehabilitation measures has been a concern of the Peace and Justice magistrates since their early decisions. This has been also the case with regard to collective material reparations, such as the reconstruction and putting into operation of damaged infrastructure (including health and education premises) and the establishment of income generating projects.

In its first decision (March 2009), the Peace and Justice Chamber of the Bogotá Superior Tribunal ordered the Ministry of Social Protection and the CNRR to design a rehabilitation program. In a similar line, in its December 2010 decision the Tribunal ordered the Ministry of Social Protection and the Mayor of the city Cúcuta to establish an 'integral center for the recovery of the victims of the armed conflict' in the city or, the adaptation for that purpose of an existing department within a local public hospital. The Tribunal expressly ordered that the services should be provided by health personnel with expertise in armed conflict related attention.

However, the Supreme Court of Justice struck down, among others, the rehabilitation orders given by the Tribunal in its December 2010 decision, considering that a criminal judge cannot impose *obligations* to the Executive (either at the national or local levels). The Court explained that, in this regard, the competence of a criminal judge also significantly differs from that of national or international courts dealing with state responsibility (such as the Inter-American Court of Human Rights).

The doctrine adopted by the Supreme Court clearly illustrates the challenges of putting into practice the ideal of integral reparations within criminal justice procedures – even if conceived of as special, transitional justice mechanisms. Those individually responsible cannot be reasonably sentenced to provide rehabilitation and education benefits to the victims. The provision of those measures necessarily requires an active role of the national and local executive authorities. If criminal judges are not entitled to authoritatively provoke the action of the executive, then their real power to grant effective integral reparations is restricted.

Expressly complying with the Supreme Court's precedent, in its subsequent decisions the Peace and Justice Chamber of the Bogota Superior Tribunal opted for exhorting national and local executive authorities rather than imposing them specific obligations. In other instances, the Tribunal has maintained the ordering language, without specifically naming the authority that should carry out the order. Using both strategies the Tribunal continued including concrete rehabilitation and collective reparations measures responding to proven harm and, moreover, it has made progress in further detailing the content and form of those reparations provisions.

In the case on forced recruitment, for example, it ordered the implementation of an individualized and sustained psychological rehabilitation program. The program should address the specific needs of victims, according to individual diagnosis; which should be carried out taking into account gender, age, disability, ethnical and national origin, and life-project related criteria. The Tribunal also indicated that the rehabilitation program should provide for the participation of beneficiaries in deciding the approach of their treatment.

With regard to satisfaction measures and guarantees of non-repetition, the December 2011 judgments included some measures specifically addressing differentiated harm experienced by women and the gender dimension of the crimes. In the decision dealing, among many other crimes, with the two cases of rape, the Tribunal ordered CNRR to document sexual crimes that occurred in the course of the armed conflict in Colombia and amounted to war crimes and crimes against humanity. The results of the inquiry should be published within a year from the date of the judgment. The Tribunal also exhorted the Office of the Prosecutor General to adopt a policy in order to prevent, protect and serve women and girl victims of the armed conflict, paying specific attention to cases of gender-based violence.

In a similar vein, within the judgment on forced recruitment the Tribunal ordered the Office of the Prosecutor General to further investigate sexual crimes, forced marriages and the gender dimension of torture and other physical harm suffered by the identified victims in the case. This order responds to the fact that the Tribunal was not able to attribute criminal responsibility to the perpetrators related to sexual crimes committed against child recruits because the Office of the Prosecutor did not present any charge in that respect, despite the evidence available. The Tribunal also exhorted the Office of the Prosecutor General to investigate the incidence of sexual crimes in all future cases of forced recruitment.

Addressing collective harm experienced by communities due to the destruction of infrastructure, the dislocation of local economic production and the breaking of social tissue, has been a concern of the Peace and Justice Chamber of the Bogotá Superior Tribunal and other Peace and Justice players since the early stages of the process. This has been also the case with regard to preexisting extreme poverty and exclusion that has rendered victims, and entire communities, vulnerable to war related violence. Collective material reparation provisions have specifically responded to both.

In the judgment concerning the responsibility of the Bloque Vencedores de Arauca for example, the Tribunal exhorted the Education Secretary of Arauca province to assess the extent to which children were effectively accessing education services in the villages where the paramilitary bloc operated. As suggested by the Tribunal, a report should be completed examining the conditions of the infrastructure, whether schools are actually open, how many children are enrolled and safety conditions there, in order to adequately guarantee the right to education. The measure responds to the fact established in the case that the paramilitary bloc used several schools as operation centers, closing down all educational services and partly damaging the infrastructure.

Contrary to what we found with respect to rehabilitation, satisfaction and non-recurrence measures, the experience on gender aspects of economic compensation within the peace and justice criminal proceedings has not been very positive. In both cases, rape and forced recruitment, only moral damages were awarded. No form of material harm was acknowledged for the purpose of economic compensation. In the cases of rape, the Magistrate expressly affirmed that the representatives of the two victims did a poor job in identifying the harm and, in fact, only requested moral damages. The Magistrate indicated that, according to the law, she could not award any damages beyond those specifically requested. She encouraged victims' representatives to take into consideration in future cases the 'vida-en relación' and 'life-plan'[30] related damages associated with rape.

In the case of forced recruitment, the limited scope of damages awarded seem to be associated, on the one hand, to the reading by the magistrates of certain current international literature stating that, for a series of reasons, child victims of forced recruitment should not receive monetary payments. The Tribunal emphasized that children should receive the money awarded for moral harm only having completed all the phases of the official reintegration program, so that they can understand that 'the only way to be wealthy is through labor and individual effort'. On the other hand, the limited scope of economic compensation is linked to traditional legal rules on economic compensation and evidentiary standards. In the case of the more than 100 victims of illegal recruitment, the victims' representatives did request 'life-plan' related damages. Many of them also requested the recognition of lost earnings. They argued that having been recruited as child soldiers compromised their dreams of being lawyers, doctors, football players and models (actual interviews were conducted with the victims).

The Chamber affirmed that the 'life-plan' damages doctrine requires that lost opportunities and prospects are not mere eventual and unrealistic expectations, but highly probable events. With respect to the lost earnings, the Chamber argued that it was proved that the children did not even earn, as paramilitary combatants, a sum equivalent to the officially established minimum monthly salary and that, in any case, Colombian law proscribes that form of child labor. Thus, by awarding lost earnings damages the Tribunal would have been acting against the law. While some of the arguments by the Tribunal actually reflect dominant legal doctrine and interpretation, the treatment that the victims of child recruitment were given in terms of economic compensation amounts, from our perspective, to further punishing them for having been born among the most discriminated against and poor communities in the country.[31] In the context of deprivation, violence and exclusion where they grew up, it was of course not very probable that they would have completed the ordinary education cycle and accessed well-paid jobs. In fact, there was abundant evidence at hand about the specific reasons why they ended up joining the paramilitary group.

---

30 The Inter-American Court of Human Rights has developed the notion of 'life-plan' associated damages in the context of gross human rights violations. For a detail analysis of its jurisprudence see Rubio-Marin, R., Sandoval, C. and Diaz, C. 'Repairing Family Members: Gross Human Rights Violations and Communities of Harm' in Rubio-Marín, R. (ed.), *Gender and Reparations* (Cambridge University Press, Cambridge, 2009).

31 For a critique of the usage of legal paradigms on reparations in the context of massive and systematic human rights violations see De Greiff, P. 'Justice and Reparations' in De Greiff, P. (ed.) *The Handbook of Reparations* (Oxford University Press, New York, 2006).

Finally, any analysis of a criminal justice scheme addressing reparations for victims of mass violations should take into account structural features of judicial criminal procedures, such as its slow pace. Even though the Peace and Justice Unit of the Office of the Prosecutor General has been able to register 314,383 victims in almost five years of operation (up to November 2010), only 36,133 victims have been formally acknowledged as such within specific criminal procedures by the prosecutors. From those 36,133 victims, not more than 3,000 have received judicial reparations. This means that in five years, only a very small percentage of the registered victims have accessed judicially ordered reparations. This delay is disproportionately affecting women given the fact that around 70 percent of the registered victims are women; moreover the majority of these women has a very low income while significant percentages of them head their households and are in charge of several children and other dependant family members. This is one of the reasons why administrative-based reparations schemes should be considered in the context of mass violations.

The administrative reparations program

Almost three years after the enactment of PJL, on April 22, 2008, the then President of the Republic, Álvaro Uribe Vélez, established an 'administrative reparations program for individual victims of illegal armed groups' through executive decree 1290. In the official brochure distributed in the launching event, the Government explained that even though according to PJL the ones responsible for providing reparations were those criminally responsible, the Government 'cannot be indifferent to the dramatic situation of the victims'.[32] In fact, within the text of the decree, the Government expressly refers to the international principle, according to which 'when the one responsible for the violation is unwilling or unable to fulfill her obligations, the State should make an effort to provide reparations to the victims'.[33]

In the course of the drafting process, CNRR conducted a series of consultation sessions with civil society organizations, academics and women's rights groups. The draft program was also presented – not really consulted – in huge gatherings in various cities of the country, where hundreds of victims attended. Civil society commissioners and those representing the ombudsman office and the Office of the Procurator General (Procuraduría

---

32 Ministerio del Interior y de Justicia. Cartilla Informativa-Programa de Reparación por vía administrativa, Preguntas frecuentes de las víctimas en las más de 10 Consultas Sociales en todo el país, abril de 2008, p. 7.

33 UN General Assembly, 'Basic Principles and Guidelines on the Right to a Remedy and Reparation for Victims of Gross Violations of International Human Rights Law and Serious Violations of International Humanitarian Law', Resolution 60/147 of December 16, 2005.

General de la Nacion, PGN) pushed hard for the inclusion of several provisions addressing several concerns raised by civil society organizations and women's rights groups. Some proposals made it to the final version, others did not.

Based on the idea of 'solidarity with the victims' the decree provided for the distribution of lump sum awards (ranging from US$5,000 to US$9,000) among the surviving victims of various violations and among the family members of the killed and the forcibly disappeared. According to the decree, restitution, rehabilitation, satisfaction and non-repetition measures should be adopted by the National Council on Economic and Social Policy (CONPES).

The program included the following human rights violations as triggering economic compensation: forced disappearance, assassination, kidnapping, torture, physical and psychological injury leading to permanent impairment, physical and psychological injury not leading to permanent impairment, 'crimes against sexual liberty and integrity', 'illegal recruitment of minors' and forced displacement. According to the Colombian Criminal Code, 'crimes against sexual liberty and integrity' include rape, violent sexual acts (other than rape), induction to prostitution, human trafficking and pornography with minors.

The lump sum amount for torture, physical and psychological injury not leading to permanent impairment, crimes against sexual liberty and integrity and illegal recruitment of minors is approximately US$6,750. The sum for assassination, forced disappearance and injuries that led to permanent impairment is US$9,000.

According to the decree, victims and family members had two years to submit their reparations requests filling in an officially adopted format. The format consists of two pages requiring basic information and it has been widely distributed among national and municipal authorities. The format can also be downloaded from the internet.

Due to pressure by the Ombusman Office and PGN (both represented in CNRR at that time by very competent and empowered women), the documentation required to support the compensation request was very flexible. Claimants can attach to their request whatever evidence they have of the violation that occurred (from newspaper articles, reports by NGOs, international organizations or official agencies, Ombudsman office certificates, to criminal records and proceedings). If they lack documentation, the Reparations Committee can conduct a personal interview.

Many civil society and victims' organizations lead campaigns with their affiliates for large-scale filling in of the forms. In fact, the previous work of women's groups supporting victims of sexual violence was a key factor in the registration process of those women and girls.

The presidential agency administering the reparations program (Presidential Agency for Social Action and International Cooperation, 'Social Action') reported that as of November 30, 2010, 333,970 compensation requests had been submitted throughout the country.[34] The majority of the requests referred to homicide and forced disappearance (78 percent) and were submitted by women (75 percent). According to the new governmental Unit for the Integral Assistance and Reparations of Victims, by December 2011, there were 440,819 compensation claims.

For the first phase of lump sum distribution, the Government decided to prioritize the provision of financial compensation to victims of anti-personnel landmines, sexual violence and minors demobilized from the ranks of armed groups (who were still underage). However, there is no up to date public consolidated data about the number of reparations requests that have been resolved, the number of lump sum awards distributed or the number of claims dismissed. As reported by PGN, by December 2009, 10,593 petitions had been processed, all of them with a successful outcome. According to informal information from officials at the Victims Unit in Accion Social, by the end of 2010, 51,101 reparations requests had been approved and 50,331 rejected. As reported by the new governmental Unit for the Integral Assistance and Reparations of Victims, out of the total 440,819 claims, Social Action had subjected to the assesment by the official Administrative Reparations Committee, 265,044 claims.

Even though the distribution of lump sum awards constitutes a positive step to alleviate the precarious and urgent situation of victims in Colombia, the program was problematic in many ways. First of all, it was explicitly based on a notion of 'social solidarity' rather than on the recognition of state responsibility for the crimes committed. In the speech given in the public event where the first lump sums were distributed, the President of the Republic stressed that the reparations program was a component of the 'democratic security policy'.[35] In fact, one of the checks was given to a female victim by the local military commander of the area in order to show 'the commitment of the armed forces with the security policy and the commitment of the military with efficacy and transparency [aims]'. At the highest levels, the official discourse supporting the lump sum awards excluded any form of public recognition of the illegal and unjust character of the violations, of the various forms of harm experienced by the victims and of the responsibility of the state in what has happened to them.

In connection with its philosophical foundation, the reparations program expressly excluded victims of violations committed by state agents. President Uribe Vélez strongly opposed any form of recognition for victims of state agents, without a judicial decision declaring criminal responsibility. This

---

34 The figure was reported on the official website of Acción Social, see www.accionsocial. gov.co. The information is, however, no longer available since the Agency was replaced by a new Unit by virtue of express disposition of the victims' rights statute.

35 Presidencia de la República, 'Palabras del Presidente Uribe en la [segunda] entrega de indemnizaciones por vía administrativa a víctimas de la violencia'. Montería, 12 de julio de 2009. See http://web.presidencia.gov.co/sp/2009/julio/12/03122009.html.

form of discrimination can be attributed to the political stance of President Uribe denying allegations of human rights violations committed by state agents in the context of the internal armed conflict. In his speech at the public event where compensation checks were distributed, Uribe explained that victims of state agents could not be included within the reparations program or any other administrative-based benefit scheme, because it would amount to equating members of the legitimate armed forces with members of criminal groups that by definition violated the law.[36]

Finally, the administrative reparations program only focuses on monetary compensation, leaving all other forms of reparations to be developed by the National Council on Economic and Social Policy. But, the administrative reparations program was not the full stop in the struggle for justice. Even before its final adoption, the Liberal party was already crafting draft legislation aiming at a comprehensive and very ambitious regulation of the rights of victims. As we will discuss below, what ultimately became the statute on victim's rights was to incorporate a series of provisions creating specific rehabilitation, restitution and satisfaction programs.

The comprehensive statute on victims' rights (Law 1448/2011)

On June 10, 2011, President Juan Manuel Santos (2010–2014), in the presence of the UN Secretary-General, signed the statute on reparations for victims and land restitution (Law 1448/2011), through which 'attention, assistance and integral reparations measures for victims of the internal armed conflict are adopted'. Widely known as the 'victims' law', it was the result of four years of collaboration and hard work by civil society, the international community and governmental institutions.

The discussion of the victims' rights statute was marked by an interesting process of civil society participation and wide public debate. In the course of the first debate on the draft legislation a series of public hearings were held around the country in which more than 3,000 victims participated, the great majority of them women.[37] Under the auspices of UNDP, throughout nine hearings held around the country victims presented their proposals as well as moving testimonies before Congress and government delegates.[38] Following a suggestion by UNIFEM (now UN WOMEN), women's groups were invited to all sessions. Overwhelmingly, victims insisted on the adoption of

---

36 Presidencia de la República de Colombia, 'Palabras del presidente Álvaro Uribe Vélez al iniciarse la reparación por vía administrativa de las víctimas de la violencia'. See http://web.presidencia.gov.co/discursos/discursos2009/julio/victimas_05072009.html.

37 According to the reports of the workshops prepared by UNIFEM, between 70 and 80 percent of victims who participated in hearings held in the provinces of Huila and Meta were women.

38 For a complete report of the hearings' process see Gil, L. and Gaviria-Betancur, P. *La agenda de las víctimas en el Congreso 2007–2009: Aprendizaje para la incidencia desde la sociedad civil* (Fundación Social, Bogotá, 2010).

simple procedures to access justice, non-discrimination by the law toward victims of crimes committed by state agents and giving credibility to testimonies and evidence presented by victims. Women also asked for psychosocial care both in cases of sexual violence and other kinds of violence.

With active involvement of UN bodies (UN WOMEN in particular) and women's rights groups, in the course of the second round of debates specific space was open for discussion around the incorporation of women's demands into the draft legislation. In October 2010, a public hearing was held where official delegates, civil society and UN representatives spoke before Congress. Moreover, about 200 women from all around the country attended a special hearing organized by the congressional women's caucus. Finally, a 'Joint Statement' about the incorporation of the rights of women into the draft legislation was submitted by women's and human rights organizations.[39] Most of the proposals were adopted by parliament and incorporated as specific clauses into the victims' rights statute.

Women's groups presented general analysis of the draft legislation as well as specific proposals with regard to women's needs and rights. A first series of suggestions had to do with overcoming narrow understandings of gender-based violence as sexual violence. In consequence, many groups asked for the inclusion of provisions responding to other forms of gender-based violence for the purpose of reparations. With regard to the provision of reparations for victims of sexual violence, UN WOMEN called for the adoption of more comprehensive approaches including measures for addressing the immediate and long-term health, social and economic consequences of the crime. Specifically, it called for the establishment of gender-sensitive psychosocial services. UN WOMEN, human rights NGOs and women's groups also suggested recognizing as beneficiaries of the reparations program, children who were born as a consequence of sexual violence.

The importance of having non-judicial reparations mechanisms was stressed, due to frustrating experiences that some victims and women's groups have had within PJL criminal procedures. There was also a call to take into account not only women as a whole but to recognize the differences among them. In this regard, many participants argue that the bill should consider the specific needs of Afro-Colombian women, indigenous women, girls, elderly women and women with disabilities.

---

39 'Declaratoria conjunta de las organizaciones sociales sobre aspectos fundamentales con relación a los derechos de las mujeres para ser tenidos en cuenta en el trámite legislativo del proyecto de ley No. 1077/10 Cámara – 213/10 Senado', signed by Corporación Sisma Mujer, Mesa de Incidencia Política de las Mujeres Rurales, Comité de América Latina y el Caribe para la Defensa de los Derechos de la Mujer – Cladem, Corporación Humanas, Corporación Grupo de Trabajo sobre Protección, Centro de estudios de Derecho, Justicia y Sociedad – Dejusticia, Colectivo Mujeres al Derecho, Instituto Latinoamericano para una Sociedad y un Derecho Alternativos – Ilsa, Liga de Mujeres Desplazadas, Comisión Colombiana de Juristas, Corporación Casa de la Mujer, Alianza Iniciativa de Mujeres Colombianas por la Paz – IMP.

With regard to property restitution, many participants coincided on the need to include affirmative action measures directed to women in order to guarantee their effective access to land. Furthermore, it was suggested that property restitution should include not only land, but also housing, livestock and farm machinery lost as a consequence of the war. Participants insisted on strengthening official protection programs so that they adequately address women's specific needs within the property restitution process.[40] UN WOMEN specifically backed this request. In 2008, the Constitutional Court had already ordered the Government to adopt a gender approach in the design and implementation of protection programs (decision T-496), but the decision has not been fully implemented.

Many participants formulated demands relating to health, education and microfinance. But, at the same time, they emphasized that reparations measures should be distinguished from the ordinary social services that citizens are entitled to. Poverty alleviation programs should not be offered as reparations measures, they argued. In this respect, human rights organizations, women's groups and UN WOMEN coincided on the need to review the classical legal definition of reparations as the restitution of the victim to the *status quo ante*. They argued that, most of the time, restoring a female victim to her previous situation could be counterproductive since they experienced discrimination even before the occurrence of the crime. Therefore, human rights and women's groups and UN WOMEN stressed the need to incorporate a 'transformative approach' to reparations.[41] This means reparations measures should contribute to correcting, when possible, previous gender-based discrimination. In fact, UN WOMEN suggested implementing

---

40 Acording to several sources, since the adoption of the comprehensive victims' rights statute, 17 community and victims' leaders have been killed. A total of 52 peasant and victims' leaders have been assassinated in the last three years. See Jiménez, A.M. 'La amenaza de los ejércitos antirestitución', Periódico El Espectador, March 31, 2012. Many of the targeted victims' leaders are women. MH-CNRR included, for example, the story of community and peasant leader Yolanda Izquierdo killed on January 31, 2007 in Montería in its report on 'Women who make history'. MH-CNRR, *Mujeres que hacen historia: Tierra, cuerpo y política en el Caribe colombiano* (Ediciones Semana y Editorial Taurus, Bogotá, 2011).

41 Ideas on a 'transformative approach' to reparations have been developed by scholars and practitioners in Colombia and abroad. Ruth Rubio-Marin formulated it in her 'Introduction: A Gender and Reparations Taxonomy' in Rubio-Marín, R. (ed.), *The Gender of Reparations* (Cambridge University Press, Cambridge, 2009). A 'transformative' notion of reparations was included into the 'Nairobi Declaration on women's and girls' right to a remedy and reparations' adopted by an important group of women's rights advocates and activists, as well as survivors of sexual violence in Nairobi in March 2007. In Colombia, the theory of 'transformative reparations' has been developed by researchers of the Centro de Estudios de Derecho, Justicia y Sociedad – DeJusticia; particularly by Rodrigo Uprimny Yepes, Maria Paula Saffón, Nelson Camilo Sánchez and Diana Esther Guzmán. See, for example, Uprimny, R. and Saffón, M.P. 'Reparaciones transformadoras, justicia distributiva y profundización democrática' in Díaz, C., Sánchez, N.C. and Uprimny, R. (eds.) *Reparar en Colombia: los dilemas en contextos de conflicto, pobreza y exclusión* (ICTJ and DeJusticia, Bogotá, 2009).

temporary special measures aimed at guaranteeing equality between men and women with regard to land, housing and property restitution processes, using as reference the UN Principles on Housing and Property Restitution for Refugees and Displaced Persons (the Pinheiro Principles).

UN WOMEN also suggested the incorporation into the draft legislation of concrete non-repetition measures such as educating public servants, the armed forces, the police and society in general, on the nature of gender and gender stereotypes and on women's human rights – starting with reformulating educational curricula at all levels. Along the same lines, a joint statement by human rights NGOs and women's groups proposed, as a concrete satisfaction measure, the understanding of physical and sexual violence against women as constituting part of a widespread or systematic attack against women in Colombia. The establishment of a policy of zero tolerance for sexual exploitation and abuse in the Armed Forces was also suggested as non-repetition guarantee. As a way to get data about the magnitude and specific impact of the armed conflict on women, many participants also suggested to – at least – disaggregate official statistics according to sex.

Guaranteeing equal participation and full involvement of women in decision-making processes and institutions was a recurrent point. The participants offered specific ideas about participation of women within the various institutions established by the draft legislation and the setting up of special participation mechanisms including the required official consultation with indigenous and Afro-Colombian peoples.

The victims' rights statute incorporated most of the suggestions made by human rights NGOs, women's groups and UN WOMEN. A major achievement was the widening of the definition of victim, in order to include those who had been victimized by state agents. As discussed before, the Government of President Uribe Velez (2002–2010) strongly rejected any form of inclusion of victims of state agents into administrative-based reparation schemes.

Following UN sets of principles on the right to obtain reparation and the fight against impunity, the statute defines as victims those people who have suffered harm as a consequence of a human rights violation or an International Humanitarian Law infraction committed after January 1, 1985.[42] Nevertheless, as is also the case in Peru, the law does not consider as victims those who have been members of illegal armed groups even if they have suffered sexual violence, torture or forced disappearance. This exclusion has been severely criticized by civil society groups as well as by the UN.[43] In the case of victims of forced recruitment, a victim can only claim reparations if she decided to leave the armed group before reaching the age of 18 (art. 3).

---

42 With respect to persons who lost their property as a consequence of the armed conflict, the Statute protects victims for acts that occurred after January 1, 1991 (art. 75).

43 UNOHCHR, 'Declaración de la Oficina en Colombia del Alto Comisionado de las Naciones Unidaspara los Derechos Humanossobre la Ley de Víctimas y Restitución de Tierras', Bogotá, June 7, 2011.

Following the Peruvian experience, the statute also recognizes as victims children who were conceived as a consequence of sexual violence (art. 181).[44]

Law 1448 finally incorporated into domestic law specific ICC rules on evidence and procedure for sexual violence cases – previous attempts to adopt the rules within PJL had been frustrated. The statute also included confidentiality rules for giving testimony as well as for the purpose of legal and psychological services in the course of the criminal proceedings.

Another major step in the incorporation of the Colombian gender justice agenda into the victims' rights statute was the adoption of a specific and separate chapter on land restitution for female beneficiaries. The statute included specific provisions to guarantee the access of women to the restitution procedures. Protocols to facilitate access to women's organizations and networks should be adopted and restitution claims submitted by women must be processed with priority (arts. 114 and 115). Specific provisions were adopted in order to guarantee the expedition of property titles in the name of both, man and wife or partner, and to effectively ensure the possession of land by women. In addition, the statute stipulates that, notwithstanding that only the man (or the wife/partner) files the property restitution claim, the property must be restituted to both of them (art. 118). Additionally, the statute ordered the administration to safeguard the possession of restituted property by female beneficiaries (art. 116). Finally, Law 1448 gives women priority in obtaining a series of benefits stipulated by the Statute on Rural Woman (Law 731/2002), such as loans, land allocation, social security, education, recreation, family subsidies and participation in campaigns to register women who do not have an identity card, among others (art. 117).

Specifically responding to a series of assassinations of female leaders of collective land restitution claims[45] and echoing specific indications by the Constitutional Court, the Statute gives six months to the National Government to review the existing personal safety and protection programs in order to make them gender sensitive. The Law orders that protection measures should be specifically designed so as to take into account the different types of aggression usually suffered by women, the special risks that women have to face and their particular vulnerability before the aggressor.

---

44 Entire villages and communities in various Colombian regions were under de facto paramilitary authority. These regimes included in certain cases the power of having women and girls 'at their disposal'. Hernán Giraldo, the demobilized paramilitary commander of the Bloque Resistencia Tayrona, for example, accepted in his 'free version' hearing that he had had at least 24 children conceived by girls under 14 years old in peasant communities in the areas of the Sierra Nevada de Santa Marta under his control. In the Cauca province, there is an entire generation of girls and boys called by people as 'paraquitos', because they are sons and daughters of members of paramilitary groups. See MH-CNRR, *Mujeres y Guerra: Víctimas y Resistentes en el Caribe Colombiano* (Ediciones Semana y Editorial Taurus, Bogotá, 2011). The purpose of including those children as victims is to recognize their rights and the damage suffered by them. However, every effort should be made not to reinforce their identity as a product of the sexual violence suffered by their mothers.

45 See note 39.

Meeting the demand by human rights and women's groups and the instructions given by the Constitutional Court (decision T-45/2010), Law 1448 ordered the establishment of a Rehabilitation Program aiming at restoring the physical and physiological condition of victims. According to the Law, the program has to be designed with a gender-sensitive approach. Specifically, victims of sexual violence must be assisted by professionals with specific training. The program must have also a component designed expressly for female victims (art. 139).

Within the chapter on memorialization (chapter IX), the Statute specifically mandates to advance truth seeking initiatives oriented toward preserving in the collective memory of Colombian society the human rights violations against women (art. 145). The Statute also includes a chapter on non-repetition guarantees (chapter X). Specifically, it states that prevention measures have to be free of gender stereotypes and must be designed taking into account the particular risks that women face in the context of internal armed conflict (art. 149d). The Statute also ordered the adoption of an education strategy about human rights and international humanitarian law addressed to law enforcement officials, incorporating a differential approach as well as a policy of zero tolerance for sexual violence. Moreover, the Statute orders the implementation of national campaigns to reject violence and discrimination against women (art. 149s).

Finally, another significant development of Law 1448 lies around the incorporation of concrete mechanisms for victim participation. The Statute created a quite complex edifice of new implementing institutions and procedures including national and municipal-level Committees for Victim participation. By virtue of the Statute, victims' organizations and networks will appoint their delegates to the municipal committees, who will then represent victims from all over the country in the various new implementing bodies. Victims' representatives will sit, among other governing and implementing bodies, in the Local Transitional Justice Committees, on the Board of Directors of the Special Administrative Unit for the Restitution of Dispossessed Land and on the Board of Directors of the Executive Committee for Victims' Assistance and Reparation. The statute expressly established that the Committees for Victim participation must seek the participation of female delegates.

Translating all the principles, rights, institutions and mechanisms into actual effective services operating throughout the country, constitutes a major challenge. First of all, the new bureaucracy will need to change a dominating historical institutional culture of ill-treatment and discrimination against victims. In terms of gender justice specifically, the challenge is to go beyond certain understandings of female victims only as especially vulnerable subjects, in order to empower them as transformation agents and equal citizens. Affirmative action measures could be used indeed as a means for recognizing historical discrimination against women. But, at the same time, if not carefully implemented it could rather reinforce stereotypes about female vulnerability, more than emancipatory ideas of women as decision-making agents.[46]

In fact, the very implementation process could be seen as a significant opportunity to empower women and their organizations, at the top national as well as at more local and community levels. Every effort should be made in order to ensure that female victims actually take advantage of the special seats reserved for them within the Committees for Victims' participation. The official consultation processes to indigenous communities and Afro-Colombian peoples would also need to adequately include women. Women should also be appointed to high-level positions within the new institutions. This is advisable in order to guarantee that women's needs do not remain as second-order demands, as well as to raise the empowerment of women. A positive sign in this regard was the appointment of Paula Gaviria, the former director of one of the leading civil society groups involved in the drafting of the Statute, as the Executive Director of the new reparations and assistance governing and implementing body.

Conclusion

The reparations component of the transitional justice arrangement in Colombia has shown sustained progress in the incorporation of the women's needs and rights agenda. While the controversial PJL (2005) included a few dispositions specifically addressing certain suggestions made by women's rights organizations, the victims' rights statute (2011) took into account much broader discussions about the rights of women as victims. The great majority of the proposals advanced by women's groups were adopted and the Statute incorporated specific women's issues into several key new programs, institutions and mechanisms, such as the ambitious land restitution scheme, the rehabilitation program, memorialization initiatives, non-repetition guarantees, victims' protection programs and participation mechanisms.

The women's needs and rights movement can also be clearly observed in the peace and justice criminal judgments. While the first decision by the Peace and Justice Chamber of the Bogota Superior Tribunal in the case of the assassination of local female leader Aida Cecilia Lasso and her daughter

---

46 Some specific dispositions of Law 1448 provide for a 'special treatment' in the case of women, based on the mere fact of being a woman, but without identifying a specific discrimination factor. Such approach could end up in reinforcing, rather than reverting, social stereotypes of women as vulnerable persons. Nancy Fraser discusses the risks of affirmative action measures. According to Fraser, the measures that emphasize the distinction between men and women do not transform gender dichotomies themselves. Such measures tend to focus just on the results of discrimination, but they do not take into account the causes of gender discrimination, which lay, according to Fraser, in the lack of recognition. Fraser says that, in the long term, those measures reinforce the identity of women as vulnerable persons. Fraser, N. Iustitia Interrupta: Reflexiones críticas desde la posición post socialista (Siglo del Hombre Editores, Universidad de los Andes, Bogotá, 1997).

constituted a major lost opportunity, the last group of judgments issued in December 2011 showed significant progress. The decisions specifically address two cases of rape and the gender dimension of the crime of forced recruitment of children. In both cases, female magistrates made conscious efforts to, on the one hand, expose sexual crimes as generalized and systematic patterns of violence within the armed conflict in the country, constructing the facts as crimes against humanity. The judgment on forced recruitment particularly, gives voice to the victims and authoritatively acknowledges their experiences. On the other hand, the judgments delved into the differentiated dimension of harm that women and girls suffer, not only associated with sexual crimes. Finally, specific rehabilitation, satisfaction and non-repetition measures addressing those particular gender-related harms were adopted. However, as clearly evidenced by the judgments, economic compensation still remains an area of judicially based reparations where dominant legal doctrine operates as an obstacle for adequately addressing the consequences of crimes as linked to preexisting forms of exclusion and discrimination.

The Colombian peace and justice arrangement has been a very much domestically owned process. Instead of automatic incorporation of international formulae, the specific forms and content of the transitional justice mechanisms have been the result of intense public debate where civil society organizations have played a significant role. In contrast to what has been the experience in other latitudes,[47] the donor community, intergovernmental bodies and foreign experts have not played dominant roles in shaping the transitional legislation and designs, but have backed a series of domestic players in creatively struggling against impunity. The role that UNDP and UN WOMEN played around the consultation process and the drafting of the victims' rights statute clearly illustrates this trend.

Substantive progress toward engendering the assistance and reparations legal framework has been associated with the increasing participation of women's groups within public and parliamentary debate. Civil society organizations also served as a quite successful platform to contribute to the legislative drafting process. Well-positioned national-level groups channeled specific demands and proposals by victims' organizations and women's groups.

Progress in the crafting and designing of concrete programs and mechanisms responding to women's needs, is also associated with a cumulative process of strong appropriation by domestic players of the gender justice agenda. The Colombian Constitutional Court has played a particularly important role therein. In the last years the Court has issued a series of decisions, on the one hand, aiming at protecting women within the persisting

---

47 Fletcher, L. and Weinstein, H.M. with Rowen, J. 'Context, Timing, and the Dynamics of Transitional Justice: A Historical Perspective' 31(1) *Human Rights Quarterly* (2009), pp. 163–220.

armed conflict and, on the other, specifically addressing the needs of displaced women (Order 092/2008, T-045/2010). Gender justice discourse and its concrete manifestations with regard to the crimes against humanity character of sexual crimes, the differentiated harm suffered by women and the gender dimension of forced recruitment of girls has also significantly penetrated Peace and Justice criminal proceedings. In addition to the body of jurisprudence by the Constitutional Court, decisions by the Inter-American Court of Human Rights and the use of expert witnesses have contributed to mainstreaming gender justice agendas.

Finally, the case of Colombia also exemplifies how domestic players have resisted the limitation of transitional justice to a narrowly constructed corrective justice exercise and have demanded the inclusion of more ambitious distributive justice goals and schemes to be incorporated into the transitional arrangement. The development of the reparations component illustrates well this move. Reparations ideas and designs have been influenced by the 'transformative approach' to reparations. This approach was originally articulated in Colombia to go beyond traditional legal understandings of reparations as merely 'restitutive'. Under the transformative approach, the traditional aim of reparations of restituting victims to the *status quo ante* is complemented by distributive justice goals. While, in Colombia, the 'transformative reparations' idea was originally conceived of for the formulation of a property restitution program, its proponents quickly realized the potential of the approach for engendering reparations.[48]

Applied to the arena of gender justice, the approach implies that reparations should not just restore the victim to the original situation in which she saw herself before the occurrence of the crime, but that reparations should also correct and transform the conditions of discrimination against women existing before the crime. The victims' rights statute expressly adopted the notion of transformative reparations into the definition of the right to reparations; the notion was also used in the parliamentarian debates for the incorporation of specific provisions on property restitution for female victims. A major challenge, however, is to put into actual operation throughout the country the series of new principles, rights, institutions, programs and mechanisms, specifically in those regions facing high poverty indicators, weak local democracy and ongoing armed confrontation.

---

48 Guzmán, D.E. 'Reparaciones con enfoque de género: el potencial para transformar la discriminación y la exclusión', in Fondo de Desarrollo de las Naciones Unidas para la Mujer, UNIFEM, *'Justicia Desigual' Género y derechos de las víctimas en Colombia* (UNIFEM, Bogotá, 2008).

9 The Peruvian case

Gender and transitional justice

Julissa Mantilla Falcón[1]

Introduction

Gender and women's experiences and stories have frequently been neglected in transitional justice processes. Truth commission, ad hoc tribunals and reparations programs have usually been articulated without considering gender differences and the different impact of them on men and women.

Despite some recent advances, women are still missing in peace negotiations, transitional legal framework, human rights agendas and directive positions of the transitional justice entities. In fact, usually gender and women's human rights have been restricted to sexual violence leaving aside the complete dimensions of their rights.

This chapter presents an example of a transitional justice process that has incorporated a gender approach in order to show the importance of this perspective and its real impact on women victims.

---

1 Julissa Mantilla is a Lawyer and Professor of the Pontificia Universidad Católica of Perú (PUCP). She has a Gender Diploma by the PUCP and a LLM in International Human Rights Law at the London School of Economics (LSE) of the London University. She is also an international consultant on Gender, Transitional Justice and International Human Rights Law. She was the Gender Director of the Peruvian Truth and Reconciliation Commission. She was a lawyer of the Peruvian Ombudsman Office and participated in the investigation of the cases of forced sterilization during the Fujimori regime. She has given lectures around the world in universities and organizations like the IADB, the OAS, the World Bank, American University, Hunt Alternatives, George Washington University, George Mason University, University of Santiago de Compostela, University of Buenos Aires, University of Peace of the United Nations in Costa Rica, Iberoamericana in México, Universidad San Carlos de Guatemala, among others. She has also published several articles and documents on issues like sexual violence, armed conflict, truth commissions, transitional justice, gender and human rights. Currently, she is a Consultant on Gender Justice at UN Women in Colombia, where she advises the Truth, Justice and Reparation Program for women of this UN agency. She is also a member of the Criminal Policy Commission created by the Minister of Justice in Colombia. She is a Professor of the Academy of Human Rights and Humanitarian Law of the Washington College of Law at American University in Washington DC.

A gender approach to the international framework: recent advances

Feminism has developed strong criticism to the law, which is considered androcentric[2] because it devalues women's experience and does not take women's rights seriously. Law's apparent neutrality is cause and consequence of social and cultural constructions that reinforce stereotyped and discriminatory models. This criticism includes legal theory, institutions and juridical methods.[3] Law is a result of patriarchal societies; thus, even when it means to protect interests and needs of women, its application is in charge of patriarchal institutions and women's rights remain unprotected.[4] In this sense, gender is a tool for challenging this traditional and conservative approach and to incorporate different perspectives to the law.

In this point it is important to understand that *gender* should be understood as the socially constructed roles of women and men that are ascribed to them on the basis of their sex, in public and in private life. Thus, gender roles depend on a particular socio-economic, political and cultural context and are shaped by other factors, including age, race, class and ethnicity.[5] Each society elaborates gender roles in a different way, but traditionally they diminish women's rights, limiting them largely to the family and preventing them from assuming roles in the public sphere. Thus, gender approaches allows us to identify women's subordination and to implement measures to improve their situation. This is why gender is usually associated only with women or women-based approaches.

In fact, gender refers to the social construction of masculinity and femininity, not to the sexual differences between men and women. The purpose of emphasizing gender relationships is to highlight the particular manner in which women have been subordinated and oppressed through socially constructed differences.[6]

In this sense, applying a gender perspective to international human rights law requires that treaties and international documents should be drawn up taking account of gender differences, and calls on international bodies to take account of gender in choosing their membership. A gender perspective also allows us to see that human rights violations often affect men and women differently. Using this perspective makes it clear that there has not been the same degree of attention to human rights violations that affect women as to those that affect men, making it less likely that women will receive justice or appropriate reparations.

2 Facio, Alda, "Towards other critic theory of law," www.equidad.scjn.gob.mx/IMG/pdf/FACIO_ALDA_Hacia_otra_teoria_critica_del_derecho.pdf.

3 Jaramillo, Isabel, "Feminist criticism to the law," in: R. West, (*Gender and Law Theory*, Uniandes, Instituto Pensar, Siglo del Hombre), 2000, p. 13.

4 Jaramillo, op. cit., p. 13ff.

5 HRI/MC/1998/6, Geneva, September 14–18, 1998, "Integrating the gender perspective into the work of United Nations human rights treaty bodies," Report by the UN Secretary-General, p. 16.

6 Gender and the Truth and Reconciliation Commission, "A submission to the Truth and Reconciliation Commission," Prepared by Beth Goldblatt and Shiela Meintjes, May 1996.

A gender approach also helps to understand that there are violations of human rights that affect women simply because they are women. The judgments from the International Tribunals for Yugoslavia and Rwanda show that sexual violence against women was expressly organized and that women did not have access to justice. Moreover, those Tribunals concluded that sexual violence could be considered torture and may constitute genocide in some circumstances.

To apply a gender perspective to the law implies to identify when differences between men and women impedes them to exercise and to demand their rights.[7] It also highlights that there are cases where victims are mostly women such as domestic violence, and where consequences are specific for women such as pregnancy after rape.

In the case of international human rights law, many international documents such as the Universal Declaration of Human Rights (1948) or the International Covenant for Civil and Political Rights (1966) have been elaborated without a gender perspective and employ a "neutral" language that does not distinguish between men and women. Actually, they only refer to the principle of non-discrimination. However, in 1993 the UN Second Conference of Human Rights in Vienna declared the rights of women and girls as human rights. Since then, international documents and case law have included references to women's human rights and the need for a gender perspective, although there is still a lack of understanding by international community of the importance of the gender perspective to the investigations of human rights violations and the processes of post-conflict reconciliation.

There has been increased attention to the need to include the human rights of women in general human rights activities since the World Conference on Human Rights in 1993. The Beijing Declaration of 1995 created a commitment to mainstream a gender approach in all UN programs. In 1997, the United Nations Economic and Social Council (ECOSOC) adopted agreed conclusions on "mainstreaming a gender perspective into all policies and programs in the United Nations system," which provided a workable definition of the concept of mainstreaming as well as a set of principles and specific recommendations for action by intergovernmental machinery (1997/2). These were reviewed and reaffirmed by the ECOSOC in 2004.[8]

Concerning treaties, in 1979 the Convention on the Elimination of All Forms of Discrimination Against Women (CEDAW) was passed.[9] The Convention defines discrimination against women as any distinction, exclusion or restriction

---

7 Céspedes, Lina, "Gender and the law," in: PROFIS, *To Make Visible Gender Violence: Systematization of Gender Experience*, Colombia, PROFIS, 2011, p. 20.

8 E/2004/INF/2/Add.2, Resolution 2004/4, "Review of Economic and Social Council conclusions 1997/2 on mainstreaming the gender perspective into all policies and programs in the United Nations system," www.un.org/womenwatch/daw/documents/ecosoc2004/eres2004-4Mainstreaming.pdf.

9 Convention on the Elimination of All Forms of Discrimination Against Women (CEDAW), 1979, article 3, www.cajpe.org.pe/rij/.

made on the basis of sex which has the effect or purpose of impairing or nullifying the recognition, enjoyment or exercise by women, irrespective of their marital status, on a basis of equality of men and women, of human rights and fundamental freedoms in the political, economic, social, cultural, civil or any other field. CEDAW establishes several obligations for state parties such as:

- to incorporate the principle of equality of men and women in their legal system, abolish all discriminatory laws and adopt appropriate ones prohibiting discrimination against women;
- to establish tribunals and other public institutions to ensure the effective protection of women against discrimination; and
- to ensure elimination of all acts of discrimination against women by persons, organizations or enterprises.[10]

In 1992, the Cedaw Committee elaborated the 19 General Recommendations[11] that state that gender-based violence is a form of discrimination that seriously inhibits women's ability to enjoy rights and freedoms on a basis of equality with men.

During the 1990s violence against women was recognized as a form of discrimination and a human rights issue. In fact, in 1994 the Inter-American Convention on the Prevention, Punishment and Eradication of Violence Against Women ("Convention Of Belem Do Para") was passed. This Convention defines violence against women as any act or conduct, based on gender, which causes death or physical, sexual or psychological harm or suffering to women, whether in the public or the private sphere. Moreover, it states that violence against women shall be understood to include physical, sexual and psychological violence:

- that occurs within the family or domestic unit or within any other interpersonal relationship, whether or not the perpetrator shares or has shared the same residence with the woman, including, among others, rape, battery and sexual abuse;
- that occurs in the community and is perpetrated by any person, including, among others, rape, sexual abuse, torture, trafficking in persons, forced prostitution, kidnapping and sexual harassment in the workplace, as well as in educational institutions, health facilities or any other place; and
- that is perpetrated or condoned by the state or its agents regardless of where it occurs.[12]

---

10 See www.un.org/womenwatch/daw/cedaw/cedaw.htm.
11 Committee on the Elimination of Discrimination against Women, General Recommendation 19, 1992, UN Doc. HRI\GEN\1\Rev.1 at 84 (1994), www1.umn.edu/humanrts/gencomm/Sgeneral19.htm.
12 InterAmerican Convention on the Prevention, Punishment and Eradication of Violence Against Women "Convention of Belem do Para," articles 1 and 2, 1994, www.cajpe.org.pe/rij/.

Finally, the Convention recognizes that every woman has the right to be free from violence in both the public and private spheres.

Despite these advances in recognizing gender and human rights of women, the impact of the structural inequalities women face needs more research. As the UN Report on integrating women into human rights treaties states, "there is not yet a clear acknowledgement or understanding that gender is an important dimension in defining the substantive nature of rights."[13]

It is important to remember that to consider violence against women as a human rights violation implies the recognition of reinforced state obligations[14] to prevent, to investigate, to punish and to repair these facts. There is also a *due diligence duty* that should guide state actions not only when the perpetrator is a state agent but also when particulars commit crimes.[15] Due diligence also includes the state obligation to transform values and social institutions that reinforce gender inequality.[16]

On the other hand, it is important to mention that recently the Security Council has passed several resolutions on the matter such as:

- SCR 1325 (2000) that recognizes the disproportionate impact of armed conflict on women and the important women's contribution to conflict prevention, peacekeeping, conflict resolution and peace-building.
- SCR 1820 (2008) that recognizes that sexual violence in conflict is a tactic of war and a matter of international peace and security and requests that the Secretary-General provide a report on the implementation of this Resolution.
- SCR 1888 (2009) that urges the consideration of sexual violence within peace processes and calls for the appointment of a Special Representative of the Secretary-General on this matter.[17]
- SCR 1889 (2009) that requests measures to improve women's participation on peace processes and urges Member States to ensure gender mainstreaming in all post-conflict peace-building and recovery processes and sectors. It also called for a report submitted by the Secretary-General to the Security Council on the participation and inclusion of women in peace building and post-conflict planning.
- SCR 1960 (2010) that creates institutional tools to combat impunity on sexual violence and for prevention of and protection from sexual violence in conflict.

---

13 UN Secretary-General 1998.
14 Inter American Court of Human Rights, Cotton Field Case, Sentence of November 16, 2009.
15 Inter American Court of Human Rights, Case Velásquez Rodríguez, Sentence of July 29, 1998, párrafo 172.
16 Ibid.
17 In February 2010 Margot Wallstrom was appointed as the Special Representative of the UN Secretary-General for Sexual Violence in Armed Conflict.

This group of Resolutions has an important significance, since they imply that the Security Council understands the enormous impact that sexual violence has on peace and security. Thus, the Council urges states, UN agencies and parties in a conflict to give special importance to this issue.

Transitional justice and gender approaches: still little advances

On transitional justice, the androcentric perspective has been the rule although some recent advances have been identified. However, they are not enough to guarantee the incorporation of a gender perspective.

In this sense, it should be mentioned that in the Report on the Rule of Law and Transitional Justice in 2004 the UN Secretary-General (UNSG) included amongst its conclusions and recommendations a section on negotiations, peace agreements and Security Council mandates. The UNSG rejects any endorsement of amnesty for genocide, war crimes or crimes against humanity, including those relating to ethnic, gender and sexually based international crimes. Moreover, the UNSG reaffirms its recognition and respect of the rights both of victims and of accused persons in accordance with international standards, with particular attention to groups most affected by conflict and a breakdown of the rule of law, including women and minorities. Additionally, the UNSG expressly recognized the differential impact of conflict and rule of law deficits on women and children and the need to ensure gender sensitivity in restoration of rule of law and transitional justice, as well as the need to ensure the full participation of women. Finally, the UNSG exhorted the UN system to develop approaches for ensuring that all programs and policies supporting constitutional, judicial and legislative reform promote gender equality.[18]

This report embraces other UN initiatives that reflect an improvement in the incorporation of a gender perspective and women's human rights. In 2005, the Report of the Updated Set of Principles to Combat Impunity made several references to gender and women rights. For example, in Principle 7 on Guarantees of Independence, Impartiality and Competence, the Report states that commissions of inquiry, including truth commissions, should respect some guidelines such as the adequate representation of women as well as of other appropriate groups whose members have been especially vulnerable to human rights violations. Principle 12 on the Advisory Functions of the Commissions states that the terms of reference should ensure that the commissions incorporate women's experiences in its work, including its recommendations. Moreover, Principle 32 on Reparation Procedures establishes that concerted efforts should be made to ensure that women and minority groups participate in public consultations aimed at developing,

---

18 Report of the Secretary-General S/2004/61623 August 2004, "The rule of law and transitional justice in conflict and post-conflict societies."

implementing and assessing reparations programs. Finally, on Guarantees of Non-Recurrence of Violations, Principle 35 states that adequate representation of women and minority groups in public institutions is essential.[19]

However, despite international standards, transitional justice still lacks a real understanding of a comprehensive gender approach. It does not mean simply to add women to existing processes

> but to develop a broader gender strategy that includes peace building, an understanding of the multiple identities of women and the gendered nature of conflict, institutional and legislative reforms, gendering of strategies for disarmament, demobilization and reintegration (DDR) and security sector reform, strategies to prevent and redress continuities of violence in the post-conflict period, access to services, human security and social justice.[20]

In fact, a gender approach allows any transitional justice mechanism to highlight diverse issues that are common in situations of gross human rights violations, such as:

- the unequal status of women pre-conflict;
- the use of sexual violence as a deliberate strategy by parties to armed conflict;
- the widespread nature of sexual violence during the conflict;
- the generalized impunity that surrounds crimes against women such as sexual violence against women;
- the stigma and underreporting that accompany these crimes;
- lack of access to justice for women due not to inadequate policy, but rather to the absence of substantive measures to ensure that justice processes meet the needs of women victims.[21]

As it has been said, gender is often neglected in transitional justice processes and mechanisms such as truth commissions, since most of them have failed addressing gender issues and human rights of women.

As is well known, truth commissions have been created in post-conflict situations around the world to research and report the massive human rights violations that have occurred in a context of armed conflict or under repressive regimes. They confront and acknowledge the truth about past human rights abuses "with the hope of contributing to reconciliation, healing, and

---

19 Commission on Human Rights, Sixty-first session, "Report of the independent expert to update the set of principles to combat impunity," Diane Orentlicher, E/CN.4/2005/102/Add.1, February 8, 2005.
20 Valji, N., "Gender and transitional justice programming: a review of Perú, Sierra Leone and Rwanda," UNIFEM, August 2010, p. 2.
21 Valji, op. cit., pp. 2 and 3.

reform."[22] Each country has developed a model of how its Truth and Reconciliation Commission should proceed according to its own reality. For example, Argentina and Chile installed truth commissions after repressive military regimes, while Guatemala and Peru set theirs up after internal armed conflicts.

Although there is no standard model for all countries, truth commissions share some common characteristics related to their objectives of investigating human rights abuses in order to prevent them from occurring again. And many truth commissions share another feature: they have not implemented a gender perspective although there are important exceptions, such as South Africa, Guatemala, Peru, Sierra Leone, Morocco, East Timor and Liberia.

According to Nesiah, truth commissions have taken three broad approaches in this matter:

a   gender mainstreaming, having gender as a crosscutting theme in all operations, from the recruitment and training of staff onward;
b   the establishment of a special unit that is tasked exclusively with a focus on gender;
c   gender as a crosscutting theme as well as a specific-focus area.[23]

In general, it is common that gender was not among the main issues to be discussed in the design and establishment of transitional justice mechanisms. This is changing in recent experiences but still is not enough development in this matter. The Peruvian case is an important example in this sense.

The Peruvian Truth and Reconciliation Commission (PTRC)

The Peruvian armed conflict started in 1980 when Shining Path appeared in public burning electoral material in Chucchi (Ayacucho), one of the poorest regions of the country. At that time, nobody could imagine that that was the origin of the most cruel and difficult period in Peruvian history.

For years, the population suffered the effects of the actions of Shining Path and the State forces involved in the conflict. Later, another subversive group – the MRTA (Tupac Amaru Revolutionary Movement) – appeared. As a result, thousands of people disappeared, were tortured, executed and condemned without due process. There was no accurate assessment of the

---

22 Hayner, P. B., "International guidelines for the creation and operation of Truth Commissions: a preliminary proposal," *Law and Contemporary Problems*, Fall, 1996, p. 174.
23 Nesiah, V., "Truth commissions and gender: principles, policies, and procedures," International Centre for Transitional Justice, Gender Justice Series, New York, 2006, p. 5.

true dimensions of the human rights violations that occurred during this bloody period, even though national and international institutions brought many of these cases to light. In particular, very little attention was given to violations of women's human rights.

In 2000, after President Alberto Fujimori left the country to Japan and due to the intense work by human rights NGOs, the transitional government of President Valentin Paniagua decided to create a Truth Commission[24] to investigate the crimes and human rights violations that had occurred during the armed conflict. President Alejandro Toledo, elected in the same year, renamed the Commission including the word "reconciliation" and increased the members from seven to 12. There were only two women among the commissioners.[25]

The PTRC's main purpose was to investigate cases of gross human rights violations, including torture, forced disappearance, arbitrary executions and kidnappings, among others. The mandate of the PTRC did not specifically include cases of sexual violence committed against women, in part because it was thought that such cases were not very common. It did not recognize the importance of working with a gender perspective. However, in carrying out its charge, the PTRC consulted the final reports of the Truth Commissions of Guatemala and South Africa as international precedents, and some changes were made, among them the decision to adopt a broad definition of sexual violence, which it defined as:

> the realization of a sexual act against one or more persons or when a person is forced to realize a sexual act by force or threat of force or through coercion caused by fear of violence, intimidation, detention, psychological oppression or abuse of power used against that person or other persons, or taking advantage of a coercive environment or the inability of the person to freely consent.
>
> (PTRC Final Report 2003)

This definition allowed the investigation of cases including forced marriage, forced abortions, forced nudity, sexual blackmail and sexual slavery in addition to cases of rape.

Following through on the intent to examine these cases was not an easy task. The lack of awareness of the gender dimensions of the conflict and the lack of necessary information on cases posed a difficult challenge which the PTRC developed some specific strategies to address. These included: setting up training sessions on gender and sexual violence for the PRTC's personnel; establishing a gender unit to supervise the incorporation of the gender perspective in the PTRC; using flyers, posters and radio programs to explain that sexual violence is a human rights violation and should be denounced;

24 Supreme Decree No. 065-2001-PCM.
25 Supreme Decree No. 101-2001-PCM.

and creating a support group for women, including representatives of human rights groups, academics and women's NGOs.[26]

The Final Report of the PTRC was released on August 28, 2003. It included a chapter on Gender and a chapter on Sexual Violence against Women.[27] The Report recognized that the conflict had transformed gender roles as women assumed responsibility for family survival and for dealing with the displacement of entire populations escaping from the conflict.[28]

Concerning the cases of sexual violence, the PTRC recognized that often victims did not denounce instances of sexual violence due to feelings of shame and fear. Moreover, the cases of sexual violence often happened in the context of other human rights violations (such as massacres, arbitrary detentions, summary executions and torture), which tended to overshadow their sexual dimension.

Although previous reports on the conflict had not mentioned the magnitude of sexual violence in Peru, the PTRC concluded that sexual violence against women was widespread. The evidence from Guatemala and South Africa made the PTRC aware of the likely statistical under-representation of these cases, as victims often feel guilt and shame, and are often lost in the context of other human rights violations, as noted above. The Final Report concluded that sexual violence happened in at least 15 rural towns and cities. Ayacucho, where Sendero originated, had the most cases of sexual violence, followed by Huancavelica and Apurimac, the poorest regions of Peru. As is often the case, the victims were often illiterate or had only primary education. Most of the victims belong to the rural sectors and spoke Quechua; they were farmers or housewives.

Concerning the perpetrators, the Report found that, although the insurgent groups did commit acts of violence against women, forcing them to marry if pregnant or have abortions, most were committed by agents of the state, that is the army and the police, and that most were concentrated in two years of the conflict: 1984 and 1990. The PTRC also found that the main objective of sexual violence was to punish, to intimidate and to pressure, humiliate and degrade the population. In some cases its purpose was to make the detained women blame themselves. In addition, there were many

---

26 Mantilla, J., "The Peruvian Truth and Reconciliation Commission's Treatment of Sexual Violence Against Women," *Human Rights Brief* 12(2), 2005, pp. 1–4.

27 In Final Report of the Peruvian Truth and Reconciliation Commission, Chapter VIII, Second Part: The factors that cause violence: Chapter 2 "The different impact of violence," and 2.1 "Gender inequality"; and Chapter VI, Fourth Part: Crimes and Human Rights Violations: Chapter 1 "Patterns of Crimes and Human Rights Violations" and 1.5 "Sexual Violence Against Women," www.cverdad.org.pe/ifinal.index.php.

28 Report to the Secretary-General, Sr. F. M. Deng, "Further promotion and encouragement of human rights and fundamental freedoms, including the question of the programme and methods of work of the Commission: human rights, mass exoduses and displaced persons," Human Rights Commission, ECOSOC, 52º Session, E/CN.4/1996/52/Add.1.

cases of sexual abuses that had no direct link to the armed conflict. Sexual violence was always an exercise of power in a context where the aggressors had control of the situation.[29]

It also concluded that rape was not the only form of sexual violence. Cases of sexual mutilation, sexual molestation, sexual humiliation, forced prostitution, forced pregnancy and forced nudity were not uncommon. The perpetrators of sexual violence had enjoyed impunity, not only because women were afraid to denounce them but also because the national authorities failed to provide support. The PTRC did hand over some cases of sexual violence to the National Prosecutor, and these are currently being investigated. The Final Report includes a proposal for reparations to take account of victims of rape and their children.

Finally, the PTRC provided evidence to show that sexual violence against women was a widespread practice in the context of massacres and arbitrary executions that had been organized by the army and the police. Rape was a repeated and persistent practice within a general context of sexual violence, which fits one of the criteria for the definition of a crime against humanity in the Statute of the International Criminal Court.

The impact of the PTRC on women's human rights

In February 2004, the High Level Multisectorial Commission for the following up of the actions and state policies on peace, collective reparation and national reconciliation (CMAN)[30] was created. Later, the Integral Plan of Reparations and its Regulations[31] was passed and the National Council of Reparations (CNR)[32] was established with the objective to elaborate a Register of Victims as the only instrument for identifying the victims of the armed conflict.[33]

Victims of rape have been included and they will receive economical and symbolic reparations as well as health, housing and education if they comply with some requirements. Likewise, children born due to rapes are considered indirect victims and will have access to education, health, housing and symbolic reparations. Victims and their children could also be part of collective reparations. However, the Reparations Law excludes other forms of sexual violence such as forced sterilizations, sexual slavery and forced pregnancy. Currently, there are some initiatives for changing the law but there is still a lot of work to do.

---

29 Mantilla, op. cit.
30 The CMAN was created by DS No. 011-2004-PCM, and modified later by D.S. No. 024-2004-PCM and D.S. No. 031-2005-PCM.
31 Law 28592 of July 29, 2005. Supreme Decree No. 015-2006-JUS of July 6, 2006.
32 Regulations No. 28592 that creates the Comprehensive Program of Reparations, Supreme Decree No. 015-2006-JUS.
33 Interview to Sofia Macher, former Commissioner of the PTRC and current member of the CNR, December 2007.

As happened during the PTRC's process, there are still many problems collecting information on sexual violence. In some cases, women do not identify themselves as victims of human rights abuses and they are also afraid of the social condemnation of the community. Cultural differences are another relevant issue.

Concerning the human rights cases, from the 47 cases turned over to the National Prosecutor by the PTRC, two of them deal with gender violence. This may seem to be a small number, but it is symbolically important and a success in that the PTRC did not plan to include cases of sexual violence in its investigation when it began its work.

The first of these cases is that of a student detainee who was raped and became pregnant in 1992. The case was originally closed "temporarily" by the prosecutor because the rapist could not be identified, a situation that lasted for more than ten years, and the victim, Mrs. Magdalena Monteza, approached the PTRC. The second case deals with the systematic sexual violence committed against women from the towns of Manta and Vilca in the province of Huancavelica, one of the poorest areas in Peru where the military conducted anti-insurgent operations there in 1984 (Vilca) and 1998 (Manta). As a consequence of the sexual abuses, several children were born who do not know who their fathers are. In 2009, the District Attorney accused ex-members of the Army as being responsible for sexual violence as crime against humanity. This is the first sexual violence case formally denounced as crime against humanity in Peru.[34]

Currently, several NGOs[35] are filing cases on sexual violence that happened during the armed conflict that involve approximately 46 victims.[36] This is a big step forward as few NGOs dealt with those cases during the 1980s and 1990s. In fact, it could be said that this is an example of the impact of the PTRC since it showed the reality of sexual violence against women and the lack of national reports on the matter.

However, serious problems remain that make it difficult for victims to have access to justice, including the lack of resources available for legal aid. In addition, the Peruvian criminal code lacks an adequate definition of sexual violence, which it defines narrowly as rape. There was a project underway now supported by the International Committee of the Red Cross and some human rights and feminist NGOs to update the Criminal Code in order to incorporate sexual violence as a crime against humanity. But the process of gender inclusion is uneven. For example, the protocols for the exhumation of mass graves do not include a gender perspective and there are not guidelines to look for or analyze cases of sexual violence.

34 Fourth Supraprovincial Criminal Court, March 25, 2009.
35 Including the Association Pro Human Rights (Aprodeh), the Commission of Human Rights (COMISEDH), the Legal Defense Institute (IDL), Aprovida and the Study for Human Rights of Women (DEMUS).
36 This number is not confirmed yet but it was discussed in a meeting with the American expert Rhonda Copelon in Lima, Aprodeh, June 19, 2007.

Despite the work of the PTRC, women remain reluctant to file complaints because the judicial authorities are unresponsive and have not incorporated gender sensitivity into their work. In some cases, for example, judges have requested that women get medical exams for rapes that happened during the 1980s and 1990s. In other cases, rape victims do not want to tell their stories because they are in new personal relationships that would be threatened by disclosure and a public legal process. Not all communities support rape victims who want to file complaints. However, the work of the PTRC had important impact not only at the national level but also in the international arena.

Conclusions

As we have seen, there is a growing trend toward incorporating a gender perspective in the processes and mechanisms of transitional justice. Moreover, past investigations and cases are being reopened so far.

For example, in April 2007 the Argentine Prosecutor, Federico Delgado, requested the investigation of cases of sexual violence that happened in detention centers during the Argentinean dictatorship, based on the testimonies of rape victims. This is the first time that sexual abuses against Argentinean women were investigated independently from other human rights abuses.[37]

In 2003, Chile created the National Commission on Political Prison and Torture (Valech Commission) to investigate the cases of people that suffered these abuses by state agents, from September 1973 and March 1990. The final Report did not include the real dimension of sexual violence against women. In 2009, Chile reopened this Commission and women's organizations pushed to include cases of sexual violence against women. Some cases were filed but efforts still are not enough.

In Colombia, the Victims and Land Restitution Law (1448 Law) was passed in 2011 including several references to gender and human rights of women, such as: rules of evidence on sexual violence; attention of sexual and reproductive rights of victims, including AIDS, sexual transmitted diseases and voluntary interruption of pregnancy; psychological attention of victims of sexual abuse; national campaigns against violence against women, especially widows, women in charge of their families and orphans. In this point, it is important to explain that the original version of the law did not include references to gender and women's rights. It was after the impulse and work of women's organizations that the Congressmen decided to include those measures.

As we can see, some efforts have been developed and some advances are being incorporated on gender and human rights of women. However, there is still a long way to go before it will be possible to better protect women's

37 See, www.mujereshoy.com/secc_n/3700.shtml.

human rights. Thus, it is necessary to recognize that the incorporation of a gender perspective produces better protection of the rights of men and women. This will require a new vision of international human rights law and a better understanding of the real challenges to human rights around the world.

Conclusion

This book has attempted to illustrate that transitional justice is a dynamic and flexible principle of international law and relations that is constantly evolving in pursuit of post-conflict justice. It doing so, the book has embraced what is increasingly recognised as a symbiosis between academic research and practical experience in the context of international law, politics and relations, rather than adopting a single methodological lens. This, in turn, has been achieved by bringing together a group of women both from academia and from the field of transitional justice practice who have employed a mix of academic and non-academic, legal, political and sociological methodologies in order to provide a fresh and unique perspective on a topic for which the literature largely bypasses the practitioner perspective. This group of women has sought to provide some insight into the extent to which women are active and effective participants in transitional justice, including as field workers, protagonists, participants, observers, victims and beneficiaries.

The work was focused around practitioner contributions while the content drew on the theoretical field of gender and transitional justice. Broader, implicit issues raised throughout the works included the future relevance of theoretical scholarship driven by academics, given the invaluable insight provided directly by practitioners or indirectly, such as the pieces that were based on interview testimony; and how do the contributions and knowledge of practitioners challenge the assumptions and arguments presented in more theoretical work in gender and transitional justice, including at times within this book? Ultimately this book has sought to illustrate that there is a relative absence of women's issues from transitional justice debates and forums but that by engaging in the debate at a more grassroots and less theoretical level, there is the scope for greater understanding of what these issues are and thus more potential that these issues will in turn be dealt with. This is more explicitly illustrated in considering each chapter individually.

The engagement of civil society has been recognised by the UN Secretary-General as a fundamental factor in the success of transitional justice and the overview given of New Zealand's experience in Chapter 1 illustrated that the participation of many elements of New Zealand society in terms of negotiating and implementing the settlement process is key to the achievements thus far. Yet, it cannot be doubted that the roles played by Maori women were often overlooked, marginalised or the women in question had to be forceful in seeking recognition for their views. It will remain speculative whether greater recognition of the Maori system of equality between genders, during the transitional justice process, would have led to a reduction in the scope of Maori grievances because women were ultimately afforded the chance to speak and to a greater extent given formal roles in the settlement process. But it can be stated that while New Zealand is an effective example of non-traditional transitional justice to be studied for consideration in other conflict situations, it likewise serves as a reminder that the participation of women is an essential component of transitional justice.

Barrow focused specifically on the transition of recognising women as victims to recognising the role women can play in peace-building and other transitional justice mechanisms. She argued that there is legal space for this shift pursuant to soft law mechanisms such as SCR 1325, which theoretically should enable women to take a more active role in addressing the aftermath, rather than just as passive victims, of conflict. Barrow explored the room within SCR 1325 that theoretically allows greater movement for women to participate in a more substantive fashion than simply by fulfilling a gender quota. However, she notes that SCR 1325 remains soft law and like all soft law mechanisms it is subject to the goodwill of parties in terms of its implementation. Without express mechanisms for active enforcement Barrow notes that any of the equality women ironically achieve during conflict (due to the extreme circumstances presented) may be lost and women can find themselves in a worse position post conflict. Barrow also raised the issue of the negative peace paradigm into which transitional justice mechanisms must infiltrate. She highlights that focusing on the absence of military warfare, peace agreements and high-level negotiations as a means of addressing the aftermath of conflict is outdated and counter-productive to a more nuanced understanding and inclusion of other parties such as women and children. It is in such an argument that we can see the more fundamental theme throughout many of the works, that transitional justice cannot be confined to traditional approaches to conflict response and that the role of women in transitional justice processes (from identifying an appropriate mechanism to its implementation) is essential to ensure this shift. Ultimately Barrow argued that while the inclusion of women in transitional justice processes is clearly essential, and is recognised as such, the role of women must be more than just cosmetic. Women are needed as practitioners, protagonists and participants and given the opportunity to facilitate and promote gender sensitive outcomes in a gender inclusive environment. The problems that must be addressed are more systemic than simply addressing a deficit in numbers. Evidence exists that SCR 1325 can be useful for this purpose, as in Nepal, however its soft law quality inherently limits its application and reliance remains firmly on external parties to agitate for active implementation of the Resolution, namely to 'confront the perceived absence of gender in post-conflict transitions'.

Walsh concluded that 'international criminal justice institutions have not adequately considered gender specific differences between girls and boys in the recognition, investigation and ultimately prosecution of crimes committed against children as well as the participation of girls in these processes'. She argued that such institutions must adopt the guidance given under the Convention on the Rights of the Child to ensure that girls' age and gender specific experiences, needs and rights are addressed. The importance of specifically focusing on children is highlighted as Walsh, in the same vein as other contributors, recognised that many of the developments seeking to ensure gender protection are cosmetic such as requiring greater female representation amongst officers of the Court, rather than addressing systemic inequalities within international criminal justice that operate to the detriment of all women. The priority is instead for consistent involvement to ensure the perspective of girls, in addition to women, men and boys is acknowledged.

Walsh argued that the lack of active protections for girl children in the context of international criminal justice inhibits their participation and that this in turn undermines the transitional justice process for example if they cannot act as witnesses in trials for crimes against them then it undermines the validity of the criminal trial, unless the trial is used along with other mechanisms that do provide some form of redress. Failure to integrate and protect girl children within the international criminal justice framework risks long-term consequences associated with their perception of a world of injustice and immorality. She argued that any justice that emerges from an international criminal justice framework that marginalises or at least overlooks girls risks further marginalising girls from any notion of justice obtained during the transitional justice process and in addition girls may become disenfranchised from their community in an invidious, sustained and long-term manner.

Maddox likewise took a long-term perspective of the problems faced by women in the short term, namely the context of displacement and refugees. She highlighted that the interrelationship between causes of displacement and conflict are so vast and context dependent that it is rational to view those affected by displacement/conflict as key stakeholders in both determining the nature of and implementing the relevant transitional justice mechanisms. In particular, she noted that the experience of women is significantly different from that of men and is often capable of being characterised as more violent or at least separately characterised due to the different – often sexual – forms of violence. The difference in experience, and the fact that women's experience was often a directly related consequence of the structural inequalities that existed prior to the conflict, necessitate that the voice of women is heard independently from that of men in the aftermath of conflict, in order for the solutions identified and adopted to be long term and sustainable. Maddox further highlighted that in the aftermath of conflict, women are often faced with a disproportionate burden to that of men given that they may find themselves the head of households or communities but without the resources that had been available to their male predecessors prior to the relevant conflict, in order to fulfil their obligations.

Despite these observations, the practitioners that Maddox interviewed indicated that they had seen little evidence of engaging those affected by the conflict in the transitional justice process. Potential obstacles were not however unsurmountable with awareness and provisions accordingly made. For example, a lack of time and awareness of the transitional justice process or confidence to participate were cited, yet responses such as education and publicity as well as compensation for participation were just a few potential solutions identified. According to the practitioners interviewed for this work, engaging with the individuals directly affected suggests that priorities tend to lie with the essentials of security and survival being met before notions of justice and accountability are dealt with. Another consistent theme was that the use of international criminal trials was not perceived as being of great success or providing much certainty or satisfaction for the individuals affected. The question often left unanswered was what these large-scale justice initiatives could realistically hope to achieve.

Maddox argued strongly for the inclusion of women in all aspects of transitional justice – not just women affected by the conflict but women as practitioners of transitional justice. In both cases it is the unique perspective that women bring to these processes that can be instrumental in developing a process that is more engaged with the needs of the transitioning community. For the so-called victims this is due to their personal experience and interest in the process but for those women working as practitioners, Maddox contended that there is something idiosyncratic to the female perspective, that all women have experienced discrimination and injustice at some stage which gives them 'an ability to perceive inequities where their male counterparts cannot, to understand the potential outcomes of those inequities, empathise with those who have experienced them and the experience necessary to chart a way beyond them'.

Turning to a more academic perspective the following contributors focused on developments within the law that have sought to recognise women both as victims of conflict and as necessary participants in the transitional justice process.

Fournet argued that the rather basic, textual approach to the inclusion of sexual crimes in criminal law is at odds with a robust judicial approach that exists at the international courts (independent of gender). She showed that it was the latter that has heralded progression in terms of punishing sexual crimes. Her work covered the progress made both in terms of the broader inclusion of sexual crimes within the statutes of the various international courts, while emphasising that it is in practical steps such as the more accommodating rules of evidence and procedure that the real progress is made as in the ongoing *Bemba* case. Ultimately Fournet considered that gender is relevant in the successful prosecution of sexual crimes as an effective tool of transitional justice but that this is a factor inherent to the nature of the crime. She does not draw any link between the preponderance of female scholars or lawyers who work in this field instead concluding that the developments that have occurred are unrelated to the gender of the proponent and should continue to be so.

Similarly, Pégorier highlighted that within the context of international criminal law there has been growing recognition that women are made the victims of conflict due to their gender. Accordingly, there has been necessary progress in terms of international criminal law as a transitional justice tool to attain recompense in the form of criminal convictions of the perpetrators. Pégorier argued that despite many of the jurisprudential developments in recognising various forms of sexual violence as crimes punishable under international law, there are limitations in terms of effective outcomes for women. These include the limited number of convictions and the fact that the adoption of criminal trials was the result of a state dominated negotiation process focused on peace-building with little or no consultation with the affected communities. Pégorier highlights the impact of politics noting for example that in the context of the former Yugoslavia it was only Srebrenica that was classified as genocide so that other incidents of sexual violence were instead reclassified for example as crimes against humanity, thus the political interest led to a denial of justice for victims therefore contradicting the objectives that underlie transitional justice principles of recognition and truth.

Pégorier implicitly highlights that solely viewing women as victims within the transitional justice process is insufficient as it locks the role of women within a very traditional and non-gender-sensitive framework which authors such as Barrow in Chapter 2 have argued are ineffectual. For example where there is reliance on international criminal processes as the sole means of transitional justice then women's experiences are reduced to testimony given in court. This exposes those women who testify, to relive their experiences, to admit to violation – all of which entrench women's positions as victims and risk exposing women to further abuse such as the rejection of the community from where they came or more literally in relation to the verbal and character attacks that may be expected from defence counsel. It is without doubt important that sexual violence be recognised as a crime but its utility in terms of transitional justice must continue to be challenged. Pégorier highlighted the problems that attend criminal tribunals which expose certain of the limitations that apply to international criminal law as a transitional justice mechanism, and show that although vital to such processes, international criminal tribunals must necessarily exist as part of wider programme of measures.

Fielder's work recognised that regardless of its merits, transitional justice can be a tool to both empower and disempower women, a theme repeated throughout the book. However she argued that when active steps are taken by transitional justice practitioners then the role of women in the relevant community can be changed for the better. Practitioners, she cautions, must not seek to promote the role of women to the detriment of values relevant to the transitioning community; illustrated with reference to the African context. Being African is as much part of these women's identity as being female and the challenge identified was to balance the two aspects of identity. Fielder went on to discuss and provide insight into how the African constitutional courts have attempted to strike the balance with the view that promoting women's equality is one of the best ways to action effective transitional justice outcomes.

Mantilla Falcón argued that despite increasing recognition of gender approaches in international law, transitional justice lacks an 'understanding of a comprehensive gender approach' outlining the various characteristics that may need to be recognised including the unequal status of women pre-conflict. Using the example of the Peruvian Truth and Reconciliation Commission, Mantilla Falcón illustrated the steps taken to ensure gender issues were also achieved including the definition of 'sexual violence' and the provision of reparation for rape victims. Despite some progress, gender inclusion is uneven citing for example the ongoing reluctance of women to file complaints due to the lack of gender sensitivity.

Díaz and Marin demonstrated that the Colombian peace and justice arrangement, which was very much a domestically owned process, is an example of progress in engendering an assistance and reparations legal framework; and largely due to the participation of women's groups and networks in the country. They argued that domestic players did not prescribe to traditional perceptions that limited transitional justice to being a narrowly constructed corrective justice exercise, instead prioritising the inclusion of more ambitious distributive justice goals and schemes. As an example, it was noted that the reparations process could seek to not only restore victims to their original situation prior to the crime, but that reparations also sought to 'correct and transform the conditions of discrimination against women existing before the crime'.

The authors in this book collectively argue that it is the need to address the inequalities faced by women before the conflict as well as in the aftermath of conflict that will ultimately bring the greatest change in terms of the role played and the effectiveness of the transitional justice process for women. The authors have consistently highlighted that gender is a relevant factor in the development and success of transitional justice regardless of the context thus in accordance with the advice of the Secretary-General more emphasis needs to be placed on the role of women and space given for women to actively participate and their unique status to be recognised.

Bibliography

Articles

Abbot, K.W. and Snidal, D. 'Hard and Soft Law in International Governance' (2000) *International Organisation* 54(3), 421.

Aguirre, D. and Pietropaoli, I. 'Gender Equality, Development and Transitional Justice: The Case of Nepal' (2008) *International Journal of Transitional Justice* 2(3), 358.

Aolain, F. and Hamilton, M. 'Gender and the Rule of Law in Transitional Societies' (2009) *Minnesota Journal of International Law* 18, 380.

Banda, F. 'Global Standards: Local Values' (2010) *International Journal of Law, Policy and Family* 17, 1.

Bell, C. 'Transitional Justice, Interdisciplinarity and the State of the "Field" or "Non-Field"' (2009) *International Journal of Transitional Justice* 3(1), 5.

Bell, C. and O'Rourke, C. 'Does Feminism Need a Theory of Transitional Justice: An Introductory Essay' (2007) *International Journal of Transitional Justice* 1(1), 35.

Bell, C. and O'Rourke, C. 'Peace Agreements or Pieces of Paper? The Impact of UN SCR 1325 and Peace Processes and their Agreements' (2010) *International and Comparative Law Quarterly* 59.

Bigge, D. and von Briesen, A. 'Conflict in the Zimbabwean Courts: Women's Rights and Indigenous Self-Determination in Magaya v. Magaya' (2000) *Harvard Human Rights Journal* 289.

Bond, J. 'Gender, Discourse, and Customary Law in Africa' *Southern California Law Review* (2010) 83(3), 509.

Bronstein, V. 'Comments on the Evolution of Customary Succession Laws in South Africa' (2006) *South African Journal on Human Rights* 22, 99.

Campbell, K. 'The Gender of Transitional Justice: Law, Sexual Violence and the International Criminal Tribunal for the Former Yugoslavia' (2007) *International Journal of Transitional Justice* 1(3), 411.

Charlesworth, H. 'The Women Question in International Law' (2010) *Asian Journal of International Law* 1–6, 33.

Charlesworth, H. 'Transforming the United Men's Club: Feminist Futures for the United Nations' (1995) *Transnational Law and Contemporary Problems* 4, 448.

Cohn, C., Kinsella, H. and Gibbings, S. (2004) 'Women, Peace and Security' *International Feminist Journal of Politics* 6(1), 137.

DeGuzman, M.M. 'Giving Priority to Sex Crime Prosecutions: The Philosophical Foundations of a Feminist Agenda' (2011) *International Criminal Law Review* 11, 515–528.

Fletcher, L. and Weinstein, H. with Rowan, J. 'Context, Timing, and the Dynamics of Transitional Justice: A Historical Perspective' *Human Rights Quarterly* (2009) 31(1).

Franke, K., 'Gendered Subjects of Transitional Justice' (2006) *Columbia Journal of Gender and Law* 15(3), 813–828.

Graycar, R. 'Book Review: Gender and the New South African Legal Order' (1996) *South African Journal of Human Rights* 12, 669.

Gross, A. 'The Constitutional, Reconciliation, and Transitional Justice: Lessons from South Africa and Israel' (2004) *Stanford Journal International Law* 40, 47.

Haffar, W. 'Emergent Peacemakers: Cataloguing New Patterns of Activity in Post-Cold War Conflict' (2002) *PEPS* 8(2), 32.

Koenig, D. 'Women and Rape in Ethnic Conflict and War', (1994) *Hastings Women's Law Journal* 5, 129–142.

Laplante, L. 'On the Indivisibility of Rights: Truth Commissions, Reparations and the Right to Development' (2007) *Yale Human Rights and Development Journal* 10, 141.

Linos, N. 'Rethinking Gender-based Violence during War: Is Violence against Civilian Men a Problem worth Addressing?' (2009) *Social Science and Medicine* 68, 1549.

McKay, S. 'The Effects of Armed Conflict on Girls and Women' (1998) *Peace and Conflict: Journal of Peace Psychology* 4(4), 381.

Mouthaan, S. 'The Prosecution of Gender-based Crimes at the ICC: Challenges and Opportunities' (2011) *International Criminal Law Review* 11, 775–802.

Ni Aolain, F. 'Women, Security and the Patriarchy of International Transitional Justice' (2009) *Human Rights Quarterly* 31(4), 1057.

Ni Aolain, F. and Rooney, E. 'Underenforcement and Intersectionality: Gendered Aspects of Transition for Women' (2007) *International Journal of Transitional Justice* 1, 350.

O'Regan, H. 'Post-Colonialism: "Ko Te Mate Kururpopo – The Festering Wound"' (1995) *Womens Studies Journal* 11, 1.

Otto, D. 'The Exile of Exclusion: Reflections on Gender Issues in International Law over the Last Decade' (2009) *Melbourne Journal of International Law* 11.

Pitea, C. 'Rape as a Human Rights Violation and a Criminal Offence: The European Court's Judgment in *M.C. v. Bulgaria*' (2005) *Journal of International Criminal Justice* 3, 447–462.

Sadat, L.N. 'Avoiding the Creation of a Gender Ghetto in International Criminal Law' (2011) *International Criminal Law Review* 11, 655–662.

Shepherd, L. 'Power and Authority in the Production of United Nations Security Council Resolution 1325' (2008) *International Studies Quarterly* 389.

Udombana, N. 'Interpreting Rights Globally: Courts and Constitutional Rights in Emerging Democracies' (2005) *African Human Rights Law Journal* 47.

Books

Ambos, K., Large, J. and Wierda, M. (eds) *Building a Future on Peace and Justice: Studies on Transitional Justice, Peace and Development* (Berlin: Springer, 2009), 217–236.

Ballantine, K. and Sherman, J. (eds) *The Political Economy of Armed Conflict* (Lynne Rienner Publishers, London, 2003).

Binney, J. and Chaplin, G. *Nga Morehu the Survivors* (Auckland: Oxford University Press, 1986).

Boon, K. *Whina Cooper* (Wellington: Kotuku Publishing, 1993).

Boon, K. *Whetu Tirikatene-Sullivan* (Wellington: Kotuku Publishing, 2006).

Brown, A. (ed.) *Mana Wahine Women Who Show the Way* (Auckland: Reed Books, 1994).

Charny, Israel W. (ed.) *Encyclopedia of Genocide*, 2 vols (Santa Barbara, CA: ABC-Clio, 1999).

Cockburn, C. *From Where We Stand: War, Women's Activism & Feminist Analysis* (London; New York: Zed Books, 2007).

Díaz, C., Sánchez, N.C. and Uprimny, R. (eds) *Reparar en Colombia: los dilemas en contextos de conflicto, pobreza y exclusión* (ICTJ and De Justicia, Bogotá, 2009).

Enloe, C. *The Morning After: Sexual Politics at the End of the Cold War* (Berkley, CA; London: University of California Press, 1993).

Hinton, A. (ed.) *Transitional Justice: Global Mechanisms and Local Realities after Genocide and Mass Violence* (New Brunswick, NJ: Rutgers University Press, 2010).

Kelsey, J. *Rolling Back the State: Privatisation of Power in Aotearoa* (Wellington: Bridget Williams Books, 1993).

King, M. *History of New Zealand* (New Zealand: Penguin, 2003).

McKay, S. and Mazurana, D. *Where are the Girls? Girls in Fighting Forces in Northern Uganda, Sierra Leone, and Mozambique: Their Lives During and After War* (Montreal, Canada: Rights & Democracy, 2004).

Meertens, D. 'Mujeres en la guerra y en la paz: cambios y pemanencia en los imaginario sociales' in Museo Nacional (ed.) *Mujer, nación, identidad y ciudadanía, siglos XIX y XX* (Bogotá: Museo Nacional, 2005).

Memoria Histórica de la Comisión Nacional de Reparación y Reconciliación, *Trujillo: Una tragedia que no cesa* (Bogotá: Editorial Planeta, 2008).

Middleton, S. and Jones, A. (ed.) *Women and Education in Aotearoa* (Wellington: Bridget Williams Books, 1992), Glossary.

Mikaere, A. *The Balance Destroyed: The Consequences for Maori Women of the Colonisation of Tikanga Maori* (Auckland: International Research Institute for Maori and Indigenous Education, 2003).

Neier, A. *War Crimes: Brutality, Genocide, Terror and the Struggle for Justice* (New York: Times Books, 1998).

Ofner, S. *New Zealand Women in the 19th Century* (Auckland: Macmillan, 1993).

Parmar, S., Roseman, M., Siegrist, S. and Sowa, T. (eds) *Children and Transitional Justice: Truth-Telling, Accountability and Reconciliation* (Cambridge, MA: Harvard University Press, 2010).

Ra, M. *Wahine Ma Tapu a Io: The Role of Women in Leading Maori through the Twenty First Century* (Te Kauwhata: Mitaki Ra Publications, 2000).

Raj Upreti, B. *Armed Conflict and Peace Processes in Nepal: The Maoist Insurgency, Past Negotiations and Opportunities for Conflict Transformation* (New Delhi: Adroit Publishers, 2006).

Rei, T. *Maori Women and the Vote* (Wellington: Huia Publishers, 1993).

Rettberg, A. *Reparación en Colombia: Qué Quieren las Víctimas?* (Bogotá: GIZ, Fiscalía General de la Nación, Universidad de los Andes and Embassy of the Federal Republic of Germany, 2008).

Schabas, W. *The International Criminal Court: A Commentary on the Rome Statute* (Oxford: Oxford University Press, 2010).

Smith, L. 'Maori Women: Discourses, Projects and Mana Wahine' in Middleton, S. and Jones, A. (eds) *Women and Education in Aotearoa* (Wellington: Bridget Williams Books, 1992), Glossary.

Upenga, V, Rata, R. and Nepe, T. 'Whaia Te Iti Kahurangi: Maori Women Reclaiming Autonomy' in New Zealand Planning Council (ed.) *Puna Wairere: Essays by Maori* (Wellington: New Zealand Planning Council, 1990).

Documents/reports

Bell, C. and O'Rourke, C. 'Peace Agreements or Pieces of Paper: UN SCR 1325 and Peace Negotiations and Agreements' (Research Paper No. 11-01, Transitional Justice Institute, University of Ulster).

Comité Interinstitucional de Justicia y Paz, 'Informe Mensual: Matriz Comité Interinstitucional de Justicia y Paz', March 2011.

Henare, M. 'Nga Tikanga me nga Ritenga o Te Ao Maori' in 'Report of the Commission on Social Policy', Ministry of Social Development, New Zealand (1988).

Michels, A. 'Psychosocial Support for Children: Protecting the Rights of Child Victims and Witnesses in Transitional Justice Processes' (2010) *Innocenti Research Centre Expert Paper Series on Children and Transitional Justice*, 6.

'Report of the Secretary-General on the Rule of Law and Transitional Justice in Conflict and Post-Conflict Societies' UN Doc S/2004/616 (2004).

Robson, B. 'Economic Determinants of Māori Health and Disparities (A Report for the Public Health Advisory Committee)' *Te Ropu Rangahau Hauora a Eru Pomare* (2004), www.nhc.govt.nz/phac.

'The Administration of Justice and the Rights of Prisonners' United Nations High Commission of Human Rights, Economic and Social Council, UN Doc. E/CN.4/Sub.2/1997/20/Rev.1 (1997).

Other

Barton-Prescott v. *Director-General of Social Welfare* [1997] 3 NZLR 179.

Case Velásquez Rodríguez, Inter American Court of Human Rights, Sentence of 29 July 1998.

Fondo de Desarrollo de las Naciones Unidas para la Mujer, UNIFEM, *'Justicia Desigual' Género y derechos de las víctimas en Colombia* (UNIFEM, Bogotá, 2008).

Goldblatt, B. and Shiela Meintjes M. 'Gender and the Truth and Reconciliation Commission', a Submission to the Truth and Reconciliation Commission (1996).

Hayner, P. 'International Guidelines for the Creation and Operation of Truth Commissions: A Preliminary Proposal, Law and Contemporary Problems' (1996).

Huakina Development Trust v. *Waikato Valley Authority* [1987] 2 NZLR 188.

McRitchie v. *Taranaki Fish and Game Council* [1999] 2 NZLR 139.

Nesiah, V. 'Truth Commissions and Gender: Principles, Policies, and Procedures', International Centre for Transitional Justice, Gender Justice Series, 2006.

Ngati Apa v. *Attorney General (Attorney General v Ngati Apa)* [2003] 3 NZLR 643.

Orange, C. 'The Treaty of Wāitangi: A Study of its Making, Interpretation and Role in New Zealand History' (Thesis submitted for PhD, University of Auckland, 1984).

PROFIS 'To Make Visible Gender Violence: Systematization of Gender Experience', 2011.

Rubio-Marín, R. 'Gender and Reparations: Setting the Agenda' (2006) *Reparations for Women Victims of Human Rights Violations: Case Studies*, Social Science Research Council, New York, 21.

Shilubana and Others v. *Nwamitwa and Other* [2009] (2) SA 66 (CC).

'Speaking from my own Experience: Nga Mea I Whakairongia e Nga Tau Ki Toku Hinengaro' (New Zealand Runanga Kuia Proceedings, 1993).

Spees, P. 'Gender Justice and Accountability in Peace Support Operations' (2004) *International Alert Policy Briefing*.

'The Status and Autonomy of Māori Women as Viewed through Selected Kaupapa Māori Narratives' (MAOR 480: submitted by M. Henderson, Te Tari Māori, Te Whare Wānanga o Otāgo, Ōtepoti).

Valji, N. 'Gender and Transitional Justice Programming: A review of Perú' (Sierra Leone and Rwanda, UNIFEM, 2010).

West, R. 'Gender and Law Theory', (Uniandes, Instituto Pensar, Siglo del Hombre, 2000).

Yates-Smith, A. 'Hine! E Hine! Rediscovering the Feminine in Maori Spirituality' (unpublished PhD Thesis, University of Waikato, 1988).

Websites

Arthur, P. 'Identities in Transition: Developing Better Transitional Justice Initiatives in Divided Societies' (2009) *International Centre for Transitional Justice*, http://ictj.org/sites/default/files/ICTJ-Global-Divided-Societies-2009-English.pdf.

Ferris, E. 'Internal Displacement, Transitional Justice and Peacebuilding: Lessons Learned' (2008) Summary Report of the Internal Displacement and the Construction of Peace Seminar, Bogota, Colombia, 42, www.brookings.edu/speeches/2008/1111_internal_displacement_ferris.aspx.

'Formal Apology to Te Uri O Hau (5 July 2004), www.beehive.govt.nz/release/formal-apology-te-uri-o-hau.

International Committee of the Red Cross, 'Women facing War: ICRC Study on the Impact of Armed Conflict on Women', October 2001, 2, www.icrc.org/eng/assets/files/other/icrc_002_0798_women_facing_war.pdf.

Office of Treaty Settlements, www.ots.govt.nz/.

Walrond, C. 'Fishing Industry' (2006) *Te Ara: the Encyclopedia of New Zealand*, www.teara.govt.nz/en/fishing-industry/7.

Index